**Harvard Historical Studies · 155**

Published under the auspices
of the Department of History
from the income of the
Paul Revere Frothingham Bequest
Robert Louis Stroock Fund
Henry Warren Torrey Fund

# France after Revolution

*Urban Life, Gender, and the*
*New Social Order*

Denise Z. Davidson

Harvard University Press
Cambridge, Massachusetts
London, England
2007

*Library of Congress Cataloging-in-Publication Data*

Davidson, Denise Z., 1967–
France after revolution : urban life, gender, and the new social order / Denise Z. Davidson
p. cm.—(Harvard historical studies ; 155)
Includes bibliographical references and index.
ISBN-13: 978-0-674-02459-5 (hc : alk. paper)
ISBN-10: 0-674-02459-1 (hc : alk. paper)
1. Social change—France—History.   2. Sex role—France—History.   3. City and town
life—France—History.   I. Title.
HN425.D39   2007
307.760944'09034—dc22        2006049724

# Acknowledgments

It is a great pleasure to be able to express my gratitude to the many friends and colleagues who have offered their advice and assistance over the years that I have been working on this book. The parameters of the project, its form, and its argument have evolved a great deal since I first began my research nearly fifteen years ago. However, the initial inspiration for studying the postrevolutionary period remains the same: to understand how ordinary people came to terms with the significance of the French Revolution in its immediate aftermath. I wanted to trace the emergence of new ideas about gender and class, ideas that would remain influential throughout the nineteenth century and well into the twentieth. In the course of my research, I became convinced that everyday life and the dynamics of visibility in urban spaces went a long way in explaining the growing comprehension of ideological constructions relating to the "natures" of men and women and the behavioral expectations of the various classes. Finding evidence for these kinds of quotidian experiences required an ambitious research plan and wide reading across disciplines, and thus I sought advice from a diverse group of scholars, archivists, and librarians.

My first intellectual debt goes to the professors I studied with at the University of Pennsylvania and other institutions. Lynn Hunt was, and continues to be, a model mentor, reading countless drafts without complaint and always listening and offering advice, even when we are thousands of miles apart. Lynn Hollen Lees served as a mentor as well, offering valuable advice on just about every subject imaginable. Others who offered support and encouragement during the early stages of my research include Lenard Berlanstein, Roger Chartier, Alain Corbin, Gay Gullickson, and Donald Sutherland. In more recent years, the many friends and colleagues who have read and offered advice on various parts of this book include Christine Adams, Michelle Brattain, Anne Brophy, Craig Calhoun, Lauren Clay, Duane Corpis, Malcolm Crook, Ellen Evans, Ian Fletcher, Carol Harrison, Carla Hesse, Jennifer Heuer, Jeff Horn, Doris Kadish, Martin Lyons, Sarah Maza, Krystyn Moon, Joe Perry, Jeremy Popkin, Jeff Ravel, Michael Stevens, and Victoria Thompson. In a particularly appreciated show of goodwill and generosity, both Sheryl Kroen and Judith Miller read the entire manuscript in its near-final stage, catching some errors and improving the text overall. I must also express my gratitude to Patrice Higonnet, editor of the Harvard Historical Studies Series; Kathleen McDermott, editor at Harvard University Press; and the anonymous readers whose careful readings and thoughtful suggestions were vital to making this book what it has eventually become. Virtually all of my colleagues in the history department at Georgia State University have offered informal advice on a wide range of topics. Though I cannot name them all here, I hope they know how much their support has meant to me. I nonetheless feel I must mention by name the current chair, Hugh Hudson, and his predecessor, Diane Willen, whose patience and willingness to listen and provide advice have been invaluable. Finally, two particularly able research assistants, Laura Corazzol and Rosemary McClellan, helped enormously with the last stages of preparing the manuscript to go to press.

Numerous institutions have provided financial support for this project, and I am happy to be able to acknowledge their assistance here. A Bourse Chateaubriand from the French government funded a full year of research in France; the Mellon Foundation provided funding for research and writing for another year; and both the University of Pennsylvania and Saint Lawrence University supported research trips to archives as well as giving me the chance to attend conferences where I received valuable feedback. Since joining the faculty at Georgia State University, I have received summer funding on two occasions as well as a much-needed semester leave from teaching to complete the time-consuming work necessary to complete this book.

Historians cannot accomplish anything without access to libraries and archival collections, as well as the guidance of experts in these places. The warm and enthusiastic welcome I received from archivists in France made the many months I spent in these various settings both profitable and enjoyable. I would like to acknowledge the invaluable assistance I received from the archivists and staffs at the following institutions: the Bibliothèque

Nationale de France; the Archives Nationales; the Bibliothèque Historique de la Ville de Paris; the Bibliothèque de l'Arsenal; the Archives Départementales du Rhône, de la Seine-Maritime, and de la Loire-Atlantique; the Archives Municipales in Lyon and in Nantes; the Bibliothèque Municipale de Lyon; and the Médiathèque de Nantes. Without their knowledge and expertise, the research for this book would have been much more difficult, if not impossible. A slightly different version of Chapter 1 appeared as "Women at Napoleonic Festivals: Gender and the Public Sphere during the First Empire," *French History* 16, no. 3 (2002): 299–322. Portions of Chapter 3 appeared in "Making Society 'Legible': People-Watching in Paris after the Revolution," *French Historical Studies* 28, no. 2 (Spring 2005): 265–296. I am grateful to Oxford University Press and Duke University Press for permission to reprint this material. In addition, I wish to thank the institutions that provided the figures and maps that appear in this book, as well as the permission to reproduce them: the Bibliothèque Nationale de France, the Photothèque des Musées de Paris, the Réunion des Musées Nationaux / Art Resource, the University of Kentucky Libraries, the Archives Municipales de Lyon, and the Archives Municipales de Nantes.

Finally, I thank my family: my husband, Georges Alameddine; our children, George, Caroline, and Leila; and my mother, Marguerite Davidson. You have all helped me to keep my work life in perspective and to remember that what matters most in the end is love. This book is dedicated to the memory of my father, Richard Davidson, who died in September 2004 at the age of eighty-seven. He was the first feminist I encountered; I'll never forget the many times throughout my childhood and later that he told me that I could do and become anything I wanted. The self-confidence that came from his unconditional love helped me accomplish many personal and professional goals.

# Contents

# Illustrations

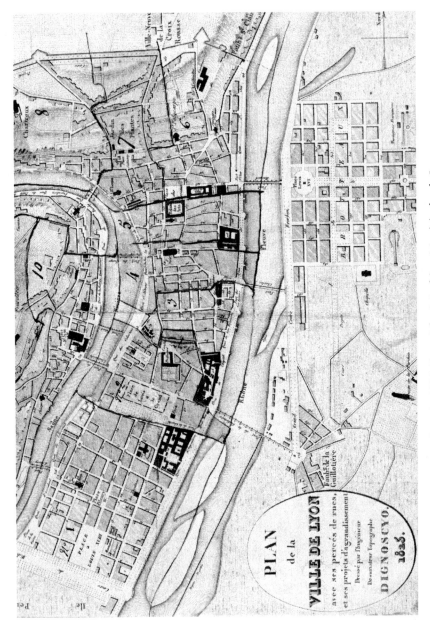

**Map 1.** Lyon in 1825. Copyright © Archives Municipales de Lyon.

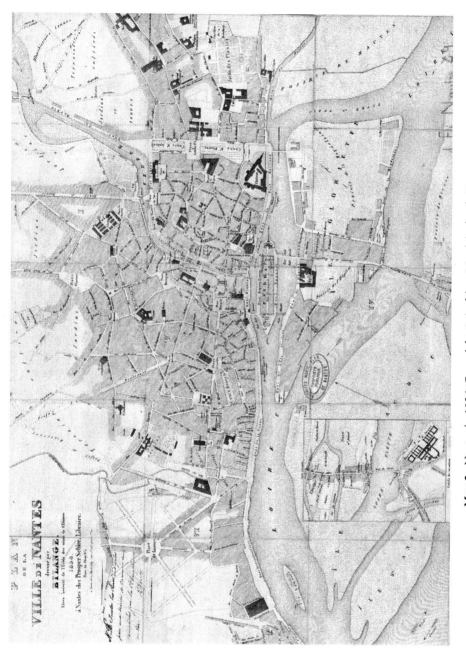

**Map 2.** Nantes in 1836. Copyright © Archives Municipales de Nantes.

France after Revolution

# Introduction

In 1822, the Academy of Sciences, Letters, and Arts of Lyon awarded a prize for the best essay treating "the moral influence of theaters and particularly secondary theaters on the *peuple*." The winning essay, Jean-Baptiste-Louis Camel's "De l'influence des théâtres et particulièrement des théâtres secondaires sur les mœurs du peuple," begins by insisting that the "people" were at risk because of their impressionable and "simple natures," which left them open to morals that were "sometimes close to depravity."[1] Camel's essay recounts the tale of a family that was ruined because of an uncontrollable passion for the theater. The father (a shoe repairman) and his wife had always lived honestly and "happily in their mediocrity." However, their children, a boy and a girl, used every cent they earned to attend Boulevard theaters, an experience that in turn inspired them to try to dress and behave as though they did not come from such a humble background. Although they did not even know how to read, "the girl dressed herself far above her *état* and the boy appeared at [upper-class] *promenades*."[2] Their passion for the theater led to their taking off days from work so as not to miss a single premiere. Then they resorted to lying to their parents. As the story continues, Camel implies that both became trapped in the immoral worlds of crime and prostitution. The theater could lead to dangerous, if not criminal, behavior as it made spectators believe they could emulate those more well-off than themselves. Later in the essay, Camel includes another anecdote in which he describes his surprise at realizing that an elegantly dressed young lady he saw on the street was actually his laundry woman![3] Camel's essay no doubt won the contest because it articulated widespread concerns about the social, political, and moral ramifications of postrevolutionary cultural practices.

1

The Revolution of 1789 created uncertainty about the expression and meaning of social hierarchies. In the eighteenth century, the French populace knew how to interpret and convey markers of social position and deference, even as these markers increasingly came under attack.[4] The Revolution dismantled these hierarchies and the symbolic system that allowed them to function. At one point the Revolutionaries even experimented with eliminating the use of the word *vous,* the formal form of "you" in French. In the aftermath of this destabilizing experience, a new set of social distinctions began to emerge. For this system to operate, people needed to develop an understanding of the social markers that evolved along with it.[5] Urban cultural practices aided in this process as various kinds of venues attracted diverse participants who put themselves on display in public as they were amusing themselves. People could then compare and categorize those around them, observing how the new hierarchies forming in postrevolutionary France would function. This familiarity with the framework of their society could then lead to a variety of behaviors, from the most submissive to the most radically subversive. By the end of the Restoration, the new markers had become legible. Though the hierarchies they represented were not necessarily more stable than those of any other period, people had learned to read them in everyday life.

Postrevolutionary confusion about whether birth, wealth, or merit would determine one's place in society also made gender distinctions particularly salient. Because gender seemed more "natural" than other categories of differentiation, women's dress, morals, education, and comportment emerged as central to the processes of observation and categorization that helped build a sense of how postrevolutionary society would operate. In a recent study of the artist David's work after the Terror, art historian Ewa Lajer-Burcharth came to similar conclusions. She describes "the emergent centrality of gender as a paramount factor in the cultural definition of the self after Thermidor" and argues for "women's enhanced social and cultural visibility in the late 1790s."[6] In the first decades of the nineteenth century, too, women stood out among the strollers on the streets and the spectators in theaters, and commentators referred frequently to their behavior. Women were also the most enthusiastic supporters of the newly returned Catholic Church, with religion often furnishing a central theme in their activities. It was during this period that the association of women with the Church and men with secular society emerged as a widely held assumption with long-term political repercussions.[7] In these different contexts, women filled public spaces; their presence was noted by others and became part of the overall experience for all involved.

Both class and gender norms were in a process of transformation in the late eighteenth and early nineteenth centuries. During the Old Regime, elite men and women participated together in many forms of cultural activities, particularly at salons, which were typically hosted by women and attended by both men and women.[8] Among the lower classes, men and women went to cabarets where they drank watered-down wine, and they attended street fairs and Boulevard theaters, locations that attracted not only the popular classes but also many from the bourgeoisie and aristocracy as well.[9] Scholars have argued that in the nineteenth century, men and women led increasingly separate lives, as "domestic ideology"—a set of beliefs regarding women's "natures" which argued that for the sake of society women needed to devote themselves to quiet, domestic pursuits as opposed to seeking the pleasures of *le monde*, or fashionable society—grew dominant.[10] "Separate spheres," a related concept, represented an elaborate justification based on "nature" for women to remain in the private realm of the family, whereas men's "natures" favored their participation in the "public sphere" of business and politics.[11] Although most working-class women could never afford to devote themselves solely to "domestic" concerns, the ideology shaped workers' sense of gender norms and their political and social goals as well.[12]

Historians have increasingly questioned the utility of "separate spheres," however, both as an analytical tool and as a reliable reflection of women's lives. For example, Elizabeth Colwill argued that "the assumption that men and women constituted 'separate spheres' was not universally accepted" in the early nineteenth century, and she found that women could assume "prominent roles in lycées, scholarly societies, salons, and the press." Similarly, in examining Parisian entertainments popular around 1800, Jann Matlock argued that "women's place in the public sphere was not so firmly disrupted by the Directory years as has been imagined. . . . Significant possibilities for women's political enfranchisement were very much available by the early years of the Consulate, and . . . one of the most significant spheres of that enfranchisement related to women's ability to reposition themselves in visual space."[13] Going further, Mona Ozouf made a case for French "singularity": that unlike the "Anglo-Saxon" countries, French men and women continued to spend their leisure time together, and this mixing explains the more moderate form of feminism that developed in France.[14] In order to build a contrast between the French case and the British and

American ones, Ozouf overgeneralized both sides. Behavioral models based on separate spheres never took as complete a hold over British and American society as she makes it seem, and gender stereotypes put limits on women's participation in French society as well. In addition, French feminists were capable of making demands as radical as their peers anywhere else.[15] Ozouf's argument inspired sharp criticism and debate, in part for its privileging of heterosexuality as the matrix for society. Where Ozouf views "gallantry" as a mechanism for easing relations between the sexes, others view it as a form of male domination.[16]

Although my findings confirm Ozouf's and others' arguments against the power of separate spheres as an ideology that steered male and female behavior in early nineteenth-century France, it is important to remember that the many mixed-sex gatherings analyzed here took on a normative function with regard to sexuality and the family, as well as gender and class. Postrevolutionary cultural practices placed great weight on heterosexual norms, and as Suzanne Desan has recently argued, the family became central to creating a sense of stability after earlier revolutionary experimentation. According to Desan, "marriage, heterosexual love, and gender complementarity held the political power to underpin patriotism."[17] Mixed-sex sociability went hand in hand with the desire to build a new social and political order, and it helps to explain why women's participation in public life was essential: this heteronormative function could not have operated without women. Confusion about gender, class, and sexuality, as well as the political and social significance of the family, reverberated through French society in the wake of the Revolution. As a result, men and women from across the social spectrum struggled to comprehend these notions in print and in their everyday interchanges. It was desirable, even necessary, for women to appear in public along with men so that all could act out and observe—and through these mechanisms, construct—new postrevolutionary social norms. Women's association with monarchism and the Church would make imagining their place in later nineteenth-century republican politics problematic. However, in the immediate postrevolutionary period, other kinds of political structures facilitated women's potential engagement with a politicized public sphere. Neither men nor women could form political parties or hold meetings; the more informal settings in which political views could be expressed, spaces like theaters and cafés, were not officially closed to women.

All of this suggests that women were not excluded from public life and even politics in the aftermath of the Revolution. The concept of the "bourgeois public sphere," as developed by Jürgen Habermas, has been influential among historians of women who often contrast the eighteenth century, when elite women supposedly had extensive influence in politics through informal channels and salons, to the nineteenth century, when the clear separation between a political public realm and an apolitical private sphere theoretically kept women from having political influence.[18] The dominant argument has been that the Revolution brought about women's exclusion from the politicized public sphere, as evidenced by the 1793 law banning women's clubs, and by women's subordinate status in the family as defined by the Napoleonic Code.[19] One recent synthetic work comments on the "unprecedented degree to which separate spheres ideology was propagated and diffused in post-Revolutionary society, in direct response to the Revolutionary experience."[20] One goal of this book is to work through why and how this ideology came to dominate during the postrevolutionary period and to determine the extent to which the discourse of separate spheres reflected common perceptions and beliefs about male and female natures and roles. In many cases, women's appearance and behavior in public spaces visibly contradicted such prescriptions. At the same time, the particular ways in which they chose to engage with public life suggest that women were consciously negotiating increasingly well-defined behavioral norms for the genders and the classes.

Newer historical work has begun to question the view that we can or should separate the public and the private. Scholars have shown, for example, that women continued to run salons well into the nineteenth century, and that so-called private or familial concerns as well as gender norms had strong connections to political developments after 1793.[21] Others have taken issue with women's assumed exclusion from the public and from politics in the nineteenth century, as well as the very idea of separate "public" and "private" spheres.[22] In an essay exploring historians' use of Habermas, Harold Mah has posited a new way of conceiving of the public sphere, not as a literal spatial entity but as a phantasmic or normative construction. "The simple spatialization of the public sphere—as a domain that any group can enter or leave—fails to address the way in which the public sphere constructs itself as a unified entity."[23] People always enter the public sphere as part of a particular group, but the normative nature of the public sphere requires universality, a claim that some groups have been able to make with greater success than others. Gender and sexual norms, among other categories of difference, structure access to the public sphere, which, as Mah emphasizes, takes on a normative function in determining who can enter this "sphere," in what contexts, and under what limits. Taken together, these debates regarding postrevolutionary understandings of public and private, and of gender and sexual norms, suggest that discursive analysis of prescriptive, political, and legal discourse relating to these issues can only tell us so much. A history of *practices*—women's and men's everyday activities—allows us to explore the mechanisms through which the postrevolutionary social and political order took shape in the minds of ordinary people. Urban social spaces provided the context for this growing comprehension.[24]

Many of the spaces examined here cannot be described as either purely public or private, if we take public to mean open to all and private to mean limited to family and friends.[25] When a female spectator was seated in her loge overlooking the audience, for example, the space was, at least temporarily, hers, and thus private. Yet it was a public space: it was not in someone's home and members of "the public" were around her; and of course she was on display in this public space while reacting to the play and to other audience members. As postmodern geographer Henri Lefebvre argued, people and their practices construct spaces themselves through their "assembly at a single point."[26] Social spaces, whether they are perceived as private or public or somewhere in between, took on certain characteristics as a result of the people who created them. They could be masculine, feminine, or gender neutral; they could be affected by the subject matter treated within them, the class composition of those who filled them, the kinds of relationships that existed between the people who inhabited the space, and politics, violence, sexuality, and so on. To quote Lefebvre once again, "Space is political and ideological. It is a product literally filled with ideologies."[27] Interactions between people and ideas in urban social spaces enabled heterogeneous groups to observe each other, learn from what they saw, and thus construct notions of their own identity and how that identity differed from that of others around them. The chapters that follow are organized around particular social spaces and the activities that took place in them: city squares, theaters, clubs, cafés, and dances. The spaces are organized from those that appealed to the most diverse groups to those that brought more narrow segments of the population together. Strengthening and clarifying individual and collective forms of identity, the shared experiences in these urban spaces contributed to people's growing comprehension of the new postrevolutionary social and political order taking shape around them.

At the same time, these ordinary people were in constant interaction with three powerful forces and institutions working to shape society and politics: the state, the Church, and various "producers of culture," including novelists, playwrights, journalists, and others whose views were disseminated through print and on stage. These other "actors" play a prominent, though less emphasized, role in my story—appearing at different moments and in different contexts. So, for example, although the state organized and staged festivals to communicate its desired messages, spectators at such events interpreted those messages as they wished and, in acting out their desired social and political roles, had the potential to reinforce, undermine, or reconfigure the official messages of festivals. We know a fair amount about these larger forces and institutions during this period, but we know almost nothing about provincial urban social, cultural, and political life from the ground up. In emphasizing the power of ordinary people, I hope to make clear how these "hidden actors" could shape and construct social norms and political attitudes. However, we must keep in mind that this process was one of negotiation with larger, more "visible" social and political forces.

Despite deep political divisions between those who had supported the Revolution and those who wished to return to the Old Regime, a desire for order and stability dominated French society during the first decades of the nineteenth century. Writing in 1900, historian Henri d'Alméras described the atmosphere that reigned in 1801: "Everyone was disgusted with everything, even hatred. After years of civil discord, Parisians wanted only appeasement. From their new government, they wanted order, material well-being, prosperity, and the embellishment of their city."[28] At every level of society and across the political spectrum, people hoped for an end to civil war, violence, and death. Napoleon Bonaparte's 1799 coup d'état closed the chapter on the moderate Directory regime that had been governing France since the end of the Terror. He succeeded in building support for his new government (first the Consulate and then the Empire, starting in 1804) in part because he satisfied the desire for order. Napoleonic policies, including the Concordat with the Pope in 1801, the Civil Code of 1804, and military efforts designed to turn attention away from internal discord by drawing it toward external enemies, all represented responses to these wishes for prosperity and an end to civil discord. In part because of his harsh clampdown on all forms of dissent, Bonaparte appeared to succeed at finally reunifying French society.[29]

When the Bourbons returned to the throne, the Restoration government also worked to guarantee stability and the relative satisfaction of the people, albeit with different tactics. The execution of Louis XVI in January 1793 had left a deep scar on the French political conscience. When his brother, Louis XVIII, took the throne after Napoleon's defeat by the allied powers in 1814, the new monarch tried to minimize the divisions between those on opposing political sides. However, this cooperative approach no longer prevailed after the period known as the Hundred Days, when Napoleon escaped his place of exile and returned to France in the spring of 1815, quickly gathering supporters for one last great battle, Waterloo. With the "Second Restoration," when Louis XVIII took the throne once again, this time with allied troops occupying French territory, political hatreds came to the surface and a phase of "White Terror" (as opposed to the "Red Terror" of 1793–1794) ensued. When Charles X, who was known for his political and religious conservatism, inherited the throne in 1824, political tensions escalated again.

Historians of Napoleonic France and the Restoration have mapped out the political, military, and administrative developments of these periods in great detail.[30] However, little has been done to link ordinary people's practices and experiences to these state-sponsored efforts at building order. This book's bottom-up approach to the construction of order represents a corrective to these tendencies. The social and cultural history of the Napoleonic period lags far behind that of the eighteenth and later nineteenth centuries.[31] Although some good work in these areas has been accomplished for the Restoration, it is usually with a view looking forward toward the later nineteenth century rather than thinking of the Restoration as part of a larger "postrevolutionary" phase during which time people came to terms with the significance of the Revolution.[32] By treating these two regimes together, despite their very real differences in form and philosophy, we can see that both represented responses to a common concern: how to build a stable political and social order that would survive despite the post-1789 recognition that governments, if unpopular or unsuccessful, could be toppled.

Although relatively little social and cultural history has been devoted to the first decades of the nineteenth century, several significant works have been enormously helpful, both for the background information they provide as well as their analytical frameworks. The evolution of social identities and their relationship to political structures has been treated by several scholars. On working-class consciousness during the early nineteenth century,

William Sewell's *Work and Revolution in France,* Jacques Rancière's *The Nights of Labor,* and Cynthia Truant's *The Rites of Labor* all discuss the language and practices of workers that helped them create a sense of identity before and after the Revolution.[33] On bourgeois class consciousness (or its absence), Sarah Maza's *The Myth of the French Bourgeoisie* and Carol Harrison's *The Bourgeois Citizen in Nineteenth-Century France,* as well as the large number of studies on the Parisian bourgeoisie by Adeline Daumard, provide different perspectives on bourgeois lifestyles and attitudes.[34] This book differs from these studies in its focus on spaces that brought together many different social groups whose sense of identity evolved in good part from their interaction with other groups they defined as different from themselves. Other works that help shed light on bourgeois identity and perspectives are studies of the concept of honor by Robert Nye and William Reddy.[35] Like Maza and Sewell on class, Nye and Reddy focus largely on language, on how discursive constructs—like honor or the concept of class itself—helped to define new social groups and shaped conflicts emerging in the postrevolutionary period. Building on these valuable studies, this book's emphasis on practices rather than discourse aims to demonstrate that discourse alone cannot explain the emergence of the new postrevolutionary social and political order. Without denying the power of language, I propose to read and analyze behavior and the *experience* of social life in ways similar to the more familiar analysis of linguistic constructs.[36] The book also contributes a new perspective by focusing on not one social group or institution across a broad period but rather a multiplicity of forces and groups studied over a relatively narrow period.

We know little about the social and cultural history of France during the first decades of the nineteenth century, and we know even less about provincial life during these years. Much of this book focuses on provincial cities, mostly Lyon and Nantes, but with material from other cities as well. Moving beyond Paris brings an important perspective on the evolution of French society and politics after the Revolution. Paris, like every other place, was unique; Parisian trends were not generally representative of national ones.[37] Paris's size and complexity make it less than ideal for the kind of detailed analysis I hope to accomplish here. In addition there are insufficient sources of information on this period because of the 1871 burning of the Hotel de Ville's archives during the Paris Commune. Provincial cities, in contrast, provide an opportunity for analysis on a smaller scale, and they often have incredibly rich, largely untapped resources in their archives and libraries. One recent study opens with the fact that "local history remains an underdeveloped field in Napoleonic historiography."[38] The same could be said of the Restoration. Despite their distinctiveness, provincial cities shared many traits, and the experiences of their inhabitants were more representative of national trends than those of the capital. In bringing to light the details of urban provincial life, this study provides a fresh perspective, from the ground up, of the complex processes involved in restructuring society after Revolution. Because so little is known (and to a certain extent can be known) about provincial life in the first decades of the nineteenth century, the individual chapters provide general information about cultural life and practices in these places. The limited nature of extant sources has left frustrating gaps in our knowledge of the period. I have attempted to fill as many of those gaps as possible, while focusing on the issue of urban social interaction and its relationship to emerging class and gender norms.

As France's "second city," Lyon was an obvious choice as I began my research into provincial city life. I then searched for another city, one that would serve as a valuable contrast to Lyon and whose archives house the type of material needed for this kind of project. Nantes satisfied these criteria. Both Lyon and Nantes played significant roles in French politics, and both made important contributions to the French economy. In 1821, Lyon's population was 131,000, whereas Nantes' was about half that size.[39] Lyon was famous for its silk production and the *canuts*, the thousands of silk workers who lived in and near the city and who staged massive revolts in 1831 and 1834. Nantes' fame came from its position as one of France's busiest ports in the eighteenth century, particularly in the triangular trade with Africa and the Caribbean colonies. With the abolition of the slave trade during the Revolution, and again in 1815, Nantes' economy suffered though French ships continued to transport Africans throughout the 1820s.[40] Of course Nantes, like Lyon, also suffered for political reasons during the Revolution. Both cities were important centers of counterrevolution: Lyon as the capital of southern federalism and Nantes as the nearest big city to the largely rural uprisings of western France.[41] In addition, both cities' inhabitants experienced firsthand the bloody consequences of political division, as some of the worst excesses of the Terror transpired in these places. Local political and economic realities shaped the options available for inhabitants to fill their leisure time and affected the atmosphere of particular locations for socializing and amusement.

The social spaces created by people enjoying cultural activities in these cities provided opportunities for interaction, observation, and categorization among participants. These sorts of everyday activities were important in shaping people's understanding of French society, what Maza has recently termed the "social imaginary," as ordinary people performed their identities in public and watched others as they did so.[42] Such practices contributed to the evolution of postrevolutionary society and culture. Michel de Certeau's influential study *The Practice of Everyday Life* provides a methodological and theoretical synopsis of the idea of practices. Building on the theories of Michel Foucault and Pierre Bourdieu, de Certeau explains that the goal of his work is to treat "everyday practices, 'ways of operating' or doing things" as no longer simply in the "background of social activity."[43] De Certeau's work makes clear the power of cultural practices: seemingly nonproductive activities, such as sitting in a theater or reading a book, create ideas about society that are in large part constitutive of society itself. As Bourdieu's work emphasizes, cultural practices involve more than simply soaking in passively that which is offered.[44] They entail choices about what to consume and often rely upon interaction with others. For Bourdieu, "cultural capital" (a person's familiarity and comfort with certain forms of art, for example) determines and solidifies social status as much as more concrete forms of capital.

Cultural practices also produce knowledge of culture and of society, not just through the subject matter absorbed but also through the experience of seeing oneself and others reacting in various ways. For social identities to have meaning, people must know what they signify. In the wake of the Revolution, the mechanisms and markers through which social distinctions operated had become vague, in part because they existed in a wide range of competing forms—some old, some new. James Scott's work on resistance demonstrates how familiarity with social structures and hierarchies, what he terms "public transcripts," is necessary both to those who wish to maintain hierarchical structures and those who would prefer to dismantle them. The latter make use of "hidden transcripts," which can include "speeches, gestures, and practices that confirm, contradict, or inflect what appears in the public transcript."[45] The spaces or sites in which these hidden transcripts can be articulated and performed are those in which "subordinates" gather, including among others, the working-class tavern, or cabaret.[46] But comprehension of the "public transcript" is a prerequisite for the emergence of any "hidden transcripts." Social spaces and the cultural practices that take place within them create knowledge of society through interaction

among and between the different classes. In the process, they permit ideological constructions, such as "domestic ideology," the "public sphere," "class,"
and other kinds of social identities, to have meaning. A greater understanding of how the new social order functioned made it possible to organize full-
fledged movements seeking to overthrow that order. This improved comprehension helps to explain the Revolution of 1830 as well as the reemergence of
socialism and feminism around the same time.[47]

Urban visibility and display, performance and observation are at the heart
of such experiences and are central to the creation of these new conceptions of
the social order. Scholars in various disciplines have devoted a great deal of attention to the issues of performance and visibility in recent years, debating for
example the nature of "the gaze." Building on Foucault's examination of the
expert's "gaze" turning a prisoner or a psychiatric patient into an object of
study, some feminist scholars have emphasized the way that the male stroller,
the *flâneur,* turns women into objects when he exercises his gaze; others have
argued that women too can exercise the gaze.[48] I would add that "being
watched" is not always as passive as the phrase suggests and that often men
and women alike chose to put themselves on display in public, and they enjoyed the experience. Urban life, in all times and places, is largely about the
enjoyment of watching and being watched.[49] In the early years of the nineteenth century, with social distinctions and the markers of social position and
deference unclear, visibility and observation helped people understand how
their society was supposed to operate and how they were expected act within
it. The spectatorial quality of urban life reinforced and gave meaning to ideological constructs like class, gender, domesticity, and the public sphere.

As much as possible, I use class terms the way they appeared in the early
nineteenth century to express categories that described and differentiated
people's positions in society.[50] No true class consciousness existed this
early in the nineteenth century, and the significance read into terms such
as "peuple" and "bourgeois" was constantly evolving. When I use "working-
class" or the "working classes," I mean literally those in society who had to
work with their hands in order to survive. Contemporaries used similar
terms and distinguished between the "peuple," and the "leisured classes."
Such language suggests a two-tiered system, when in fact French society was
much more complicated. As is often the case, the most complex situation
was that of those in the middle.[51] In this book, I usually include the middle
classes with the "upper" or "leisured" classes because when it came to culture, the middle classes defined themselves against the "popular" classes.

Middle-class men and women were literate and saw themselves as within reach of a leisurely lifestyle; many were already there. However, some toward the bottom of the middle may have actually been much closer to the workers. Writing in the early 1830s, the Saint-Simonian social observers A. Guépin and E. Bonamy divided the population into eight classes: "wealthy *(richesse)*, upper bourgeoisie *(haute bourgeoisie)*, comfortable bourgeois *(bourgeois aisés)*, constrained bourgeois *(bourgeois gênés)*, poor bourgeois *(bourgeois pauvres)*, comfortable workers *(ouvriers aisés)*, poor workers *(ouvriers pauvres)*, [and] miserable workers *(ouvriers misérables)*."[52] This formulation makes clear that class was not yet defined purely in economic terms but along other lines related to lifestyle, education, and family background. The things people did—their everyday practices—defined their class position just as their class position largely determined what they did.

This book has three parts, each with two chapters. The first part treats political festivals, with one chapter on the Napoleonic period and a second one on the Bourbon Restoration. Festivals provide an excellent opportunity to explore the interplay between state and society, as their explicit goal was to communicate the strengths of the political system to as large an audience as possible, and the spectators themselves constituted part of the message. The larger the crowd the more "successful" the festival, as people's presence alone signified their support for the regime, regardless of their actual political views. Festivals allowed both the regimes and the participants to display and build the political and social order, with the different members of French society performing their designated roles. The events staged for various social groups contributed to a growing awareness of the makeup of the social order and the accepted (and expected) political roles of each group. By reading these chapters together, it is possible to draw some interesting comparisons. At Napoleonic festivals, publicly sponsored marriage ceremonies explicitly connected the family and the state, with working-class women as the pivot between the two, whereas in upper-class gatherings little distinguished men's and women's presumed roles. Under the Restoration, women of all classes became central figures at festivals, as they represented model faithful subjects and citizens due to their image as supporters of the Bourbons and of the Church.

Part two of the book moves to theaters, another space in which the social and political order was put on display, both on the stage and off. Its chapters show spectators interacting with both the state, through its censorship and the heavy police presence in theaters, and with the "producers of culture" (playwrights and reviewers) who were working to mold postrevolutionary society through their moralistic tales and their representations of various social groups. Chapter 3 analyzes spectators at Parisian Boulevard theaters where melodramatic plays, which tended to have plot lines that reinforced the concept of birth-based social hierarchies, elicited voluble emotional responses from their audiences. Ostensibly written "for those who cannot read," melodrama appealed to virtually the entire social spectrum, with women appearing as its greatest enthusiasts. In sharing the space of these theaters, audience members acted out the social order while observing a version of it represented on stage. Whereas Chapter 3 focuses on social issues, Chapter 4 returns to politics, as theaters emerged as the site par excellence for expressing political opposition, especially during the Restoration. Provincial theaters became more politicized than Parisian ones because of less effective policing. Spectators in these theaters enacted the political, social, and sexual order as they drew attention to themselves in frequent disorderly episodes. In both these Parisian and provincial contexts, women's presence and behavior in theaters received great attention—particularly their sensitivity (sensibilité), morality, and sexuality.

Part three focuses on urban social life in the provinces. Chapter 5 deals with various kinds of associations, and the last chapter turns to drinking establishments and dancing. Both the Church and the state were involved in regulating the activities that could take place in these spaces; in many cases the two powerful institutions disagreed about what should be permissible. Participants had to negotiate with these two forces and sometimes played them against each other. Associational life represents the most class-specific activity discussed in this book. Rather than providing opportunities for participants to observe the ways in which diverse people behaved in a shared experience, associations allowed particular social groups to develop a collective sense of identity. Salons continued to bring elite men and women together long after the Revolution; clubs and reading rooms brought middle-class men together; and charities allowed women of the upper classes to socialize together while demonstrating their organizational skills and interacting with the "deserving poor." Unlike organizations with a specific membership, drinking establishments had the potential to bring together far more diverse groups of people. However, most cafés drew a predominantly male and bourgeois clientele, whereas cabarets were viewed as working-class spaces.

Dancing, a widespread practice across the social spectrum, also encouraged specific groups to amuse themselves together. The upper classes gathered at formal balls where mothers worked to marry off their daughters, whereas workers spent Sundays dancing in public squares to the sound of a violin. Moral issues became increasingly prevalent with the Restoration, as both religious and secular authorities denounced what they saw as "debauchery" among working-class revelers. Organizing and regulating sexuality became a key feature of these diverse social spaces.

As postrevolutionary social and political structures took shape, the appeal of social mixing began to wane. In the 1820s, middle-class women began to separate themselves from urban popular culture in response to growing fears of the "dangerous classes" and as middle-class men became more politically engaged.[53] According to one historian, "a shift in bourgeois sensibilities... probably occurred in the 1820s." In the wake of romantic glorification of rural traditions, an earlier widespread fear of the peasantry was replaced by growing fears of cities, towns, and suburbs.[54] As a result, middle-class urban dwellers began to avoid the crowded city streets. Maza has also found the 1820s to be a key period in the emergence of bourgeois class consciousness, which she argues was an outgrowth of liberal opposition to the increasingly intransigent Restoration government.[55] At the same time, the separation of elite women from urban public life further intensified class hierarchies as working women's lives increasingly diverged from what was becoming a middle-class norm. To the extent that certain women chose to lead more domestic existences, class animosities caused this transition—not the Revolution or the increasingly voluble rhetoric of domesticity that emerged in its wake, though that discourse contributed to their understanding of class.

Local political and economic factors largely determined how people occupied their leisure time, practices that in turn shaped social distinctions. When the classes and the sexes mingled together as they amused themselves, they had an opportunity to observe and categorize the people around them. These experiences played an integral part in the construction of social hierarchies emerging to replace those brought into question by the Revolution's dismantling of the old order. However, as class and gender norms evolved, opportunities for such interaction became less common. Little by little, regardless of social class, "bourgeois ideals" were replacing aristocratic ones, including attitudes toward women.[56] This evolution meant that male cafés and clubs were slowly replacing salons as gathering places, that women's roles as mothers and homemakers were becoming more

highly valued, and that aristocratic "decadence" was growing less acceptable. It also meant that exclusively male venues for political discussion and
participation were replacing the more ambiguously defined forms of political activity of the Napoleonic and early Restoration periods. At the same
time, the influence of popular culture on workers, whose "simple natures"
left them open to "moral depravity," according to the prize-winning essay
mentioned at the opening of this chapter, had to be kept under control.
Both regimes were aware of the potential for political and social discord to
enliven theater audiences and other social spaces. For this reason, authorities devoted significant efforts to staging political gatherings on *their* terms,
most obviously in the state-sponsored festivals to which we now turn.

# — I —

## Political Festivals

# — 1 —

# Staging the Napoleonic State

Eight months before Napoleon Bonaparte's seizure of power, an administrator in Nantes warned the minister of the interior that ordinary people needed more in the way of festivities than the Directory government had been offering them. The festival tradition that had evolved during the Revolution was failing in its attempt to fill the void left by the dual destruction of the monarchy and the Church. The official counseled:

> The people need religion and especially spectacle; only with festivals is it possible to accustom them to wise institutions. In abolishing those with religious prestige, it is necessary to entice them with others that are more suitable to their vision, that will attract people by their novelty, and that are satisfying to the eyes. . . . The *fêtes décadaires* (the equivalent of Sundays in the revolutionary calendar) are not being celebrated here. . . . The artisan who is obliged to take off from work on the *décadi* needs to be occupied by some kind of spectacle, otherwise the day's free time is a burden for him.[1]

The authorities in Paris took his warning seriously. A note written by someone at the ministry stated that the letter should be read at the meeting of the Second Division, and the minutes of the meeting confirm that the issue of *fêtes décadaires* was brought up.[2] Although the Directory government recognized that it had failed to satisfy people's desire for "spectacle," it was unable to find a solution. Napoleon made that one of his primary goals, and in large part he succeeded where the Directory failed. Allowing spectacles that brought "religious prestige" contributed to his success.[3]

Napoleonic festivals brought back some Old Regime traditions, continued some aspects of revolutionary ceremonies, and also introduced some innovations. Continuities included the perceived need for unanimity, as well as the specific activities incorporated into the events: masses, parades, speeches, games, free food and wine, and officially sponsored wedding ceremonies. One change that came with the Revolution was the development of propaganda in festivals. One scholar has argued that it is anachronistic to talk of a propagandistic intention in the Old Regime: "Love and respect for the king were givens then."[4] Though this may be oversimplifying somewhat, it is true that after 1789, and continuing into the Napoleonic period, festivals became the primary tool for disseminating messages about the legitimacy and goodwill of the government, neither of which would be taken for granted as they had largely been prior to the Revolution. The Revolution of 1789 introduced much innovation that was later rejected, but the "tradition" of republican festivals remained embedded in memory and myth during the Napoleonic period and beyond.[5] Whereas revolutionary festivals focused on the sovereignty of the people, Napoleonic ones centered on the sovereign himself. As Lynn Hunt put it: "Eventually he replaced Marianne altogether and became himself the personification of the French nation."[6] Unabashedly directed at glorifying the image of the emperor, festivals also satisfied the public's desire for amusement and entertainment, for a break from day-to-day routines, a function they had filled long before 1789.

In an effort to explore how Napoleonic politics reverberated on a local level, this chapter analyzes material from Lyon and Nantes and also incorporates examples from Rouen because of some particularly rich sources dealing with that city. During the Revolution, Rouen remained relatively moderate, and thus its inhabitants suffered less than in the "federalist" bastion of Lyon or the "counterrevolutionary" Vendée with which Nantes was associated.[7] Rouen's proximity to Paris also distinguishes it from the more outlying and thus more independently oriented cities farther from the capital. Despite references to the "Rouennais" as a separate group, few expressions of local autonomy ever arose, and local political allegiances mirrored national and Parisian ones.[8] In the other two cities, a stronger sense of regional identity manifested itself and often overshadowed national political affiliations.[9] Particularly "lyonnais" or "nantais" concerns arose with greater frequency in those cities than in Rouen. Lyon's rich tradition of local popular and religious festivals also affected the significance and atmosphere of official Napoleonic celebrations. At *vogues* (dances organized by the youth of a particular community), religious events, and dances set up outside cabarets, men and women gathered to solidify local allegiances, to express their religious fervor, and to amuse themselves while perhaps forming various kinds of personal alliances.[10] Nantes had such traditions as well, though the outright warfare in western France had brought virtually all forms of social life to a standstill since the early 1790s.[11]

Regardless of the local variables that need to be accounted for, Napoleonic festivals followed a standard pattern nationally as the regime gave detailed instructions to local officials about how to organize the events. During both the Consulate (1799–1804) and the First Empire (1804–1814), officials devoted significant resources and efforts to staging festivals that would spark enthusiasm among the populace. At the same time, however, imperial authorities believed that too many festivals could be dangerous: they were expensive and they could encourage laziness. As the minister of religion explained in an 1806 circular sent to prefects around France, "The wholesome principle of time management must preside over the organization of festivals: distributed with thrift, they impress on the love of work a new impulsion; they renew energy and stimulate the nation's industry by providing the well-off middle classes *(la médiocrité aisée)* with an honest occasion to display some innocent luxury."[12] Festivals would stimulate people to work harder for the good of the nation, but they had to take place within well-defined limits. Controlled amusement was the ideal, with the stress on "control." As under previous regimes, this control included careful delineation of what took place and when, along with attention to the message to be communicated.

These festivals brought men and women from all classes into the public arena to observe staged manifestations of the virtues of their government, and to express their support for, and less commonly their opposition to, the regime in power. In the process, they had an opportunity to observe each other and to experience a variety of possible responses to the spectacle before their eyes—from unambiguous adoration to utter skepticism, though most probably fell between those two extremes. Regardless of their political views and level of acceptance or rejection of the government, participants at public festivals found an opportunity for amusement, nourishment, and sometimes even outright cash payments. Historical analysis of festivals provides important insights into political culture (as expressed in symbols, rhetoric, and staged events), popular reactions to particular regimes, and the mechanisms used to bring politics down to the people. And, as this chapter makes clear, the "people" included women.

Napoleon Bonaparte stands out for his efforts to limit women's public and political roles. The Napoleonic Code curtailed women's rights and cemented their subordinate status in legal terms; and Napoleon himself, in one of his characteristic statements, insisted that women "are nothing more than machines for producing children."[13] He certainly did not like women who "meddled" in politics, as the example of Madame de Staël's forced exile illustrates.[14] Despite such efforts, official festivals necessarily incorporated women into politicized events, as they had during the revolutionary and prerevolutionary periods. One of the Bonapartist regime's methods of convincing women of their domestic duties was to bring them into politicized public spaces—such as a town square filled with officials—and to convey the rewards to be reaped from leading virtuous lives focused on their duties as wives and mothers. This was far from the only function of festivals, however. They also spread messages about Napoleon's successes, his goodwill, and the unanimous support of the public for him. Of course women were among the desired recipients of these messages as well. The extent to which the government strove to convince women to participate actively at official festivals demonstrates that the emperor recognized women's role in his larger goal of creating and maintaining order. The pragmatic Napoleon realized that women's presence at festivals served his purposes: they played an important symbolic role in connecting individuals to the state through the family, and their support for the regime could prove useful as they would raise devoted citizen-soldiers. Clearly expressed gender norms and images of strong families helped build the Napoleonic state.[15]

Napoleon saw women as important enough politically and for his goal of maintaining order that in his carefully orchestrated festivals he made sure to find ways to encourage women from across the social spectrum to attend and even to participate actively. In attending festivals, women assisted the regime in at least three ways: they curbed disorderly tendencies among men; they encouraged higher rates of male attendance; and if they were won over by the propagandistic messages of the festival, then they might influence the men in their families to support the regime as well. All three were important to creating a stable political and social order. Of course women had no direct political voice; but even the men who supposedly did— through the vote—had little real impact.[16] Nonetheless, women's support for the regime could take on political significance, and encouraging their participation at festivals both fostered that support and made it visible to everyone in attendance.

Napoleonic festivities incorporated different social groups in different ways and provided them with distinct forms of entertainment and public roles to fulfill. Festivals thus put the Napoleonic social order on display and linked it to the political order. Elite men and women played two primary functions in Napoleonic festivals: as speakers at official ceremonies and as those in attendance at formal balls and other types of upper-class socializing. Important visitors to the city received prominent women, and women "garnished" elite gatherings, while putting themselves and their *toilettes* on display among others like themselves. Though discussions of their beauty and their charms may have distinguished women from men, in these elite venues both sexes played similar roles: to cement relationships between diverse groups of notables whose support was vital to Napoleon's success as a leader and to solidify images of that support. Working-class women participated in Napoleonic festivals, too, though differently than women of the upper classes. Their most prominent role came when they appeared as brides in officially sponsored marriage ceremonies. In appearing on stage as models of virtuous women ready to devote their lives to their families, these women personified the connection between order, family life, and the state. Women's appearance in public emphasized their roles in society not as women per se but as wives and mothers on the one hand and as courtiers on the other.

Looking back on revolutionary festivals from the perspective of the mid-nineteenth century, Jules Michelet believed that women and children were an indispensable element. In her influential study of revolutionary festivals, Mona Ozouf makes the case that "for Michelet, one of the major virtues of the Revolution was that it brought women and children into public life, thus providing a heart in an otherwise heartless world. . . . [He] demands that the national festivals should include something for women and children, apart from the gloomy church where a 'moral night' also reigns."[17] Anticlericalism aside, Michelet judged the success of festivals by the extent to which they brought women into the public. Like Michelet, Napoleon viewed political festivals and their specific ceremonies as providing an alternative to religious festivals, one that cemented his citizens' attachment to the state as opposed to the newly returned Catholic Church. Ozouf continues her discussion of Michelet by emphasizing the fact that for him, "women lent charm to the Revolution." The organizers of festivals in the postrevolutionary period seem to have agreed on this point. Napoleonic festivals created spaces for large crowds to gather and observe both the spectacle of the state announcing its successes and the image of a diverse populace responding to that message.

## Attracting Crowds

In 1807, the mayor of Nantes received encouragement from the prefect to be zealous in organizing activities that would draw large crowds. "[For] public gaiety [to] express itself, . . . it is simply necessary to bring together many people with public amusements; and the sentiments of admiration and appreciation for the good deeds of his majesty, which must be in everyone's hearts, can only spread. It is not necessary to spend large sums of money: free performances, evening illuminations, orchestras distributed along the promenades and in public squares will suffice to attract large crowds; widespread public joy will do the rest and will distinguish this festival."[18] The primary goal was to have as many people as possible participate, and Nantes' counterrevolutionary reputation made this even more essential than elsewhere. The larger the crowd, the stronger and more widely broadcast the message because the spectators themselves and the image of mass public support they offered were part of that message. Such events were worth the effort involved in organizing and policing them because sponsoring dances and theatrical performances was among the most effective means for authorities to ensure a good turnout at public festivals, whose draw had been diminishing since the latter years of the Revolution. Under the Empire, Napoleon's prefects wanted to ensure that the same would not be true for the regime they served.

A variety of events brought together the populace to celebrate the accomplishments of their government, but fewer than had been the case during the Revolution. Soon after the coup of 18 Brumaire Year VIII (9 November 1799), which brought Napoleon Bonaparte to power as "First Consul," the provisional consuls reduced the numerous revolutionary festivals down to only two: 14 July, to commemorate the fall of the Bastille; and 10 August, the date of the overthrow of the monarchy in 1792. According to one scholar, the decision was based on the recognition that official festivals were "falling into disrepute."[19] It was hoped that limiting the numbers of annual festivals would increase their draw. However, the problems continued: an apparent lack of interest in *fêtes publiques* served as evidence of continuing distrust in the government.[20] With the Empire, two new annual festivals replaced those of the Consulate. The first of these was "Saint Napoleon's Day" on 15 August. This date, Napoleon's birthday, conveniently corresponded to the Catholic holiday of Assumption as well as the Old Regime holiday "le vœu de Louis XIII," which dated from 1638, when the king wanted to honor the

Virgin Mary and express his gratitude to her for granting his wish for an heir to the throne.[21] The anniversary of Napoleon's coronation in early December was the other annual festival, and various other events were commemorated when suitable, such as success in battle or an imperial wedding, birth, or baptism.[22] One obvious date missing from this list is 14 July; after the formation of the First Empire in December 1804, the anniversary of the storming of the Bastille ceased to be celebrated, a change that symbolized a more general transition. As one historian has expressed it: "the dynastic festival replaced the political festival; diversion took the place of commemoration."[23] The glorification of Napoleon is especially visible in the festivities marking a visit by the emperor to a particular city. In an engraving depicting Napoleon's arrival in Strasbourg in 1806, an enormous triumphal arch topped by a statue of Napoleon majestically seated on his horse dominates the scene (Figure 1.1). Near the front of the picture, the emperor and empress receive homage from local authorities as large crowds of onlookers gather around.

Regardless of the event being celebrated, Napoleonic festivals generally followed the same pattern: speeches, parades, and various ceremonies in the morning, followed by games and distributions of food, free theater performances, and finally dances, set up in various locations, that lasted well into the night. The variety of activities permitted an entire city's inhabitants to partake in the festivities, if they so chose. Taking an explicitly propagandistic approach, official festivals both encouraged the populace to support the regime and simultaneously functioned as proof of that support through the large crowds they attracted. Thus, much of the work of indoctrination was carried out by the festival participants themselves. In all cases, women were present and helped to encourage men to attend as well, an important role in itself as every effort was made to ensure the largest number of participants possible.

One goal of Napoleonic festivals was to replace spontaneous and local events, which brought competing allegiances to the surface, with more official, controlled forms of celebration.[24] In an essay on military culture under Napoleon, Alan Forrest devotes attention to the symbolism used during early festivals, which he says "emphasized the heroism of the soldier and the glory of the cause, lionizing the person of Napoleon." In the aftermath of Brumaire, he argues, "popular spontaneity was immediately downgraded, and with it the role played by the common people."[25] While focusing on military valor, these early festivals tended to put officials, not ordinary

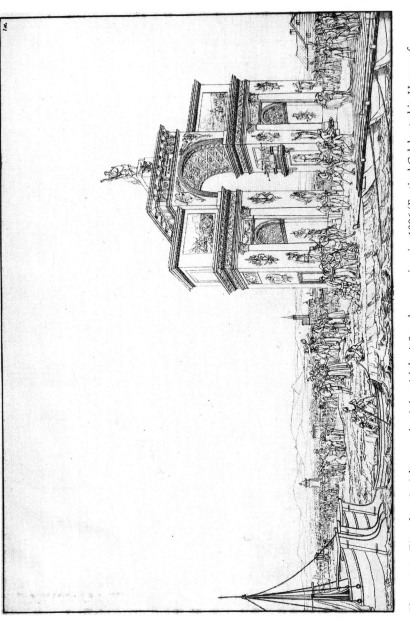

**Figure 1.1.** *Fêtes données à leurs majestés impériales à Strasbourg en janvier 1806* (Festival Celebrated in Honor of Their Imperial Majesties in Strasbourg in January 1806 [street scene]). Gravure de Guérin, d'après Six. Photo courtesy of the Bibliothèque Nationale de France, Paris.

people, in the spotlight. As the regime evolved, it used a variety of means to draw attention to national festivities. No detail was too small to escape imperial notice: in 1811 the government even went so far as to instruct printers on the appropriate typeface to use on calendars. Only the four religious holidays of Ascension, Assumption, All Saints Day, and Christmas, along with Saint Napoleon's Day, which was held on Assumption, and the anniversary of the coronation on the first Sunday in December, were to be printed in boldface, capital letters. "All the other festival days, even those we call *patronales* (patron saints' days), will be confused with the ordinary days of the week . . . and printed in the same characters; we forbid any distinctive sign designed to draw attention to them."[26] The only events deserving recognition were national festival days when everyone in the nation would, in theory at least, be sharing in a common experience that was carefully organized by local authorities to avoid disorder or any potential subversion of the official message.

A similar confusion of the superficial with the substantive occurred in the imperial desire for a large and, needless to say, attentive crowd at these scripted events. Nothing was better than a throng of obedient onlookers to demonstrate Napoleonic legitimacy. Journalists and authorities alike reported with satisfaction that their cities' inhabitants had been only too happy to line streets, press into ceremonial rooms, and line up for free food and wine, all for the glory of the Empire. Ending the day with fireworks and dancing indicated a city's wholehearted gratitude for all that the regime had brought. In a speech given at Rouen's festival marking Napoleon's coronation, the prefect explained the apparent widespread support for the regime as due to the emperor's "re-establishment of interior peace and that of the continent, that of religion, the creation of a code of law, the reconstitution of the Empire, and all the benefits which have been the result." The presence of such large crowds assembled together as well as the physical press of all those bodies reinforced the appearance of unanimity. The newspaper emphasized the fact that with the variety of events, including distributions of food and wine, "everyone was able to participate in the festival."[27] Such satisfactory accounts, exaggerated as they may have been, could only bring praise to their cities.

Lest one conclude that in a regime that glorified military bravery, women were brushed aside in these celebrations, one should note how many activities depended upon a female presence. Dancing, for instance, figured prominently at these affairs.[28] As one contemporary looking back on life in another provincial city stated, "Under the Consulate and during the Empire there was a good deal of dancing in Toulon."[29] Dancing symbolized the people's happiness, as though people could not dance if they were not sincerely joyful. At Nantes' June 1811 festival celebrating the baptism of Napoleon's son, orchestras were set up along all the promenades and squares of the city. The prefect proudly reported that "orchestras were positioned on the promenades and public squares of Nantes where dances continued until dawn. Everywhere there were abundant crowds . . . without the slightest trouble."[30] The mayor of Rouen informed the prefect of similar celebrations in his city to mark the birth of the boy. "Dances . . . formed spontaneously in different neighborhoods. The peuple indulged in noisy celebrations all night long, which we can realistically consider as a heartfelt expression of joy."[31] Women's presence in such circumstances not only increased the size of the crowd in itself but also encouraged men to attend these ostensibly "spontaneous" celebrations.

In addition to dances, festivities that drew large crowds of men and women included distributions of food and wine, especially during years when food shortages arose. At Nantes' 1805 celebrations marking Napoleon's coronation, 2,800 metric pounds of bread and 2,800 liters of wine were distributed to the poor at specific locations around the city; then orchestras paid by the city performed music in public squares for several hours in the early evening.[32] To prepare for the December 1813 festival for the anniversary of the coronation, the mayor of Nantes sent cards that gave holders the right to a three-pound loaf of bread to various "Dames de Charité," who were in turn to distribute the cards at the homes of the impoverished people they aided.[33] This system was part of an attempt to allow for an orderly distribution of food at a time of particular hardship. It also relied upon and put on display common assumptions about women's "natural" roles in charitable efforts.

Free admission to theaters, another event that presumed women would be among the participants, required even more careful planning than providing food and drink. Tickets were distributed in advance to avoid overcrowding at the theaters, which typically staged the free performances on the eve of the festival.[34] Everything was done to assure an incident-free evening. The success of such efforts in January 1805 warranted comment in a nantais newspaper: "In order not to disturb the class of citizens that normally fills the theater, the [free] performance began at 5:00 and ended at 8:00. Plays suitable for stimulating gaiety were chosen: people laughed a

lot; but they were peaceful, and not a sound, not a single outcry interrupted the pleasures of the evening."[35] Allowing spectators to attend the
theater for free permitted those who normally could not afford such an
experience to enjoy an activity that was otherwise closed to them. However, such an event also opened the door to potential disorderly behavior,
as the large group inside a closed space served as a ready audience for the
regime's detractors to make their views known. Local officials were aware
of such possibilities, and they did their best to control the crowds, including ending the performances earlier than was the case when spectators
paid for their seats.

Authorities' strategies to attract crowds varied depending on the situation at hand and the resources available to them. In 1813, the prefect of the
Loire-Inférieure wrote to the mayor of Nantes to make the surprising sug-
gestion that he put an end to the *spectacles gratis.* "I think it would be expe-
dient to abolish the free theatrical performance. Staged on the eve of the
festival, it loses its connection to the event; held the same day, it presents the
inconvenience of taking away part of the public and diminishing the concourse and the movement in the squares and on the streets: I think it would
be preferable to use the cost of the free performance [to add to] the distribution of free food and drink, which provides real assistance to poor families."[36] Perhaps because of the difficulties faced by the nation in late 1813,
crowd size was diminishing, and everything had to be done to ensure that
the largest numbers of people possible filled the streets so as to provide visible evidence for the continued widespread support for the regime. The prefect apparently believed that food and wine would do a better job of this
than the theater. The period of crisis made the priorities with regard to
staging festivals clearer than they were otherwise: first in importance was a
large, happy crowd. Authorities recognized the power of ritual, the strength
of a message delivered to an enthusiastic audience whose reaction reinforced and provided proof of the validity of any official statement about the
successes of the regime.

Official coverage of festivals and other moments when people gathered to
manifest their support for the regime emphasized the size, diversity, and fervor of the crowds. Napoleon's visit to Rouen in 1810 included a tour of a velvet factory *(manufacture de velours)* in the working-class neighborhood of
Saint-Sever.[37] The newspaper described the give-and-take between the emperor and the crowds: "The large numbers of workers who live in the neighborhood of Saint-Sever pressed in front of His Majesty, whose cherished

features could be observed as long as desired and without any obstacle. His Majesty received several addresses, and responded in a most affectionate manner, which further brought out the delirium of love and of gratitude of the multitude that lined his path."[38] Such an event served two purposes: to make the emperor appear truly interested in the concerns of all his subjects, rich or poor, male or female, young or old; and to allow spectators to express their enthusiasm while surrounded by throngs of other onlookers doing the same thing.

These onlookers were the ones who truly determined the makeup and significance of these social spaces. When officials worked to have large and "joyful" crowds appear in city squares, they were opening up possibilities for these men and women to shape the experience for participants more so than the staged events. This was (and remains) the nature of festivals: to be "successful," they needed to allow large, potentially unruly crowds to gather and to amuse themselves freely. However, this "freedom" also created spaces for dissenting voices to be heard. Napoleon risked such expressions of dissent because he knew he enjoyed support among the popular classes who composed these crowds. He was more anxious about the people he believed likely to support the Bourbons.

## Engaging the Elite

In May 1810, Napoleon and his new bride, Marie-Louise, went on a tour of several cities to introduce the citizens of France to their empress. Included in their itinerary was a visit to Rouen, an increasingly important manufacturing town, particularly for textiles. Among the numerous celebrations staged to honor the couple was a gathering held at the chamber of commerce, where their majesties had an opportunity to examine the products of Rouen's *fabriques,* which were laid out around their thrones. Then a group of thirty "jeunes demoiselles" all dressed in white entered the room and presented the empress with "a rich basket filled with samples of [the city's] most beautiful products of industrial manufacturing." One of the young ladies read a poem to the emperor who, according to the local newspaper, "deigned to listen with kindness."[39] He then presented the girl with a pearl necklace. Afterward, the demoiselles performed a little dance, as their families watched with pride and joy. The carefully staged event made Rouen's elite families, especially the women, feel as though their emperor cared about them, and at the same time it put young women in the spotlight.

Why did a man whose regime rested above all on victory in battle bother to take the time to attend, and at least pretend to enjoy, such an event? And why put young women in such a prominent place? To answer these questions, we need to reconsider Napoleonic politics and attitudes toward women.

Events staged for upper-class men and women worked to garner their support by allowing them to display themselves in luxurious, even aristocratic atmospheres while hobnobbing with the political and social elites of their cities. As one historian described it, Napoleon "wished to rally to him those who were dissatisfied [with the regime] . . . especially royalists."[40] When Bonaparte and Josephine spent two weeks in Lyon in January 1802, they made sure to attend the theater, and commentators drew particular attention to the women present. Their "dresses were sumptuous; all the ladies, even Josephine, were dressed in silk and velvet fabrics manufactured in Lyon."[41] Civic and national pride came together during these visits. When the couple returned in 1805, now emperor and empress, a courtlike atmosphere surrounded them as the most elite segments of society gathered to present their homage to the newly crowned monarchs.[42] One observer mentioned that "the lyonnais ladies making up the relief *(secours)* committee had the honor of being admitted to a reception with the empress from whom they received the friendliest welcome."[43] One of Josephine's ladies-in-waiting commented on the beauty of the women who attended a ball honoring their majesties at the Théâtre de Terreaux, usually referred to as the Grand Théâtre. "The lyonnais ladies, generally very pretty, were dressed with a great deal of taste and elegance; it was clear that they had spent large sums on their *toilettes* to pass in review before their sovereign, and this expense was not wasted, as the Emperor was very amiable."[44] Women were an integral part of these events as Bonaparte worked to encourage local notables to feel connected to his regime, an important aspect of his larger effort to construct a stable, orderly society.[45] Elite women participated in and observed gatherings that permitted them to feel connected to the "royal" family, including formal balls and other gatherings (Figure 1.2). Napoleon clearly felt it was worth his time to nurture this sense of attachment on the part of the sex meant only for "producing babies," even though these events probably bored him.[46]

Wealthy women in Rouen also relished the opportunity to mingle with "royalty" when Napoleon and Marie-Louise visited that city in 1810 as part of a trip designed to allow the foreign-born empress to become acquainted

**Figure 1.2.** *Fêtes données à leurs majestés impériales à Strasbourg en janvier 1806* (Festival Celebrated in Honor of Their Imperial Majesties in Strasbourg in January 1806 [ballroom scene]). Gravure de Guérin, d'après Six. Photo courtesy of the Bibliothèque Nationale de France, Paris.

with the country whose leader she had just married. Local officials did not fail in their efforts to bring off the visit with suitable éclat: fireworks, balls, and illuminations all figured in their plans. In the course of emphasizing the perfection of the events and the utter joy of participants, the *Journal de Rouen* provided a general account of the festivities. For example, the newspaper described the regal entry in which their majesties appeared at a ball surrounded by great dignitaries and followed by city officials, after which they, along with the king and queen of Westphalia (Napoleon's brother and sister-in-law), sat on thrones at one end of the room. Some of those in attendance then danced a few rounds, before being joined by members of the imperial family, who

> danc[ed] a few steps with each of the dancers in the midst of applause from all the spectators who were unable to contain their understandable gaiety.
>
> After this dance, His Majesty the Emperor stepped down from his throne . . . and slowly crossed the room addressing a few words to each of the ladies. His august wife at his side also spoke to several ladies. Cries of "Vive l'Empereur! Vive l'Imperatrice!" could be heard coming from all sides of the room, and it was in the midst of all the expression of general rapture that their majesties retired.[47]

According to this account from a local newspaper, all of the guests were enraptured; they all called out enthusiastically as they gloried in the presence of their beloved monarch and his spouse. The journalist made a point of emphasizing the attention the emperor paid to the women in attendance as he and his new bride spoke individually to each lady at the ball. Napoleon apparently did a good job of charming these women, prompting attendees to proclaim "Long live the Emperor!"

Thanks to some unusually rich material preserved by their descendants, extensive records exist detailing some bourgeois women's reactions to this visit, accounts that were not always as glowingly positive as those in the press. Amélie Vitet, a young woman from a prominent Rouennais manufacturing family, recounted her experiences during the imperial couple's visit in a letter she wrote to her husband, a doctor in Paris. At the opening of her letter she describes the disappointment felt by *"un peuple immense"* that lined the streets of Rouen in the hope of seeing the emperor who stayed inside his carriage as he passed them at a fast trot. She herself saw little from the apartment of a friend where they had waited "patiently," implying perhaps that the boisterous crowds below had been less patient. Then she explained that her dissatisfaction was well compensated that evening when she attended the ball organized by the city in honor of the visitors. "We arrived very early and were well positioned to see even the slightest movements that the Emperor and Empress made. And me, I especially had twice the happiness because I was dancing . . . when the Empress chose to join in and imagine the happiness of your wife who held at the same time the hands of the empress and the king of Westphalia."[48] The courtlike atmosphere and the presence of "royalty" impressed this bourgeois woman above all. Napoleon was a master of "giving the people what they want" and clearly "the people" included women. These women's political significance came from their social position, their role in making visible Napoleon's acceptance among local elites. Recognizing that women's views could be as important as men's, the emperor hoped to convince the wives and daughters of his "notables" to support his regime by staging events that flattered and impressed them, a tactic that generally worked.

That said, it was impossible to satisfy everyone all the time. Vitet added in her letter to her husband: "Since I told you about our joys, I must also speak of our displeasure." The day before the emperor's actual arrival, the theater had been prepared for him, because everyone expected him then. In the semidarkness of the theater, she and her group waited for three hours just to be told to go home; the emperor was not coming after all.[49] Even a gifted administrator and strategist like Napoleon could not orchestrate these official tours with precision, but of course such shortcomings do not appear in the official coverage of the emperor's visit.

Unfortunately for Napoleon and his unwilling bride, these visits may have only sparked greater disparaging conversation about the couple among their detractors, as few seemed to like the new empress.[50] In memoirs written later in her life, Adélaïde Bauche, a teenager in 1810, who did not go herself because she and her family were ardent royalists, reflected on the ball that Vitet attended.[51] "People said that [Marie-Louise] asked all the ladies whom she honored by addressing them: 'Do you like the countryside?' And we anti-imperialists laughed a great deal at her *accent circonflêxe* [sic] and her laconic manner. People cited some caustic reflections made by the emperor provoked by the naïve responses of certain ladies whose language contradicted their brilliant attire."[52] Her informant was evidently less than impressed by the imperial couple. In addition to her family's political leanings, Bauche had other reasons to dislike both the emperor and his new wife: like many women of her age and class, she felt great sympathy for Josephine when Napoleon divorced her after she had been unable to produce an heir to the throne. "She had been generally loved. Everyone felt sorry for her. For me, I took this affair to heart as though it had been personal. I loved Josephine before her misfortune; I loved her even more after and the Emperor became odious to me."[53] Another royalist woman who left her memoirs expressed similar views toward Josephine: "She proved that a villainous *(scélérat)* husband can have a worthy *(digne)* and virtuous wife."[54] Sympathy for Josephine gave women (and men) who opposed the Napoleonic regime further ammunition to attack the leader and his character. Though such views were far from what the regime hoped to instill through such events, these women's comments demonstrate a level of political engagement that Napoleon's efforts to win over women suggest he himself recognized. As would be expected, the official coverage provides no trace of the derisory tone contained in Bauche's version of the event or even the complaints voiced by Vitet. Despite their differences in perspective, however, all three accounts leave no doubt that elite women were seen and saw themselves as central to the activities held in honor of the emperor. Elite women's views counted in efforts to build public opinion in support of the regime.

The venues in which elites gathered as part of Napoleonic festivals included theaters, city hall, and the prefecture, spaces that could be controlled more easily than the open-air festivities at which the lower classes drank and danced the night away. Their interiors were also luxuriously decorated to provide suitable backdrops for the expensive *toilettes* of the participants. Napoleonic officials strove to provide upper-class women and men with an experience that would both solidify their attachment to the regime and minimize the social and political differences among the diverse elites whom Napoleon hoped to gather around him in an undifferentiated way. Whether or not they succeeded in winning over the hearts and minds of these men and women is difficult to say, but officials made every effort to do so. Even the proto-military dictator recognized the importance of public opinion, particularly among these influential men and women who could shape conditions on a local level.[55]

## Marriage Ceremonies: Connecting Family and State

Methods of incorporating working-class women and men into Napoleonic festivities were naturally quite different from those used to make elite women feel connected to the regime. Working-class women numbered among the spectators of many of the events staged: they danced and celebrated in various ways, and there are examples of soldiers' widows being organized to parade through city streets.[56] However, the most prominent role working women played in Napoleonic festivals was their appearance as brides in officially sponsored wedding ceremonies. At these events, typically held the morning of a festival day, one or several couples selected by local authorities gathered on a platform and took their marriage vows in public. Speeches glorified Napoleon's generosity and positioned the couple as a model of virtuous behavior and dutiful citizenship.

The December 1808 festivities celebrating the anniversary of Napoleon's coronation included publicly staged weddings of young couples who also received dowries from their cities. Propagandistic speeches preceded the ceremonies. In Rouen, Monsieur Remy-Taillefesse, *officier public,* made the following comments to the couple about to be married. The linking of personal morality and imperial politics could not have been more explicit.

> The ceremony that brings us together . . . having the goal of honoring and recompensing virtue, presents the double advantage of diffusing happy influences on morals, and at the same time, adding a new degree of interest in the solemnity of a day destined to commemorate a celebrated battle [Austerlitz] and a memorable event [Napoleon's coronation]; an event that, in reestablishing on ancient and solid bases the system of government, returned France with a burst to the lofty position that she should occupy, . . . having repaired numerous disasters and reestablished order where confusion reigned; four years have passed since the day when the brilliant and majestic ceremony placed on the throne the august Monarch who governs us; this glorious epoch . . . must be marked by a national festival and by homage paid to virtue. At this moment in the principal places of the Empire, virginal crowns are being bestowed to young girls who stand out for their prudence [*sagessee*], for the purity of their morals.[57]

Despite the length of his first sentence (even with large sections omitted!), the official spoke with clarity about the goals of this event: while drawing attention to the emperor's successes and the resulting glory of France, his speech also spread a message about the benefits to be reaped from leading a life of virtue and obedience. In addition, he drew attention to the fact that the woman was on display, and it was her virtuous behavior that made her an appropriate choice for this spectacle: "This preference that honors you, Mademoiselle, and presents you for all to see as a model young person of your sex, prescribes that in the future you will also be a model wife and mother."[58] She was the central feature of this part of the festival: all eyes were on her as an example to follow. One could contrast this role as wife and mother with the more symbolic use of women as living statues in revolutionary festivals, and with later images of Marianne during the Second and Third Republics.[59] The Napoleonic regime had dispensed with such ephemeral symbols and replaced them with a no less symbolic and politicized kind of realism.

The speaker then reiterated official views of women's and wives' ideal behavior. Once again, devotion to duty carried the most importance.

> Born with a happy penchant for that which is beneficial, accustomed since your childhood to fulfilling your duties, you will faithfully complete the task that prepares you for your new Etat; henceforth dependent upon and under the jurisdiction of a spouse who will be worthy of you, because he knew how to touch your heart, prudent *(sage)* and submissive wife, you will often rely as support for your principles upon the advice dictated by the prudence of this husband, or even better, a single sentiment, a single will will steer you both, having for a goal the accomplishment of your duties and for a result your mutual happiness.[60]

Such sentimental speeches presented an ideal image of marriage and of the roles husband and wife should play, just as the festival as a whole communicated an ideal image of the regime and of French society, as well as the roles ruler and ruled were to play. In both arenas, from the emperor to the male head of household, the lines of authority were clear, and they were to remain unquestioned.

Publicly staged weddings had a long history in France. A fashionable activity of the 1760s was for wealthy visitors to the countryside to attend *fêtes de la rose,* rustic ceremonies that brought together the prettiest girl in a village, the *rosière,* and her groom, who received a dowry from the local lord.[61] These were profoundly local celebrations, which the revolutionary government would standardize and nationalize, as such ceremonies were part of the activities during revolutionary festivals as well. Among the events staged at the Festival of the Federation at Mont-Geneviève (near Nancy) in July 1790 were "baptisms, weddings, even endowments for poor marriageable girls!"[62] In her work on revolutionary political culture, Lynn Hunt contrasts the early and later stages of the Revolution, arguing that beginning in August 1793 revolutionary festivals increasingly represented women in "distinctly motherly roles."[63] During the Directory, it appears that weddings had lost their prominence in festivals. One document described the Fête des Epoux in Rouen on 10 Floréal Year VI (29 April 1798) as "celebrated very simply in the courtyard of the town hall."[64] Under Napoleon, however, such events became a central part of festivals, more so than during either the revolutionary period or the Restoration. Despite the new system into which they had been integrated, the ceremonies retained a connection to their old-regime roots, evidenced by the fact that authorities still sometimes referred to the bride as a *rosière*.[65] However, the benevolent seigneur became Napoleon himself as represented by local authorities, who bestowed upon the couples dowries of between 600 and 1,100 francs. The prominence of these events, as well as the expense involved, suggests that the emperor saw such ceremonies as an effective method for relaying his desired message about the benevolence of his regime and the rewards to be reaped from devoting oneself to the nation. For women, such devotion took the form of being supportive wives and mothers.

The changing criteria used in selecting brides and grooms give insight into gender (and class) norms as well as the evolving priorities of the Bonapartist regime. Early in the period, grooms had to be veterans; the longer their service, the more likely they were to receive this honor. This emphasis on military service reflects recognition on the part of Napoleonic authorities that resistance to conscription represented a serious threat to the regime. They no doubt hoped that by glorifying veterans in this way, conscripts would be more likely to fulfill their duties.[66] Among the most important traits for grooms were their bravery, courage, and service to the nation. For women, the single most crucial issue was their moral status and respectability, though a connection to a fallen soldier helped too.[67] Toward the end of the Empire, particularly in Lyon, authorities increasingly searched for brides and grooms who contributed to the city's economic well-being, primarily through their roles as silk workers. This change probably stemmed from authorities' realization that with support for the wars growing thin and the economic situation worsening, it was better to express gratitude to productive workers rather than draw yet more attention to the dire military situation.

Finding suitable candidates was often quite difficult. The president of the committee responsible for selecting the couples to be married in Lyon on the festival day marking Napoleon's coronation complained that "none of my colleagues wanted to, or more accurately they did not dare to, designate individuals deserving of such a privilege; [they were] afraid of being mistaken, not about [the girls'] indigence, but about their morality." Poverty was visible everywhere; virtuous behavior was less so. Forced to name someone, he suggested two young women: Marie Nachery, *jardinière* (gardener) from Perrache (a working-class neighborhood), a seventeen-year-old orphan engaged to marry twenty-three-year-old François Ruidant, who was also a *jardinier;* the other was Jeanne Regnaud, an *ouvrière en soie* (silk worker) who was twenty-three years old and lived in Perrache, too, along with her mother. Her brother, a soldier, had not been heard from for a long time and was thought dead, a fact that made her even more attractive as a bride. She was to marry Martin Follet, *faiseur de bas* (stocking maker) aged thirty-three, who lived at the same address.[68] The fact that the future bride and groom lived at the same address, though perhaps in different apartments, did not shed a negative light on their moral uprightness.

Similar problems arose in Nantes, as evidenced by a letter the mayor sent to the prefect discussing the results of his search for *une fille sage* to be married by the city on 6 December 1807 (the anniversary of Napoleon's coronation). The woman he found, Jeanne Louise Hucet, was twenty-three years old and he asserted, "The information I have procured about her conduct has been very favorable." She was to marry François Perrotte, a veteran from the imperial army who, "though sixty years of age, has maintained all the force of this ripe age."[69] The far-from-ideal age difference again hints at the difficulties authorities faced in finding suitable couples on which to bestow this honor. The bourgeois administrators of the public assistance bureau believed it was virtually impossible to find young women workers whose morality was incontestable. The nature of working women's constant incursion into public spaces may explain bourgeois men's inability to find "pure" women. Bourgeois definitions of "proper" female behavior were incompatible with the realities of working women's lives, realities that made it impossible for these women to focus solely on domestic pursuits or to display the kind of passive submission to authority figures that officials hoped to find. Working-class and bourgeois views of public and private and of male and female roles were incompatible. Such contradictions may have undermined efforts to promote the regime's "family values" among workers.

Of course, as the following chapters demonstrate, the real lives of bourgeois women often contradicted such ideals as well.

On 29 April 1810, the day that Napoleon married Marie-Louise, communities all over France celebrated the marriages of local inhabitants.[70] Who received this honor? In Lyon, "twelve girls whose brothers or close family members [fought] in the armies of the Emperor, and [demonstrated] impeccable behavior" were to be married and to receive a dowry of eleven hundred francs. Eight of these twelve were to marry men who were employed as textile or silk workers because the city council wanted to demonstrate its consideration for "this principal branch of Lyonnais industry." The other four grooms could come from "the other most important manufacturing [sectors] of the city."[71] The selection of couples in Lyon involved evaluation of their contribution to the city's economy, suggesting recognition that supporting workers could contribute to lessening potential unrest as economic difficulties intensified. In contrast to other events, military service was not an issue in this case, at least not for the grooms. Indirectly, it was among the criteria for choosing the brides, which reinforced the regime's emphasis on women's roles in raising and supporting soldiers.

At the December 1810 festival marking the anniversary of Napoleon's coronation, the mayor of Rouen gave a speech in which he articulated the logic behind the selections. He began by addressing the bride: "Your behavior has earned you the inestimable favor which you are going to receive, which you are receiving already. You will justify this preference that you have obtained . . . and you will release the debt which it imposes upon you. Gratitude . . . will suffice, without the assistance of the good principles engraved in your heart, to remind you of your duties, as if you could forget them for a single instant." The women who received such honors were chosen for their purity and their devotion to duty. They were in turn to feel grateful and thus be even more devoted to their country and their families. The criteria for men included bravery and fidelity: "And you, young man, who honorably served your country, marching faithfully under your flags, in the ranks of the brave, you will be no less faithful to the sacred engagements you are about to contract."[72] The ideal Napoleonic woman was a wife and mother, the ideal Napoleonic man a soldier, and both carried great significance for the emperor to succeed in his domestic and military goals. Proper gender roles were directly related to the regime's larger goals of creating and maintaining order, with the family as the foundation of a stable society. The spectacle, the public enactment of an ideal marriage, accomplished more than any speech could by itself. The individual relationship involved became a part of state ritual; marital duties became associated with the duties of citizenship.

Wedding ceremonies also allowed Napoleon and the local authorities serving him to present themselves in a positive light: their benevolence included supporting local industries and helping the male and female workers whose labor kept the economy going. Their goal was for participants and spectators of both sexes to feel a greater sense of solidarity with the regime. The ceremonies held in Lyon on the day Napoleon and Marie-Louise married took place after "the fathers of families who had contributed to the selection of the dowered girls, and a great number of notable citizens of the city, were introduced."[73] Just as the brides appeared as prospective mothers, the men who chose them appeared as "fathers of families," too. Such demonstrations of paternal generosity strove to ensure that workers, convinced of the goodwill of the national government and of local officials, would occupy themselves with their work rather than with rebellions and revolts, a particular concern in Lyon. Following the marriage ceremony, the festivities continued throughout the afternoon and evening at designated locations where the city provided *mâts de cocagne* (games that involved climbing up a large greased pole), orchestras, and dancing.[74] Again, such events encouraged a good turnout, which in turn meant that large numbers of people—male and female, young and old—would receive the desired message: namely, that Napoleon's government was benevolent and just and that it had the unanimous support of the populace. Of course, it is unlikely that all the spectators interpreted the festival's various components in the same manner.[75] Their mere presence accomplished the regime's primary goal of bringing together the populace, however, regardless of how they might have interpreted the ceremonies.

The birth and baptism of Napoleon and Marie-Louise's son, "le Roi de Rome," in the spring of 1811 inspired further sets of sponsored marriages. The city of Nantes provided dowries for the marriages of ten veterans. The ceremonies were held in the city hall, in the presence of local officials and "an immense concourse of inhabitants."[76] Lyon's municipal council spent 100,000 francs on six weddings, fireworks, freeing prisoners in jail for debt, and giving food to the poor. According to a local historian, a banquet followed the wedding ceremonies, after which those gathered demonstrated "their gratitude with a well-rehearsed dialogue."[77] The language took a remarkably religious form, suggesting Napoleon's willingness to position himself at the center of people's lives where the Church had once been.

*The mayor:* "It is the emperor who is marrying you; you will dedicate [*vouerez*] your children to him."
*The spouses:* "We will dedicate our children to him."
. . . . . . . . . . . . . .
*The spouses:* "Vive l'Empereur!"
*The spouses:* "Vive l'Impératrice!"
*Everyone:* "Vive le Roi de Rome!"

Prefiguring Third Republic pro-natalism, the regime sought to encourage marriage and childbearing as a duty to the state. The importance of the family in the Napoleonic state is demonstrated as well by the government's designation of 1 January as "family day."[78] Napoleon's military techniques required large numbers of human bodies, and he worked to encourage fertility through every means available to him, including these types of propagandistic spectacles.

At Lyon's celebrations of 15 August 1813, with the Empire crumbling and the state functioning in crisis mode, a group marriage ceremony still seemed worth the effort. The mayor's speech to the future spouses stated clearly why the government chose to make so much out of these public weddings:

Young couples . . . you are about to undertake the most important commitment of your lives. The ties of marriage impose sacred duties and obligations. Your happiness depends upon the inviolable fidelity with which you fulfill them.

You will not forget that you owe your fortunate union to the festival of the Great Napoleon and that this cherished monarch was the restorer of industry and the arts in our city.

Chosen from the class of silk workers, remember that it is the exercise of this profession that brought you the flattering distinction of which you are the object, we wanted to honor your *état*, which holds the first place among the branches of Lyonnais industry.

An emphasis on the city of Lyon and its special characteristics counterbalanced the attention to the "Great Napoleon." Such attention to local concerns was absent from the speeches made at similar ceremonies in Rouen where Napoleon appeared as the person who brought order to all of France indiscriminately.

As he continued the speech, the mayor of Lyon again underlined the role of local administrators and how they, with no mention of the emperor, would protect the couples. "In taking your sincere vows, I must tell you that you will only find happiness in the love of order and of work, that you can only assure [happiness] by irreproachable conduct; in return for this [behavior], loved by your bosses and your equals, you will always have the right to the benevolence and the protection of your magistrates and the municipal corps to which you owe your establishment; neither will ever cease to hold great interest in you."[79] In addition to broadcasting the goodwill of national and local authorities, sponsoring marriages encouraged the "family values" desired by the state: the family functioned to curb disorderly tendencies, especially among men whose natural impulses seemed to make them an unruly group. One way in which women were of significance politically was that they could help maintain order by serving as models of virtuous and selfless behavior. It was thus equally important to convince women *and* men to appreciate and be faithful to the Napoleonic state.

We cannot identify with precision the makeup of the crowds that filled city streets and squares during these events. Nor do we know how they reacted to the messages conveyed, or with what degree of sincerity they expressed their attachment to the regime in power. In fact, because of the extraordinary success of the police state in the Napoleonic era, and the relative banality of most police reports, we know very little about what anyone was really thinking. As one scholar has expressed it: "The Napoleonic regime's antidote to civil disorder . . . consisted of depoliticization, partly based on governmental control of expression of opinion."[80] The goal of Napoleonic festivals was to have large, enthusiastic crowds voicing their support for their emperor, an outcome that went a long way in spreading the desired messages among those in attendance: that Napoleon had accomplished a great deal for France and that he was loved as a leader. Authorities hoped these ideas would reach women as well as men, and women's visible support for the regime was sought after as much as men's. The public celebrations that took place at these festivals played a central role in shaping the meaning of the imperial community on a local level, and women were an integral part of this process. However, the methods used and messages articulated varied according to class: upper-class women's roles were much the same as men's—to garnish elite spaces and demonstrate notable support for the regime; poorer women played more gender-specific roles in their depiction as wives and mothers, though they too simply added to the size of the enthusiastic crowds that filled theaters and public squares. Women were not represented as a single, coherent category or group. There were the "good" and "virtuous" mothers and wives defined by their reproductive role; and there were courtiers, male and female, defined by their social and political roles, irrespective of gender. Finally, there were the hidden opponents of the regime, many of them women, who no doubt existed in large numbers but not according to the official pronouncements made at festivals.

An interesting paradox emerges in the festivals' orchestration of working-class women's roles as the wives and mothers of soldiers. On the one hand, such images promoted "traditional" views toward women, ones that limited their participation in public life and focused their efforts on supporting their husbands and raising their children. On the other hand, women of all classes were encouraged to attend festivals—thoroughly public and political events—and authorities organized activities that ensured high levels of female participation. The rhetoric used also transformed women's domestic activities into service to the state and to the emperor himself. Though he may have seen women only as "machines for producing children," Napoleon recognized the political and military significance of having women of all classes support his regime. The Napoleonic state did not view women as so separate from politics as to exclude them from these public manifestations of the power, popularity, and benevolence of the regime. Women's participation in festivals reveals the impossibility, even the undesirability, of fully excluding women from politicized public spaces—despite a government and a dictator whose rhetoric made such exclusion an official goal.

Contemporary accounts made it appear that Napoleon succeeded in bringing women to his festivals, but there is evidence to suggest that some women's support may have been less than sincere. This seems to have been particularly the case in Nantes where, in contrast to Lyon and Rouen, the documents leave no record of elite women participating in the events staged for Napoleon's 1808 visit to that city. That absence becomes even more noticeable because the opposite emerges with the Restoration. In August 1815, nantais newspaper coverage of the *Fête pour le retour du roi* drew an implied contrast between women's views toward the restored Bourbon king and their attitudes under the Empire. "An enormous crowd filled the square, whose paths were all garnered with ladies *(dames)*. . . . We noticed several elegantly dressed ladies, commendable for . . . their continual attachment to the king, who opened the dances. . . . It is necessary to say that the ladies distinguished themselves in the most particular manner. . . . This day was for them a day of triumph."[81] Of course, one cannot take such accounts at face value. To varying degrees under both regimes, journalists were under pressure to stress the popularity of the current government. However, it is interesting that the press would choose to call attention to well-dressed women standing out on their "day of triumph" as the Bourbons celebrated their return to the throne. Though Napoleon was never mentioned, the implication of the article is that these women were not among the crowds that supposedly thronged the streets during Empire festivals.

# — 2 —

# Renewing Ties with the
# Bourbon Monarchy

In March 1815, at the beginning of the tumultuous period known as the Hundred Days, when Napoleon Bonaparte returned to France and tried one last time to lead his troops to victory, the mayor of Nantes published a proclamation defending the monarchy. The language he used to attack the Revolution and ensuing events, as well as his depiction of Louis XVIII as bringing order back to France, is telling of both the Bourbons' self-representation and what their supporters believed the people wanted from their government.

Tormented factions guided by a spirit of innovation overthrew the most ancient and brilliant monarchy of the universe. In its place they substituted . . . a phantom republic that could never be suitable for a state with such a large population and territory. They thus threw the most faithful and controlled people into the excesses and horrors of anarchy. . . . The desire and need for order . . . resulted in the ten-year Consulate, the Consulate for life, and finally the Empire. Some even believed they had found a monarch in the usurper.

In his hands, religion was nothing but a political instrument. He ripped out the arms of agriculture. He destroyed commerce by reducing it to an odious monopoly. . . . It seems that he was hoping to destroy civilization and the social order. . . .

[With the return of the Bourbons] already religion is returning to its ancient splendor; agriculture is blossoming; commerce is returning; the arts are supported. Each day our hopes and dreams are coming true; each day the social edifice is becoming more solid. Since the Restoration, the King has worked to heal France's wounds and to make her happy. . . . Let all the French thus rally around a prince who has given them so many signs of love, of wisdom, and of moderation. *VIVE LE ROI!*[1]

After so many years of civil and political discord, and then the military debacle of the last years of the Empire, the Restoration government worked to depict itself as bringing peace and order to France. Like previous governments, the regime also strove to represent itself as legitimate, and state-sponsored festivals played a prominent role in these efforts.

Despite such expressions of monarchist sentiment on the part of authorities, many people's political allegiances fluctuated with economic, political, and military developments. One anecdote also dating from March 1815 indicates that even Nantes' inhabitants were far from the sincere royalists depicted in many official texts. An envoy sent there to shore up support for the Bourbons as Napoleon was heading toward Paris found upon his arrival "white flags on every window," and visible support for the monarchy. That evening, when the bulletins arrived announcing Napoleon's entry in Paris, the city was transformed. "The decoration changed immediately, the white flags disappeared, the tricolor flags were displayed, and shouts of *Vive l'Empereur!* replaced the cries of *Vive le Roi!*"[2]

The monarchy's task was at once easier and more difficult than the one Napoleon faced. On the one hand, the regime's reliance on religion to bring meaning and order to society assisted in the creation of a satisfying spectacle for the people. Masses and other religious ceremonies staged in conjunction with festivals presented a clear and familiar message to the populace. On the other hand, the Bourbon desire to erase the memory of the Revolution and all that it stood for was an impossible goal, one that would limit the success of the regime's self-fashioning through spectacle and festivals. Though the Bourbons could rely on Old Regime traditions to create a sense of stability, they could not ignore all that the French had experienced since 1789. Participants at festivals brought their memories of the previous decades' political turmoil with them when they entered spaces meant to glorify the Bourbon regime and its supporters. In addition, the relationship between Church and state during this period was far from straightforward; Church-state conflict often undermined the regime's efforts.[3]

The Restoration government staged two annual festivals: the anniversary of the death of Louis XVI in January and the celebration of the king's saint day, first the Fête de Saint-Louis on 25 August and then, beginning in 1824 when Charles X replaced his brother on the throne, the Fête de Saint-Charles in October. The festivities staged in Nantes for Saint-Louis in 1818 reflect the typical scenario. The day began with a mass attended by public officials who gathered at the prefecture and walked together *(en cortège)* to the cathedral. Then they entered the church in order of their titles, starting at the top of the hierarchy. Later in the day, distributions of wine took place, with three locations announced in advance where people could gather to partake in this aspect of the festival.[4] Similar events also marked provincial celebrations of special events, which included the baptism of the duc de Berry's son in 1821 and visits by various members of the royal family to particular cities.

The activities staged during Restoration festivals paralleled those of the Napoleonic regime, with distributions of food and wine, *spectacles gratis,* fireworks, and so on. They often were organized differently, however, in part because the government had fewer resources to devote to the orchestration of festivals than the Empire had. Though the regime continued to stage festivals, the events were simpler and, to quote one historian, religious festivals "occupied an important place to the detriment of festivals of distraction."[5] Authorities also feared events that might allow the populace to get out of control, though they still needed enthusiastic crowds to portray the regime's widespread support. In September 1814, when the king's brother passed through Lyon for the second time in a week, the mayor's office published a poster encouraging the city's inhabitants to "continue to manifest for this cherished prince who is coming to spend a few more moments with us, the sentiments of love, of respect, of devotion, and of attachment that fill your hearts. . . . Redouble, if it is possible, your zeal and enthusiasm upon his return to our town. . . . [You will] thus merit even more his affection . . . and will renew for him the expression of your fidelity and thankfulness."[6] The city could not stage "successful" Restoration festivals without the cooperation of inhabitants whose presence and enthusiasm both satisfied this royal visitor and displayed his popularity and support among the populace. As under Napoleon, authorities worked to encourage large crowds to gather, but they were less confident of their ability to keep those crowds under control. Although working-class women and men participated in Restoration festivals as recipients of food and in outdoor dancing, they rarely had the opportunity to assume more active roles. Regardless of these differences, constants again prevail: women as well as men took advantage of festivals during both the Napoleonic and Restoration periods as a chance to have a day off from work and to amuse themselves as best they could.

The depiction of women at Restoration events differed from their depiction at Napoleonic ones. The Restoration government was less explicitly opposed to women's involvement in politics. In fact, because it viewed women as likely supporters, the regime worked to make women's voices more audible than they had been under Napoleon. No longer represented as the wives and mothers of soldier/citizens, they now appeared as faithful subjects and as the best organizers of newly formed charities and other royal organizations. This portrayal of women at festivals paralleled those made by Catholic writers of the period, who argued that women were "to calm and soothe, to make good the bad that had been done."[7] Women also played more prominent and diverse roles than they had at Napoleonic festivals, particularly elite women who found themselves raised as examples of fidelity to the monarchy and the Church. Restoration festivals put women at center stage *as women* because they were seen as devoted royalists whose attachment to the monarchy would convince others to support it as well. Unfortunately for the Bourbons, many remained unconvinced, and the growing class divisions of the period made a uniform portrayal of women unstable.

A nantais journalist with liberal views, Victor Mangin *fils* used what he saw as lack of enthusiasm in the carnival season of 1820 to insinuate that the French were dissatisfied with their government. He argued that the French had changed. "Winter amusements are no longer as lively and noisy as they once were. . . . Completely occupied with the larger concerns of their country, [the French] can no longer throw themselves into their pleasures while their happiness is threatened. In addition, some people have inspired strong antipathy toward the Carnival: since the Revolution they are in constant Mardi Gras, while the people are fasting for Lent." The journalist went on to recount his version of the history of the Revolution, writing that when some people "audaciously refused to accept the wishes of the nation . . . their heads covered with a horrible red bonnet, they soiled liberty." When Louis XVIII returned, and granted the Charter, "peace descended from the heavens, . . . but the monarchists . . . were working behind the scenes to destroy this Charter while it was blossoming. . . . The unhappy year of 1815 replaced '93, as they proclaimed their reign of terror; and the white clubs did as much damage to France as the tricolor clubs." Mangin concluded by stating that though the Carnival season continued, it was "painful: the French people, who have paid all these costs, are disgusted with *mascarades.*"[8] The Restoration government may have been fighting a losing battle, but it persevered. State-sponsored festivals provided the most obvious venue, with the widest possible reach, for convincing the French populace that the Bourbon regime was both legitimate and loved.

## Bringing Women to Center Stage

Soon after the first Bourbon Restoration, the *Journal de Nantes* reprinted an excerpt from a letter written by Charles Lacretelle that had originally been published in the *Gazette de France*. Lacretelle glorified the "virtues" of women: "Women have always inspired great deeds; but during the Revolution, they performed them. They demonstrated all the marks of courage, while maintaining all the graces of modesty *(pudeur)*. . . . Most of these women, whose *beaux traits* created such profound and touching admiration, have perished. We must continue to mourn at their sacred graves, or better yet, build . . . the tombs which these courageous women were denied."[9] With the Restoration, both real women and symbolic representations of women suddenly took center stage in public life. These patterns are especially visible in Nantes, where women's devotion and fidelity to the Church and the monarchy became a common subject of discussion. Women's roles as educators and organizers of charity drew greater attention, as did their ability to make sacrifices for the common good. Restoration festivals brought a drastic shift in the portrayals and perceptions of women. In contrast to Napoleonic displays of working-class women as brides and the mothers of soldiers, women of all classes now appeared as strong, courageous participants in the struggle to right the wrongs of the Revolution.

During the early days of the First Restoration, celebrations took place to mark the declaration of peace and the return of the monarchy. A nantais journalist stated that upon hearing the news of the Bourbons' return the residents of his city "spontaneously lit up their houses, and an immense crowd, crossing the city streets, shouted cries of joy to the heavens during the entire night." The next day, "inhabitants donned white cockades and hung the royal flag out their windows. . . . Games and dances were set up near the Bourse and the place Royale."[10] Two months later, further celebrations took place. "The most genuine satisfaction appeared on all the faces; all the classes of society mingled to take part in an event which not only reconciled us with the rest of Europe, but which also charges us once again with the sacred duty to forget all that might disrupt union and harmony. Let us turn our attentions away from the past, and focus instead on the future." During the evening, people "set bonfires *(feux de joie)* around which they danced and sang songs whose refrains were *vive le Roi! vive la paix!*"[11] Similarly, in August 1814, during the Fête de Saint-Louis, "inhabitants, in a spontaneous movement, built bon fires and chanted vive le Roi! Dances were established in different neighborhoods, including the place Louis XVI, where there was an orchestra. The peuple were also given the pleasure of attending the theater. An immense crowd filled the Théâtre du Chapeau Rouge."[12] The newspaper emphasized the apparent spontaneity of these celebrations with an implied contrast to Napoleonic festivities, which it suggested had been imposed from above.

Julie Pellizzone, a bourgeois Marseillaise with royalist sympathies, described in detail the atmosphere in her city during the early days of the First Restoration and recorded inhabitants' reactions to the return of the Bourbons in the spring of 1814. Pellizzone's staunch monarchism reverberates throughout her memoirs. Though far from objective, she was a careful observer of the events that took place around her. For example, she described the crowds that filled the streets of Marseille on 13 April 1814, the day before Napoleon's abdication:

> They thought that the authorities . . . were about to proclaim that it was necessary to submit to Louis XVIII. An enormous crowd gathered around [a municipal official], women of the people surrounded him to kiss him: he was almost suffocated. . . . Repeated cries of *"Vive le Roi!"* could be heard. . . . Finally, he read a proclamation from the Empress . . . announcing that she had taken refuge at Blois, that her husband was fighting at the walls of Paris to try to take them back, and that she hoped the French would support him.
>
> As this piece was read, the enthusiasm suddenly came to an end, the cries of joy stopped, and everyone separated sadly. Poor peuple, your joy *(ivresse)* was short-lived.[13]

In Pellizzone's account and elsewhere, women appear as the primary supporters of the monarchy. A similar account of women's joy at hearing about the defeat of Napoleon and the return of the Bourbons appears in the journal of a monarchist woman in Lyon, who commented on the number of women who attached fleurs-de-lis to their hats while enormous crowds shouted, *"Vive le Roi!"*[14] Women, more so than men it seems (despite the fact that men were, for the most part, the ones who were fighting and dying in Napoleon's armies), were exhausted from the emotional and economic turmoil of the nearly constant warfare with which they associated the Napoleonic regime and the revolutionary experiments that preceded it.[15]

When news came the next day that the Bourbons had been brought back to the throne, Pellizzone recorded the following observations: "All the honest people of Marseille mingled among the crowds [and] had decorated their hats with white paper cockades, . . . and holding their white kerchiefs from one end, they waved them like flags. Cries of 'Vive le Roi!' rose to the heavens, reverberating in the hearts of all true French people. . . . Everyone has a white cockade on his or her hat, men and women. No one went to bed the first night."[16] All the symbols of the monarchy reappeared instantaneously as the inhabitants of Marseilles celebrated the news. As soon as possible, supporters of the Bourbons staged a festival linking the Church and the throne. Pellizzone attended a *Te Deum* held in Saint-Martin Church on 16 April 1814: "What a difference this touching enthusiasm is after the sinister silence in churches when we sung by force the *Salvum fac imperatorem Napoléon.* Cries of 'Vive le Roi!' [and] clapping hands echoed in the church despite the holiness of the location; the cannons roared outside. This majestic noise, this complete joy *(cette ivresse si grande)* cannot be described."[17] Her comments echo other Restoration sources that contrasted the sincerity of people's feelings toward the king with the "forced" nature of Napoleonic celebrations. Pellizzone also recorded the celebrations held in Marseilles in the aftermath of the Hundred Days, emphasizing the strong attachment of working-class women to the king. "The used-clothing sellers *(revendeuses)* and fishwives staged marches while carrying a bust of the king . . . and white flags."[18] Fishwives had played prominent roles in royal festivals prior to 1789. Their outspoken expressions of support for the Bourbons harkened back to these traditions.[19]

The supposed spontaneity of these celebrations does not mean that the Bourbons took a passive approach to staging festivals. To the contrary, officials expended great effort to ensure that their festivals followed precise plans. Preparations for Louis XVIII's arrival in Paris in the spring of 1814 included heavy police activity to avoid any kinds of disorder. In her study of festivals during the Restoration, Françoise Waquet emphasizes officials' attention to detail as they prepared for this and later festivals. Unlike Napoleon, however, neither Louis XVIII nor Charles X played a direct role in such plans; they left this work to their administrators. As in Marseilles, a *Te Deum* in Notre Dame followed by a procession to the Tuileries Palace marked the king's arrival in the capital. Once in the palace, the king stepped out on the balcony several times to respond to the cries of the voluminous crowd that filled the gardens. That evening, festivities were held around the city, with illuminations, games and distributions of food and wine on the Champs-Elysées, mock battles between boats on the Seine, and a reception and ball at the Hôtel de Ville. The festivities went on until dawn.[20] All of these events required careful planning.

In addition to relying immediately on the Church and other traditions to lend legitimacy to the regime, the Bourbons wasted no time in sending members of the royal family to various cities around France. Each visit represented an attempt to solidify people's sense of connection to the throne and to bring the "royal touch" down to a local level. The Bourbons knew from the beginning that "public-relations" work would be necessary in the new post-1789 world. For example, a festival took place in honor of the duc d'Angoulême (the king's nephew) when he visited Nantes in July 1814. The prefect made a speech that described the city's destruction during the Revolution and Empire and the subsequent economic and moral renewal already in evidence since the Bourbons had returned to the throne: "the well-being of all citizens was each day becoming a more satisfying spectacle." At another celebration, the mayor began his speech by discussing "the joy that filled the hearts of all the French" after the "anarchism and despotism" that the country had lived through. Following the speeches, a military parade ensued. "An immense crowd of spectators, including a large number of ladies" thronged the streets.[21] Here again, women received special attention as spectators, something that never occurred in the coverage of Empire festivities. However, ordinary women remained pure spectators now, again in contrast to the Empire when a select few were put on display to serve as models to the rest. During the early Restoration, only extraordinary women, particularly aristocratic women and nuns, merited such display. Later, in the mid-1820s, when prizes for virtuous behavior were created, women of humble origin served as models once again. In 1814, only elite women received invitations permitting them to circle around the duke as he was eating his dessert, and an even narrower segment of this elite was presented to him later that same evening.[22] They were the ones who were written about in the official publication describing the duke's visit to the city.

Royal women too came to symbolize all that was good about the monarchy. The duchesse d'Angoulême (Louis XVI's daughter) passed through Lyon in August 1814 and was honored in a variety of ways by the inhabitants of the city. Among other sights, the duchess visited the city's hospitals and the library, where a poem was read in her honor.

> Si ces auteurs pouvoient renaître,
> Comme leurs cœurs seroient émus!
> Ils s'écriroient en la voyant paroître:
> "De graces, de bonté, d'esprit et de vertus,
> "Aucun âge n'offrit un plus touchant modèle
> "A l'amour de son Roi Lyon toujours fidèle,
> "Vit renverser ses murs et brûler nos écrits.*
> "Ah! Pour servir la Fille de Louis,
> "S'il faut combattre encore, avec le même zèle
> "Les Lyonnais, serrés sous le drapeau des Lis,
> "Sauront vaincre et mourir pour elle."
>
> > *Tous les livres de la bibliothèque ont été brûlés
> > après le siège par les soldats révolutionnaires.[23]

> [If these authors could come back to life
> How their hearts would be moved!
> They would write in seeing her appear:
> "Of grace, kindness, spirit and virtue,
> "No age has offered a more touching model
> "Of love for her King, Lyon always faithful
> "Saw her walls knocked down and our writings burned*
> "Ah! to serve the daughter of Louis,
> "If it is necessary to fight again, with the same zeal
> "The Lyonnais, crowded under the flag of the Lis,
> "Would know how to conquer and die for her."
>
> > *All the books of the library were burned after the siege
> > by revolutionary soldiers.]

The poem depicted the Revolution as purely destructive, a sentiment no doubt shared by the duchess who had been imprisoned with the royal family in 1792 prior to losing both her parents, Louis XVI and Marie Antoinette, to the guillotine. The returning Bourbon monarchy would bring back all that was good and pure, and women seemed to represent that goodness and purity better than men.

Elite women performed more significant and visible functions in the articulation of the newly returned monarchical order than they had under the Empire. In September 1814, the comte d'Artois (the brother of Louis XVIII and the future Charles X) visited Lyon. His visit, which according to one published account inspired repeated acclamations of the phrase "One God, one King, one Faith, one Law," provided another opportunity to emphasize women's special attachment to the returned Bourbons.[24] The first day of his stay, he was taken to see the triumphal arch that had been constructed in his honor, around which stood "a large number of richly attired *dames* and *demoiselles*." Among the homage he received was a speech by Mademoiselle de Cazenove, the daughter of one of the city's leaders, at the head of a group of *jeunes demoiselles:* "Who more than us should rejoice! We find ourselves at the beginning of life under a regime that protects innocence; we bring to our princes homage as pure as our hearts. . . . [We are] happy to be able to express, with all the simplicity and truth of our age, how much his august person fills us with respect and love."[25] Symbolizing purity and fidelity, young women from elite Lyonnais families took center stage in the ceremonies held in honor of this dignitary.

The count also attended the theater twice. Both times, crowds filled the theater itself and the streets around it beginning in the afternoon, though the guest of honor only appeared in the evening. Upon his arrival, he had a beautiful sight before his eyes: the theater was "decorated and lit with great taste"; those waiting inside displayed the "beauty and grace of the most fashionable and brilliant elegance, the fire of sparkling diamonds everywhere, the pleasure that shined in the eyes of everyone and which filled all our hearts. The ladies were dressed in the richest fabrics, all manufactured in Lyon."[26] Performing an economic as well as a symbolic function, these women were both walking advertisements for and consumers of the premier Lyonnais creation: silks. A ball following the performance permitted further display of elite solidarity and support for the regime. The annual fêtes du Roi provided a similar opportunity for what a history of Lyon labeled "magnificent receptions" for "le Tout Lyon," in other words Lyon's elite and fashionable set, who gathered at city hall to display both their *toilettes* and their loyalty to the Bourbons. Women decorated their hats with fleurs-de-lis, and white cockades stood out on their blue coats.[27] Fashion, as usual, was a political statement as much as anything else. In all these contexts, women provided a sense of cohesion for postrevolutionary elite society, which incorporated aristocratic and bourgeois elements.

Women's prominence during the early Restoration appeared in many forms. A poem published in 1815, which was read at Lyon's Grand Théâtre in August of that year, praised women as a group for their unfailing attachment to the monarchy, especially those who had lost their lives as a result.

> Des femmes sans défense, et n'ayant d'autres droits
> Qu'une vie exemplaire et l'amour de nos Rois;
> Des femmes, dont les noms bien chers à l'indigence,
> Sont gravés dans les cœurs par la reconnaissance,
> Ont osé, des méchans, défiant le courroux,
> Se placer avec joie, entre le Ciel et nous![28]

> [Defenseless women holding no rights
> Only exemplary lives and love for our kings;
> Women whose cherished names [brought] poverty,
> Are engraved in [our] hearts through gratitude,
> Defying the wrath of the evil ones, dared
> To place themselves joyfully between us and Heaven!]

Again, women appeared as exemplary subjects, models of fidelity and courage for both sexes to follow. The poem depicted "women" as a sociopolitical category: they were selfless, courageous defenders of throne and altar. In August 1815, at Nantes' celebrations for Louis XVIII's (second) return, *"Mesdames les revendeuses"* prepared a "superb" bonfire at the place du Bouffai, while the upper-class ladies in attendance impressed a local journalist. "The most lively and sincere amiability and gaiety seemed to lend even more new charms to this sex that dared to accuse us [men] of frivolity when it knew [how] to resist the intrigues, to conserve complete fidelity to the royal dynasty, and to show, in these difficult times, a certainty of sentiment that few men could have."[29] Because of their exemplary "natures," women received far more attention at these public festivities than they had during the Empire when their attachment to the regime was more dubious. Now, they served as models for men as well. Historian Steven Kale has argued that during the Restoration, "many upper-class women enjoyed politics and felt entitled to assert themselves in the public sphere. Noblewomen . . . openly cheered Napoleon's abdication, demonstrated for the return of the Bourbons, and routinely sat in the gallery of the Chamber of Deputies."[30] Whereas Napoleonic celebrations incorporated women into the largely undifferentiated crowd and glorified their roles as wives and mothers through the staged marriage ceremonies, the Restoration regime sought out women's participation and drew particular attention to them as a separate group within society, one that stood out for its fidelity and willingness to sacrifice.

In some cases, women actively drew this attention to themselves and their political sentiments. In January 1816, a group of "demoiselles royalistes" collected money to donate to the king. The *Journal de Nantes* devoted several columns to their efforts and reprinted the letter the mayor sent to the minister of the interior to accompany the 3,404 francs and 87 centimes that would be deposited into the national treasury. According to the mayor, women were more likely than men to have remained courageous in the face of the "usurper's" reign:

If the criminal and momentary success of the usurper unveiled much treachery, it also served to make feelings of fidelity and devotion to the legitimate monarch conspicuous. It is especially among ladies that such pure and courageous sentiments endured, and among whom, in such perilous circumstances, we noticed the noblest examples. They [these ladies] particularly gained distinction in Nantes, despite all the genres of persecution to which this town was exposed. Their daughters have followed in this heroic impulsion . . . [quoting these young women]: "Heaven, touched by our prayers for such a long time, delivered to us our illustrious Monarch; but his heart is broken by the sight of all the ailments that his forced absence has caused our unhappy country; if we are not called to contribute to repair them, we hope at least that this good prince will accept the small donation it is possible for us to offer him to aid in the needs of the state."[31]

These women functioned as symbols of Nantes' commitment to the Restoration, and of the purity of heart of the inhabitants in general. At the same time, the paltry sum they had to offer must have seemed silly in light of the real needs of the nation.

Restoration festivals accentuated elite women's roles beyond motherhood to a greater extent than had been the case during the Empire, and by the 1820s they began to acknowledge the contributions made by women of the lower classes as well. The 1823 visit of the duchesse d'Angoulême created several opportunities for the inhabitants of Nantes to express their support for the royal family and for women in particular to stand out as staunch supporters. When she spoke at the inauguration of a statue of Louis XVI, the duchess emphasized that the city had wasted no time in creating this symbol of its attachment to the monarchy: "The city of Nantes was the first among all its sisters to consecrate a statue to the beneficent martyr king."[32] The duchess also visited the Hôtel-Dieu (charitable hospital) where a large crowd obstructed the entrance to the building. According to an observer, her simple words to the crowd made the onlookers clear a path for her without causing them to feel aware of their indiscretion: "Ladies, I am not here to make a social call; I have come only to see the sick, and those (celles) who nurse them." Her words suggest that only women filled this particular crowd; they were the ones who felt such an attachment to the Bourbons that they thronged the streets to get close to the duchess. Some Nantaises would have an opportunity to address the duchess directly later during her stay when she received them in her temporary residence. At the meeting, "women from religious and charitable institutions, pious establishments which this city possesses in greater number than any other," discussed a "multitude of charitable issues with her." The duchess spoke with "the dames de la Société maternelle, the dames de Charité, the dames de la Providence, and des petites Ecoles, whose charitable solicitude procures religious instruction and work to seven or eight hundred girls, and even assures the nourishment of a large number of them."[33] She repeatedly referred to women's important contributions to the health of their community.

Drawing attention to lower-class women's attachment to church and throne, the duchess next received "the market women (dames des halles) and representatives of popular associations who had joyfully constructed the arches and altars of foliage that appeared on nearly every street of the city. . . . Some of these women fell to their knees, others burst into tears" when they saw her. At that point, the prefect reiterated to the duchess "that the oldest of these women had hidden or aided, during the country's difficult times, many priests and victims, and that the youngest had learned from the others to love and venerate her illustrious family."[34] Local and national authorities glorified women across classes as those who had supported the monarchical system against all adversity. Their actions, which required strength and bravery, prepared them for roles beyond motherhood, and the events that incorporated these women into festivals made these roles visible.

The festivals staged to celebrate Charles X's coronation in 1825 provided an occasion for wealthy women to display not only their virtues but also their beauty and good taste.[35] In Lyon, women made sure to show themselves off in Lyonnais silks. According to a newspaper article, textile manufacturers and dressmakers (couturières) were kept busy creating the ball gowns and other clothing required of the city's most elite women.[36] Here we see the broader effects of these celebrations. In reviving aristocratic conspicuous consumption, something Napoleon had tried to do as well, the Restoration government stimulated local economies and thus tried to make workers happy as well. In Nantes, inhabitants used the coronation festivities as a venue for charitable work, distributing bread and money to the indigent. In recounting these events, the mayor described the situation of one man, a porter and father of five, who found himself destitute when his horse died. Working with others, he managed to collect two hundred francs, which were used to replace the man's horse. "Here is one family that will never forget what it owes to the coronation of Charles X," he concluded.[37] The mayor also devoted attention to the city's free schools, which were operated by male and female religious orders. He visited several of them in conjunction with the festival events, distributing funds and prizes to students and reminding them of the love and respect they owed their king. He was particularly impressed at the moral lessons received by girls at these free schools, as they were taught the values of work and of instruction.

Nantes' festival marking the coronation included a wide variety of events meant to satisfy all the town's inhabitants. The day began with a march through the city by authorities accompanied by troops. That was followed by games set up outdoors for the populace while a ball and dinner was held in the large *halle aux bleds* (grain market), which had been recently renovated. Part of this event included visits by fishwives and fruit sellers, women who expressed their love for the king before the crowd of officials and other elite members of nantais society. Games, including *mâts de cocagnes* (greased poles), were set up in two city squares, where the mayor believed that crowds could assemble without danger. In the evening, the city's buildings were lit up and fireworks entertained "the entire population of Nantes at nightfall, to the great satisfaction of this large gathering."[38] The festival offered something for everyone and was meant to create a long-lasting and positive memory of a joyful day, which inhabitants would associate with their new king and with the first Bourbon coronation held in France in fifty years. In fact, the events differed little from Old Regime festivities, which included roughly the same activities. Although fishwives may have expressed their views before officials at an elegant ball, most of the spaces in which celebrators gathered were for certain classes and permitted little mixing.

Despite the separation of activities designed for elite inhabitants and the masses, some interaction did take place during Restoration festivals, and contemporaries were aware of the potential for the two groups to mingle and observe each other in the spaces created by those attending festivals. In January 1825, the president of the Société Académique de la Loire-Inférieure wrote to the prefect asking for some members of his group to receive invitations to the events being staged to mark the death of Louis XVI. He made the argument that "it would be best for all persons whose behavior could have an influence on the spirit of the masses to attend."[39] He believed that the "masses" needed to be able to observe as many "positive" models as possible. In some contexts, festivals provided an occasion for that type of observation to take place. Generally, however, organizers created separate physical and psychological spaces for the different classes. Elites wanted to shine among themselves, and fears of disorderly crowds kept the upper classes away from popular festivities, which were in the process of becoming more tightly controlled and limited.

## Controlling Popular Festivities

In addition to placing more attention on women of all classes, another change from the Napoleonic period was in the Bourbons' treatment of popular festivities, which they attempted to limit and control as much as possible. As a result, their efforts to encourage popular manifestations of support for the regime were of only limited success. According to Waquet, festivals of the mid-1820s "possessed neither the unanimity nor the spontaneity that the men of the eighteenth century defined as necessary conditions of true popular festivals."[40] Under Napoleon, authorities often bragged about pop-ular dances going on until dawn, a symbol of the people's sincere and unanimous support for their emperor. In contrast to Napoleonic officials who encouraged ordinary people to celebrate as long as they wished, the Restoration government feared the people, which was an understandable sentiment considering the preceding decades, and thus limited their merrymaking. So for example, elite balls held in Nantes to celebrate a royal baptism in 1821 went on until 3 A.M., while those held outdoors, the *danses du peuple,* ended at 11 P.M.[41] The dances held at three public squares in Nantes to celebrate the Fête de Saint-Louis in 1814 were to end by midnight, whereas in Lyon they ended even earlier: the orchestras performed from 5 P.M. to 10 P.M.[42] As time went on, authorities shortened the celebrations even more: dances held at Lyon's place Bellecour for the Saint-Louis festivities in August 1819 were required to end by nightfall.[43] Encouraging crowds of "unruly" workers to carouse in the streets until all hours of the night was not something the Restoration government felt was in its interest.

To make as wide as possible a portion of the population feel as though they were participating in Restoration festivals, local authorities organized a variety of events, with separate spaces catering to different groups. To celebrate the duchesse d'Angoulême's visit to Lyon in 1814, for example, the duchess "honored the Grand Théâtre by her presence" one evening. As she and Lyon's elite residents enjoyed the play, "dances [were held] at the promenade of the Tilleuls at the place de Louis le Grand."[44] The notables of Lyon received the honor of finding themselves in close proximity to this member of the royal family, while less elite segments of the population also received the message that they belonged to the new civic order by having a space in which to celebrate the duchess's presence: a public square with an orchestra. Though all were ostensibly there to celebrate her visit, the physical separation and the distinct amusements offered to the two groups highlighted divisions between them. Similar trends can be observed in the celebrations held in Nantes to mark Spain's return to Bourbon rule under Ferdinand VII in 1823. "In the evening, numerous illuminations, games, dances, and bonfires called the joyous population of the town to diverse public places and promenades. . . . [At each] popular gathering a symphony of songs" celebrating the event inspired applause. The day's activities "were terminated by a ball where the prefect brought together a brilliant and numerous society, at which the dancing continued well into the night."[45] Free dances and bonfires in public squares were meant to attract the popular classes, whereas formal balls appealed to wealthier men and women. Separate events took place under Napoleon as well, but at least some gatherings were meant for all to enjoy, and official coverage devoted less attention to these distinctions.

Other kinds of representations help us to understand why elites would have chosen to distance themselves from the peuple. Louis-Léopold Boilly's 1822 painting *Distribution de vins et de comestibles aux Champs-Elysées* (Figure 2.1) gives a sense of elite views of the working classes and the potential violence that the elite imagined to be ever-present wherever workers gathered. The painting's representation of disorderly crowds of people climbing over each other in the rush to gain access to food contradicts the emphasis on "controlled amusement" evident in official correspondence.[46] One Restoration official commented on the fact that the people's joy was mingled with pain, as they suffered from injuries caused by the bread, sausages, and bottles that were thrown at them from high above.[47] Whereas

**Figure 2.1.** Louis-Léopold Boilly, *Distribution de vins et de comestibles aux Champs-Elysées* (Distribution of Wine and Food at the Champs-Elysées; 1822). Musée Carnavalet, Paris. Copyright © Photothèque des Musées de la Ville de Paris. Photo by Joffre.

earlier depictions of city life by Boilly and others showed inviting, entertaining scenes of the diverse groups of people found in shared public spaces, here we see a fearful and dangerous scene to be avoided at all costs.[48] In marked contrast to earlier traditions of the female-dominated food riot, the women depicted in the image appear on the sidelines, giving the impression that they were not directly involved in such tumultuous behavior.[49] As gender and class norms evolved, their contradictory nature could undermine as well as reinforce each other. Although "women" as a uniform category were portrayed as model subjects, recognition that they could also belong to the "dangerous" working classes weakened efforts to construct such uniformity. Lower- and upper-class women led very different lives; their distinct experiences and aspirations made unstable any effort to represent them as a single, coherent social group. As the provincial theater disturbances discussed in Chapter 4 show, however, women across classes increasingly appeared as the victims of young men's anticipated violence and disorder.

Bourgeois impressions of free distributions of food evolved during the nineteenth century as well. In a late nineteenth-century history of festivals, Emmanuel Lemaire commented on such events under Napoleon and during the Restoration. He made reference to an earlier history by Philippe Le Bas, who criticized Napoleonic festivals because "they found nothing better to amuse the peuple than the shameful distributions of food that was thrown at them like at a rapacious dog; the balls, the public theaters, the fireworks, the greased poles, etc. . . . These traditions were continued by the Bourbons until the Revolution of 1830. As for the government of Louis-Philippe, . . . it at least knew to make the most ignoble of these accessories disappear."[50] Lemaire went on to argue that "every government must be concerned with the dignity of those it administers, no matter how modest their social position, and these efforts must tend towards giving them self-respect [and teaching] respect for others, which is one of the first qualities of a civilized man. This is something that the First Empire and the Restoration completely misunderstood."[51] These authors saw food distributions as dehumanizing the poor, an interpretation that agrees with Boilly's depiction as well. Elites during the Restoration wished to stay as far as possible from such "animals." As suggested by their placement in the Boilly painting, women of the popular classes could take on the role of a civilizing force among these dehumanized masses.

Boilly depicted a similarly disorderly and violent crowd in an 1819 painting of the entrance to a free theatrical performance at one of the Parisian

**Figure 2.2.** Louis-Léopold Boilly, *Spectacle gratis à l'Ambigu-Comique* (Free Performance at the Ambigu-Comique; 1819). Photo courtesy of the Réunion des Musées Nationaux / Art Resource, New York.

theaters (Figure 2.2). As under Napoleon, free performances were seen as vital to satisfying the common people. In October 1815, with the allotted funding for festivals used up, the prefect in Nantes found some emergency funds to provide 660 francs to reimburse the mayor's office for the free performance that had been held in August of that year.[52] He agreed with the mayor that the populace of the city needed this diversion, which was among the best-attended events staged at festivals. The free performance held in August 1814 drew an "immense crowd" that completely filled Nantes' Chapeau Rouge Theater.[53] Yet, as the years wore on, free performances fell from the programs of Restoration festivals.[54] The program of events staged in Lyon to celebrate the 1821 baptism of the duc de Bordeaux (the son of the duc de Berry, who had been assassinated the previous year) included publicly sponsored marriage ceremonies at city hall; a mass at the cathedral; the placing of the first stone of the pedestal for the statue of Louis XIV that would be posed in the place Bellecour; a parade from the statue to the new public hospital being built on the banks of the Rhône; and public dances, which started at 3 P.M.[55] The authorities did not provide a *spectacle gratis* on this occasion, however, or at other festivals staged after 1820. It may be that the expense became too great, but in all probability, growing concerns about disorderly and even political outbursts sparked this change. The well-dressed family Boilly included on the left-hand side of his painting who are looking with disgust at the working-class men (and a few women) climbing over each other to enter the theater reflects emerging attitudes that crowds were by nature dangerous and disorderly.

Still, the government worked to make the popular classes feel as though their government cared about them and was working to improve their lives. In preparation for the Fête de Saint-Charles on 23 October 1826, Lyon's mayor had a poster printed announcing that the king was aware of their suffering and that he was going to help them.

Having just heard about the temporary difficulties of the manufacturing class of our city, [the king] is rushing to give, through a personal act of munificence, the first impulse to restore life to such an important branch of our local industry!

Inhabitants of a town that has always distinguished itself for its attachment to legitimacy, for its pure principles, and for its inviolable honor, Lyonnais, your enthusiasm will augment the brilliance of such a beautiful festival, . . . [by shouting] *Vive le Roi!!! Vivent les Bourbons!!!*[56]

Although the mayor did not make clear exactly what the king would be doing to alleviate workers' misery, he attempted to connect these expressions of fidelity to the monarchy to the financial support inhabitants could hope to receive. Staging festivals created spaces in which to communicate such messages, though how the messages were actually received is, of course, another issue. The nature of existing source materials does not allow us to know exactly how participants may have responded. What we can say with certainty is that officials did what they could to encourage spectators to respond enthusiastically, to create at least an image of unanimous support.

One event used by Napoleon to garner popular support and to distribute funds to worthy recipients was the public wedding ceremony, but Restoration authorities apparently found this form of giving less appealing. The Bourbon regime sponsored far fewer marriage ceremonies than had the Napoleonic regime. During the celebration of the duc de Berry's marriage in June 1816, an event for which locally sponsored marriage ceremonies would seem to be eminently suitable, officials in Nantes organized a *spectacle gratis* followed by fireworks and dancing, along with distributions of wine, but no weddings.[57] At the 1821 celebrations held in honor of the baptism of the son born after the duke's death, Paris and Lyon provided dowries for brides, but Nantes did not.[58] Instead, municipal authorities found other ways to distribute funds. The city of Nantes set aside sufficient funds to provide a dowry of five hundred francs to ten children born around the time of the dauphin's birth, which would be payable when they reached their majority.[59] The selection processes followed during the Empire and the Restoration paralleled the political philosophy underlying each regime. Under Bonaparte, money was given to people who had proven their merit, whereas under the Bourbons, it was distributed at birth regardless of later conduct. It no longer seemed necessary or useful to glorify mothers; instead the Bourbons emphasized the role of God (or destiny) in determining which children would receive this gift, as chance—their date of birth—gave them this honor.

Publicly staged marriage ceremonies did reemerge during the Restoration but in a drastically different form. Internal missions of the 1820s included remarriage ceremonies that proved quite popular. Couples who had been married civilly or by priests who had taken the oath to the Constitution and had thus been excommunicated by the Pope during the revolutionary period took their vows under the auspices of the Church in mass religious spectacles. The weddings took place in the context of religious missions held around France during the Restoration. A historian of these internal missions, the abbé Ernest Sevrin, described the "regularization of civil unions" as one of the clearest successes of the missions. He cites one example in 1818, where 238 couples came forward to be married all at once.[60] The sight of all those people taking vows must have provided quite a spectacle! Though organized for different purposes, these events could easily have reminded spectators of the state-sponsored weddings organized under Napoleon and thus might have undermined the goals of their organizers. They also draw attention to the problematic, but necessary, connection between the Church and the state. The missionaries and the Catholic Church politicized and transformed the debate over marriage, making it more difficult perhaps for the state to make use of such ceremonies for its own purposes.

## Extolling the Virtues of "Virtue"

Beginning in 1820, a new feature of Restoration public statements of policy emerged: the national Prix de Vertu, an annual prize that rewarded extraordinarily selfless, virtuous behavior. The prize provided an opportunity to focus attention on women once again as most, though not all, of the recipients were female. In 1824, for example, three of the four honorees were unmarried women. Two of these were orphans and the third, a glove maker, started from equally humble origins. Each woman gave of herself to help someone in need, at the expense of her own well-being.[61] These stories circulated around the country as prefects sent copies of the year's announcements to the deputy-prefects and mayors in their departments. Local authorities were charged with "carefully searching for such pious works . . . down to the modest homes *(asyles)* where they are most often hidden." They could then report on these virtuous acts that would honor the residents of their communities.[62] Virtuous, selfless behavior seemed more prevalent among women than among men, and women's motivations for practicing virtuous behavior appeared purer than men's. Adélaïde de Dufrénoy, a prolific author of the period, explored the distinct bases for men's and women's behavior, including the origins of their "virtues." "Men's virtues are almost always the fruit of reflection and knowledge of their duties: women's virtues always come from sentiment; religion is their most important basis."[63] Sentiment grounded by religion would ensure that women led virtuous lives; men's virtues evolved out of their intellect.

The Prix de Vertu dated from the end of the Old Regime, when philanthropist Auget de Montyon (1733–1820) funded it anonymously. The Revolution put an end to the practice, which was revived in 1820 when the philanthropist provided funds for it in his will. It continues to the present day, often called the Prix Montyon.[64] Beginning in 1824, the Académie française chose to associate the announcement of the prizes with an annual speech on virtue, and that practice continues as well.[65] That year, the prizes were announced and the speeches given as part of the Fête de Saint-Louis in August. The speeches were then published and distributed around the country soon after. All of the recipients were poor, and roughly three-quarters of them were women who had performed extraordinarily selfless acts to assist those in need.

Also in 1820, the same year that the Restoration brought back the Prix de Vertu, the Academy of Lyon essay contest asked writers to "indicate the means by which to recognize true indigence to make almsgiving as useful to those who give it as it is to those who receive it." The winning study, J. M. Gérando's *Le visiteur de pauvres* equated giving with love: "To give is to love. To receive is to learn to love."[66] The sentimental, idealistic depiction of charity mirrors that found in many of the period's books, regardless of genre—essays, as well as novels, plays, and poems. Charity, virtue, and love would work together to save individuals and society as a whole. Growing recognition of the value of charity for building the social order can be seen in many contexts. It appeared in festivals, where the Bourbons were portrayed as providing help to those in need. It also inspired another essay contest, this time launched by the Académie française in 1827. The theme that year was "Charity's influence on morals *(mœurs)* and on the social organization."[67] In alleviating some misery, charity also carried the potential to make the poor feel as though their government cared about their well-being. Like festivals, "public-relations" work could be accomplished through such activities. During the Restoration, "charity" and "virtue," two accepted components of women's "nature," dominated what we would today call public policy discourse.

"Virtue" arose with regularity in less official venues as well. In the preface to her collection of stories entitled *La bonne cousine*, best-selling female author Elizabeth-Félicie Bayle-Mouillard (who wrote under the pseudonym of Madame Celnart) addressed two specific groups of readers: young girls and adult women. She advised the former to take her messages to heart and then dedicated the work to the latter, whose behavior could inspire younger readers.

My young [female] readers, I implore you not to respond to my lessons, to my examples of virtue with the banal phrase, "That is good in books"; . . . good actions, generous traits pass from the world to books, and by reaction to the latter, return to society. . . . [T]hink of me once in a while when you are hugging your happy mothers. . . . And you, my dear sisters, my amiable friends, who have lent me both your characters and your names, may this work, which I dedicate to you, serve as evidence of my strong friendship, charm your leisure time, [and] inspire my young readers to follow your exemplary sweet and solid virtues.[68]

Wishing to encourage virtuous behavior on the part of her young readers, Bayle-Mouillard hoped that her book would mold impressionable youth and entertain older readers whose personalities were already fixed. She was far from alone in extolling virtue when she published this book in 1822.

What exactly did Restoration officials and moralists have in mind when they spoke of "virtue"? In 1820, was it possible to use the term without dredging up memories of a previous regime's use of "virtue as terror and terror as virtue," as voiced by Robespierre in 1794? Certainly the meaning of the term has changed over time. The behavior selected for the Prix de Vertu involved self-sacrifice, putting someone else's well-being above one's own, whereas earlier the term conjured up notions of giving of oneself for one's nation. In conjoining national, official festivals with speeches highlighting selflessness and sacrifice, Restoration authorities accepted individualism by awarding prizes to particular people, while placing these individual acts of kindness into a national context. The prizes also drew attention away from the monarchy itself, putting ordinary French women and men on display rather than the unpopular royal family. Charitable behavior became a civic duty, one that women fulfilled as well as, if not better than, men.

A study of Third Republic festivals defines such events as "gestures destined to renew the ties of an invisible solidarity."[69] This was certainly the case during the First Empire, which can be viewed on the one hand as bringing the revolutionary period to an end and on the other hand as the first incarnation of politics as they would emerge in the nineteenth century. It was also true when a monarchical government returned to France. The forms taken by Napoleonic festivals necessarily differed from Restoration ones, but not as extensively as one might expect. Both regimes made use of distributions of food and wine, free theatrical performances, outdoor orchestras that provided music for the common people to dance to, and balls at which the elite participants gathered and danced into the early hours of the morning.[70] Both used festivals to commemorate "royal" births, baptisms, and birthdays, as well as the passage of important figures through a particular place. Finally, both were seeking the same outcomes: expressions of support for the regime and a sense of attachment to the government among participants. These continuities extend back in time, as well. Old Regime festivals used similar techniques to accomplish similar goals, and revolutionary festivals, though innovative in form and logic, still strove to bring people a sense of connection to the government.[71] Mona Ozouf argued that similarities outweigh differences among festivals throughout the revolutionary decade, despite divergent political goals.[72] The same could be said for much of the nineteenth century as even more diverse governments—republics, empires, and monarchies—made use of similar tactics to enliven public support. Although some of the specifics changed with the various regimes, many of the actual activities remained the same well into the twentieth century, as did the overall goal of staging festivals.

Another constant is the presence of women, albeit in different roles, at all the festivals staged during the Napoleonic period and the Restoration. Their prominence demonstrates the recognition on the part of both regimes that women too needed to be convinced to support the government; that they were far from nonexistent politically, if only because they could have so much influence over their husbands and sons. Women were part of the spectacles staged, and they numbered among the spectators, too. No one could have defined a festival as a success if women had not attended in large numbers.

Whereas the Empire glorified women's roles as mothers, the political culture of the early Restoration created a space for women's involvement in political discussion as they appeared as model subjects. Recognizing that large numbers of women had consistently opposed many aspects of the revolutionary project, Restoration festivals placed women on pedestals because of their presumed fidelity toward the monarchy and the Catholic Church. Only certain women received such treatment, however, primarily elite women and women who had demonstrated unflinching attachment to the Bourbons. The vast majority of women in the cities under examination here were simply part of undifferentiated crowds, which bourgeois commentators increasingly came to view as dangerous. As a result, Restoration officials did not offer the kinds of glowing reports about the enormous crowds celebrating until dawn that were commonplace (and no doubt exaggerated) under the Empire. The working classes, women included, were evolving into the dangerous classes.

These trends would have long-term repercussions. Later in the nineteenth century, the courage women had demonstrated during the Revolution, and which the Restoration regime so praised, came to be viewed as exceptional, and even dangerous, especially in the eyes of bourgeois liberals with an anticlerical bent. Finally, with the Third Republic (1871–1940), it would become very difficult for women to be imagined as political subjects of a republic that was defining itself against the monarchy and the Church, which helps to explain the lateness of female suffrage in France (1944).[73] As bourgeois liberals enlarged their spheres of influence during the 1820s and beyond, and as they increasingly set the terms of public discussion, women appeared as frivolous, delicate beings who were easily swayed by priests, among others, rather than strong, dedicated monarchists as described by Restoration authorities during the earlier period. As clearer behavioral norms emerged for women, bourgeois and working-class views toward acceptable female involvement in city life grew increasingly disparate. Whereas bourgeois women could limit their visibility in public to "safe" contexts if they so chose, working-class women had no choice but to circulate through city streets on their own, whether for work, family concerns, or amusement. Class and gender distinctions reinforced each other, and both relied in large part on women's appearance and behavior in public spaces. Such issues emerge with even greater clarity in the next two chapters, which focus on theater audiences acting out the new social order while the state and its censors on the one hand and playwrights and theater critics on the other attempted to shape and control the experiences of theatergoers.

# — II —

# Theaters

# — 3 —

# Melodramatic Spectatorship
# on the Parisian Boulevard

Although "the Boulevard" housed numerous theaters, cafés, dance halls, and other businesses geared toward entertainment, an English guidebook to Paris pointed to the crowds that circulated there as the neighborhood's central appeal.

> The chief attraction of the Boulevards . . . is the concourse of gay company and equipages that frequent them. . . . Persons chiefly intent on amusement form this motley assemblage; and their aim is accomplished. . . .
>
> The merry dance, the sprightly air of those who pass, the dazzling lights, the company, two or three deep, who line the way, seated on chairs under gay canopies reading, drinking, smoking [*sic*], and laughing, in the midst of them several well dressed ladies, of great respectability, just descended from their carriages, and these, rattling the stones, with the noise of fruit women, tumblers, footmen and their lasses, the most obsequious apologies for molesting the toes of the seated spectators, many of whom come for no other purpose than to enjoy the endless bustle; officers from a dozen countries in their respective habits, the gayest of damsels on foot, with towers and trees upon their heads, perfectly careless of their burdens; in short, such a combination as leaves far behind the descriptions in the Arabian tales, when diversity of amusement is their theme.[1]

The crowds participated in a never-ending game of display and observation. The variety of the passersby, as well as the theaters and cafés whose explicit purpose was entertainment, meant that this place provided a multifaceted spectacle, one worthy of comparison to "the Arabian tales." Of particular interest to this commentator was women's prominent visibility: "well-dressed ladies of great respectability" and "the gayest damsels" as well as

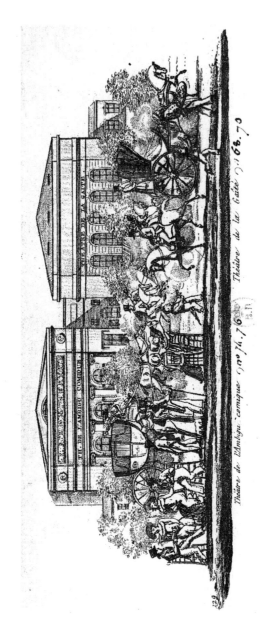

**Figure 3.1.** Anonymous, *Le boulevard du Temple* (1811). Photo courtesy of the Bibliothèque Nationale de France, Paris.

"fruit women." The sight of elite women "rattling the stones" with working women served as entertainment even before one entered a theater.

The "Boulevard" refers to the string of boulevards in northeastern Paris, particularly the boulevard du Temple, which became known as the boulevard du Crime in reference to the scoundrels who dominated the plays performed in theaters there. An engraving from the Empire (Figure 3.1) depicts the street in front of two of the most famous Boulevard theaters. Its portrayal of well-dressed men and women seated on chairs observing the crowds around them as carriages rushed to drop off more revelers mirrors the description quoted above. The Boulevard was a space that catered to the "popular classes," but in the immediate postrevolutionary period, upperclass fans of the neighborhood's many attractions mingled on a regular basis with those who came for the inexpensive, or even free, entertainment.

The most popular Boulevard plays were melodramas, a genre that owed its existence to revolutionary developments that opened up the theatrical world. As one nineteenth-century critic explained it, "melodrama was born out of revolutionary disorder, from its confusion of social positions *(états)* and [theatrical] genres."[2] First staged in 1799, melodramas evolved out of the mid-eighteenth-century genre of the *drame bourgeois,* bringing together the music, dance, and outlandish settings of eighteenth-century Boulevard theater with spoken dialogue and a wide variety of theatrical devices.[3] "Boulevard theater" refers to the indoor and outdoor forms of entertainment that had existed on and near the boulevard du Temple since the eighteenth century. First gaining popularity in the 1760s with performances that incorporated pantomime, acrobats, music and other elements, these theaters were free to add true plays to their repertoire after 1791, when the law granting freedom of the press also abolished the privileges that had determined which theaters could stage plays with dialogue. By 1800, the term "melodrama" (literally meaning plays combining music and spoken dialogue; prior to this time only operas included music) was applied to productions that followed a quickly established set of conventions more or less invented by one prominent playwright, René-Charles Guilbert de Pixérécourt, an ex-émigré.[4] According to one history of French theater, Pixérécourt wrote "with the sincere intention of drumming scruples" into an audience comprised of "half savages."[5] Though the undisputed father of melodrama stated that he wrote "for those who cannot read," he hoped to attract everyone. Women and men from virtually every level of society—from the newly returned aristocracy to artisans and shopkeepers and even laborers and servants—rushed to enjoy the entertaining scenery, music, and dances of melodramas. The plays made use of spectacular stage effects—simulating thunder and lightening was a favorite—and music to intensify the emotional responses of audiences, who frequently screamed and even fainted during performances. Few seemed immune to the phenomenon created by this innovative form of theatrical performance.

In both the plays themselves, most of which centered on the plight of a female victim/heroine, and among spectators, women's behavior emerged as a key theme. As the plays encouraged strong emotional reactions among audience members, attending these plays provided an opportunity for cross-class comparison of female behavior and expressions of female sensitivity. Class markers manifested themselves most visibly on women's bodies: their dress, comportment, and degree of sentimentality. This chapter examines the repercussions of this specularity within the specific context of the postrevolutionary period, when social structures were in flux and gender norms grew to seem particularly meaningful. Sharon Marcus has recently argued that many aspects of Second Empire urban modernity were "already in place by the 1820s, including a culture based on commodification, spectacle, and speculation, and a legible urban space easily mapped and navigable by the upwardly mobile."[6] This chapter explores the mechanisms that helped Parisians acquire this ability to read and navigate Parisian society, and the Boulevard was the primary venue for developing such skills. As the neighborhood and its theaters attracted diverse crowds, women and men from across the social spectrum found themselves in shared spaces that encouraged observation and categorization of different social groups. Over time however, as social structures became more stable and "legible," the upper classes withdrew from many forms of "popular" culture. Beginning in the 1820s, commentary on Parisian amusements emphasized less and less the interaction and observation of heterogeneous groups as a component of their appeal. By 1830, melodramatic theaters of the Boulevard were drawing more purely "popular" audiences.

## The Boulevard: Atmosphere and Social Mixing

The Boulevard's diverse crowds made it an attractive location for a prominent Parisian leisure activity, the promenade. A song from the early nineteenth century included as its refrain:

La seul' prom'nade qu'a du prix,
La seule dont je suis épris,
La seule où je m'en donne, où je ris
C'est l'boul'vard du Temple à Paris.[7]

[The only promenade that's worth it,
The only one I am taken with,
The only one where I give myself, where I laugh
Is the boulevard du Temple in Paris.]

The song continues with stanzas about the theaters, cafés, and public gardens that added to the amusement. Ostensibly a location for "popular" entertainment, the Boulevard also attracted elegant ladies and gentlemen. In 1805, the *Journal des dames et des modes* (an expensive proto fashion magazine) published an article on promenades that explained how fashion determined where upper-class strollers decided to spend their time. "There are many promenades in Paris; nothing more magnificent than the Tuileries, more vast than the Champs-Elysées, more varied than the boulevards, [or] more rural than the Vincennes woods; but . . . for [a promenade] to be frequented, it is necessary that it be à la mode."[8] The garden near the Louvre and the Tuileries palace, the Tuileries was the place where members of court would stroll. The same people who went there for their promenades could also go to the "varied" Boulevard, when fashion dictated that it was in good taste to be seen in the less sophisticated location.[9]

A young unmarried woman's letters recounting a trip to Paris in 1821 lend credence to the openness of these spaces even to women of the middle and upper classes. A member of a family that ran a glassworks company and other successful businesses in the Loire Valley and eastern Brittany, Adèle Vallois was in her late teens when she visited the capital. The letters she wrote to her cousin's wife in Nantes describe her fascination with and enjoyment of Parisian sights.

We have already visited all the stores along the Boulevard . . . , some of the cafés and restaurants, and nearly all the *jeux tortoni*. During the evening, it's off to the Palais Royal. . . . The galleries are magnificent when lit up, and it is also de rigueur to have ice cream at the café de foi. I also find amusing the bright costumes *(brillante toilette)* of the prostitutes *(grandes poupées)* who circulate in the galleries. . . . One evening, I also visited all the *petits spectacles* along the Boulevard . . . all these parades are very amusing, these cafés and gardens, among others the Jardin Turc.[10]

This young woman was free to move about and enjoy various sorts of entertainment for which Paris was known. The entire city became a spectacle for her to observe with glee, including the prostitutes of the Palais Royal whom she refers to as "grandes poupées" (literally, "big dolls"). She likened visiting the *petits spectacles* along the Boulevard to a parade, one she no doubt observed as a spectator while contributing to it herself. In most cases she used the pronoun "we," which suggests she rarely explored on her own. Still, she was free to observe the spectacle the city and its inhabitants were constantly creating for her and everyone else to consume.[11]

The businesses along the Boulevard were as diverse as the crowds that patronized them: cafés, shops, public dance halls, and a wide range of amusements attracted Parisians and visitors to the city in large numbers. Guidebooks published during the first two decades of the nineteenth century highlighted this diversity above all else. One described the boulevards of northern Paris as "bordered by a thousand and one little boutiques that [are] packed up and cleared away each evening, and where *petits spectacles* [of all sorts] shine in all their glory. . . . This is the favorite promenade for property owners *(rentiers)* of the Marais, idlers *(oisifs)*, and prostitutes *(Vénus subalternes)* of the adjacent streets."[12] Among these *petits spectacles* was, for example, a "*muséum mécanique* . . . where one could see scenes like 'the beheading of Saint John the Baptist.'"[13] As others have found for the later nineteenth century, this was a culture of spectacle, in which various businesses and their customers all became part of the show.[14]

Cafés provided one of the best ways to observe this spectacle, and the cafés of the Boulevard were as varied as the crowds.[15] Many were affiliated with one of the theaters, such as the café de la Gaîté, next door to the theater of the same name. Others were known for their outdoor gardens and terraces. The most successful of these, Frascati, on the rue de Richelieu, was the subject of a satirical newspaper article that described it as the fashionable place to "get ice cream and breathe some fresh air." Most striking for the journalist was the "imperturbable thoughtlessness of women wearing meter-long trains, and the admirable care taken by men, pushed on all sides and dragged along by the crowds, to find a means to avoid tearing the fragile tissue floating in front of them."[16] Another of these outdoor establishments was the café Turc, which an 1811 guidebook described as "the most famous of the numerous cafés of the Boulevard. . . . Its unique form, the beauty of its garden and terraces, the immense crowd that fills it, everything adds up to a spectacle of infinite variety."[17] The pleasure of such a place revolved around participating in this variety as both a spectator and person on display. One went to these cafés precisely because of the numbers of people who frequented them, and these establishments drew such large crowds because of their proximity to all the other attractions of the Boulevard. According to one provincial tourist, "It is during the intermission of a melodrama that is attracting large audiences that it is necessary to see a café of the Boulevard."[18] The interconnectedness of theaters and other businesses in the neighborhood to the genre of melodrama must not be overlooked. The new genre, which brought characters from a wide range of social backgrounds together on stage, also assembled a broad array of social actors in the streets and public places like restaurants, cafés, and dance halls located nearby.

The Boulevard attracted the largest crowds on Sundays when working people were free from their ordinary occupations. In the eighteenth century, apparently, elites frequented public promenades only on workdays. On Sundays and holidays, "people of good taste do not go out . . . they flee the promenades and the theater, abandoning them to the peuple."[19] That practice returned with the Restoration when commentators made a point of specifying that Sundays and Mondays, essentially the weekend, were for workers and their families and that the upper classes went to the Boulevard on other days of the week. Although the upper classes enjoyed the atmosphere at the Boulevard, they began avoiding it on those days when it was overrun with the peuple. In contrast to the 1805 description of elite women "rattling the stones . . . with fruit women" that opened this chapter, an 1816 article entitled "Journal d'une petite maîtresse" (journal of a [female] dandy) in the *Journal des dames et des modes* begins with a woman complaining that "last Sunday, the weather was so horrible I could not go to the country, and considering the day of the week, I could not go to the theater *(les spectacles, vu le jour, m'étoient défendus)*."[20] Such ladies may have avoided spaces for popular amusements when the "popular classes" filled them, but this was not because they disliked the plays. Melodramas appealed to everyone.

## Melodrama as a Genre

Two influential studies of melodrama provide complementary analyses of the contents of these plays and how they functioned in their social context. In *The Melodramatic Imagination*, Peter Brooks emphasizes the democratic nature of the genre, insisting that the plays presented their messages, whether liberal or conservative, in a form that was easily understood by everyone. Melodrama's function, he argues, is to uncover, demonstrate, and make "operative the essential moral universe in the post-sacred era."[21] In *L'entreprise mélodramatique*, Julia Przybos focuses on what these messages were and concludes that "classical melodrama" had a clear purpose: to strengthen social hierarchies and to convince the masses to obey their superiors.[22] Building on this work, but taking a different approach, this section considers the genre from the perspective of the spectators. For our purposes, the plays themselves are significant to the extent that they give a sense of the experiences of spectators and reflect audience preferences. Although the "messages" may have been about strengthening social hierarchies, their consumption suggests far less straightforward implications.

Melodramas drew huge audiences because they provided an image of a world in which everyone knew where they stood. The plays soothingly portrayed as constant birth-based forms of social status as well as the hierarchical relationship between male and female and master and servant.[23] They often involved cases of mistaken identity in which an innocent young woman would find herself in a terrible situation through no fault of her own. Always perfectly evil or good, by the end of the play, characters invariably revealed their "true" natures. Theorists of the genre see that "visibility" as a key component to understanding the genre's appeal.[24] In the aftermath of the Revolution, people wanted clarity and easy answers; they wanted to see villains punished and heroes (and heroines) rewarded. To quote Brooks: "Melodrama starts from and expresses the anxiety brought by a frightening new world in which the traditional patterns of moral order no longer provide the necessary social glue."[25] The explicit messages articulated by the plays were conservative, propounding the existence of "natural" hierarchies and the great benefits gained by obeying them. However, the overall experience of Boulevard theater, including participating in the shared emotions inspired by them, at times subverted the propagandistic motives of playwrights and the government censors whose approval they sought. As a result, theaters became sites in which the ambiguities intrinsic to the postrevolutionary project of recreating order were expressed and understood. Just as play-wrights negotiated with censors about what could be included in their plays, audiences negotiated with theater management by choosing which plays to see and through their vocal responses at the performances.

The genre suited the emotional needs not only of the "masses," who were assumed to be its consumers, but also of many members of the upper classes who enjoyed melodrama as consistently as the workers and artisans whom playwrights addressed. Although historians have debated the utility of attempting to analyze the mentality of ordinary people through exami-nation of culture they did not produce themselves, the particularities of melodrama's consumption eliminate or at least greatly reduce such difficul-ties.[26] Although distinctions between "folk culture" and the mass-produced popular culture of "modern" societies remain valid, spectators and readers do not passively accept whatever is made available to them. They choose how to spend their money on cultural products even if they do not produce that culture themselves.[27] With melodrama, consumers influenced the pro-duction quite directly, as playwrights frequently adjusted their plays based on audience reactions at the initial performances. According to Przybos, "The day after the first performance is a day of intense labor: the author and the stage managers adapt the play depending on the whistles, the stamping, the cries, the laughs, the tears of the public and, of course, the reviews pub-lished in the press. They readjusted the play, to season it to suit better the taste of the spectators."[28] Though not as formal, these practices resembled today's test showings of films prior to their release; consumers had a direct impact on this early form of "mass culture."

Writers and producers made use of a wide variety of devices to draw crowds to theaters; two of the most important were backdrops and settings, which apparently went a long way in determining the success of a melo-drama.[29] One critic went so far as to say the decoration alone was sufficient to assure the play he was reviewing "the hundred performances necessary to define a melodrama as a success."[30] Another article stated bluntly, "We are resolutely in the century of decorations."[31] By depicting a frightful environ-ment, playwrights could instantaneously foster tension and fear. This pro-cess was explained in a satirical pamphlet entitled *Traité du mélodrame, par MM. A! A! A!* "On the boulevards, one of the first principles is that in order to please, it is necessary to surprise.... For nothing captivates our spirit and our heart better than a prison of melodrama! ... A cavern is equally in-dispensable to the perfection of a work: placed in the middle of an obscure forest, it will be frequented by wolves, wild boar, bears, and by men one hundred times more ferocious still!"[32] Suspense, fear, and pleasure were inseparably linked in these performances. The idea was to immerse spectators in an exotic world that was both terrifying and appealing because of its contrast to daily life. Spectacular effects helped to hold the attention of audiences, and villains added to the frightening atmosphere as they personified pure evil through their victimization of innocent young women.

The most successful early melodrama, Pixérécourt's *Cœlina ou l'enfant de mystère* (first performed on 2 September 1800), defined the genre's formula for the following twenty years, including the four essential characters: the villain, the innocent and virtuous heroine, the honest man who protects innocence, and the comic character—the *niais* or fool.[33] The play revolves around the plight of a purely good young woman who finds herself in a seemingly hopeless dilemma where despite her virtue and honesty, the people around her think she is untrustworthy. In the opening scene of the third and final act she appears alone in a forest. The stage description covers every minutia and reveals the extreme care taken with décor, which worked in conjunction with the narrative. "During intermission, the distant noise of thunder is heard: soon the storm intensifies and at the curtain-rise, all of nature seems in disorder; brilliant lightning everywhere, thunder rolling with fury, the wind bellowing, the rain falling with a crash, and the multiple thunder claps, which are repeated a hundred times by the echo of the mountains, carry terror and dismay into the soul."[34] No detail could be overlooked in the production of a melodrama, even during intermission. The main character's distress had to be mirrored in nature's torment in remote, exotic-sounding locations.

Spectators cared most about backdrops, ballets, and music. Successful plays, those that managed to draw large crowds to performance after performance, created a multifaceted experience as spectators heard the music, watched the dances, and allowed themselves to get caught up in the mood of the plays. One reviewer made explicit the connection between décor and music and the likelihood of a melodrama's success (in this case Pixérécourt's *Robinson Crusoe*): "The din of the performance, the decorations, the dances, the movements of the Caribbean natives, the fireworks, the bells, the musket fire, the music, the caricature, the grimaces of Friday, the theological, philosophical and political declamations of the chief of the savages and of the Spanish captain, form an unbelievable ensemble that guarantees at least fifty performances to this new masterpiece of the boulevards."[35] Every review of a melodrama included evaluations of the decorations and dances because "on the Boulevard, everything depends on the manner . . . in which a subject is treated."[36] In comparison to the subtle turns of phrase that entertained the spectators at classical theater, popular theater relied on hard-hitting techniques, including outrageous sights and sounds. One reviewer stated: "The ordinary spectators of our Boulevard theaters fancy a sturdier genre. They want more substantial nourishment, and always prefer the sound of drums, the pomp of melodrama, and the marvels of the stage technician to the most melodious sounds."[37] What exactly was meant by "ordinary" spectators in this quotation is far from clear. Nonetheless, the importance of technical effects is echoed in the printed versions of plays, theater reviews, and every form of writing about the genre. The common assumption at the time was that for a play to succeed it had to surround the spectators with the sights and sounds of another world. Audiences thus found themselves transported to a place where emotions mattered more than money and where good always triumphed.[38]

"Goodness" most frequently took the form of an innocent young woman, and one of the most striking innovations within the plots of melodramas was this prevalence of female central characters. As emphasized by Brooks, "Virtue is almost inevitably represented by a young heroine, though in classical French melodrama . . . she need not be a virgin, for it is moral sentiment more than technical chastity that is at issue." But for goodness to function, it required its antithesis. "Opposed to virtue and innocence stands the active, concerted denial of them in the person of evil, known traditionally as *le traître,* no doubt because he dissimulates, but also because he betrays and undoes the moral order."[39] As symbols of virtue, heroines represented not only perfect goodness but also perfect women, not unlike the real women put on display as brides at Napoleonic festivals and at the "virtue" awards of the Restoration. The fact that these virtuous young women tended to take center stage in melodramas was one of the defining features of the genre. In her examination of the literature of the period, Doris Kadish argues that although women lost political rights in the aftermath of the Revolution, they were "propelled forward culturally and symbolically as political participants."[40] Gender, according to Kadish, became an increasingly visible issue, and the new focus on female characters supports her views. Although women had no direct political leverage, they became increasingly important as symbols of a healthy society. An obsession with female behavioral norms, expressed through countless publications about women's education and their roles in raising future generations, emerged out of a desire to find stability and order after so many years of chaos.[41] But that search for stability was hindered by the fact that what it meant to be a "woman" varied considerably depending on class.

Melodramatic plays presented contradictory messages with regard to ideal female roles and behavior. Far from meek and docile, melodramatic heroines demonstrate great strength and courage, but the strength of character the women display must be juxtaposed to the fact that plotlines turn around their victimization. When the villains attack them in some way that threatens to ruin their entire lives, the heroines' reactions are limited to passive acceptance of their fate until a plan emerges through which they can retrieve both their status and their innocence, usually with the help of a man who is in some way subservient to them. After recognizing that they could not simply rely upon the protection of men, their own intelligence and bravery usually saved these women; they managed to remove themselves from terrible situations exactly because they were *not* weak and powerless. Generally, however, they maintained a veneer of helplessness, and their vocabulary emphasized their intense fear despite their brave behavior.[42] In contrast to upper-class heroines, the female characters who *could* appear both outwardly and inwardly strong tended to be peasants and other working women, such as innkeepers. Although these secondary female characters possessed strong wills, even to the point of being overbearing, they still represented "good" women. One young woman, a miller's daughter in Pixérécourt's *Tékéli,* might have been described by her fiancé as emasculating, but instead he states: "They say that my wife will be the mistress, that she will do with me what she wishes, and it is for that reason that I will be the happiest of men in my little household."[43] Although some irony may have been at work here, the idea that good wives had to be passive was not a common theme of these plays. Unlike the heroines who tended to be superficially passive but strong underneath, lower-class female characters were openly strong-willed and powerful, participating in public life alongside their husbands. Unsurprisingly, the plays portrayed and reinforced divergent standards of behavior for women of the different classes.

Plays focusing on the plight of a male character tended to be less successful, which suggests that audiences were more comfortable with a woman as the heroine/victim than a man. Why might such a preference have existed? First, audiences may have felt uncomfortable seeing men made into victims and put into such passive positions.[44] Second, they may have found it easier to accept a woman as perfectly good, as all melodramatic heroines had to be. The category of "men" seemed more susceptible to subtleties, whereas "women" were viewed as either wholly good or wholly bad. In literature too, female characters appealed most to readers of the very early 1800s, whereas male characters came to dominate romantic literature of the 1820s.[45] Melodramas both shaped and responded to evolving behavioral expectations for men and women; the changing nature of these views led to frequently contradictory representations of "proper" male and female behavior.

The ambiguity of these messages results from the fact that the plays' plot-lines nearly always revolved around evil men (and sometimes evil women as well) victimizing the female lead characters even though they were "virtuous" women who had always behaved properly. These women's passivity and innocence resulted in their near-ruin, but their action and strength saved them. They were not the delicate creatures of later nineteenth-century melodramas who responded to their "ruin" by throwing poison in the faces of men who mistreated them. The sense of helplessness among heroines in these later melodramas prohibited them from improving their situations; they could only hope for revenge.[46] Despite their ability to fight to save themselves, the female lead characters of early melodramas maintained a veneer of passivity. These contradictory messages reflect uncertainties within society as a whole about women's "nature" and its repercussions. Although one could argue that these were the views of playwrights and not of the broader population represented by audiences, melodrama's contents and form reflected popular attitudes. Audiences would not have liked the plays if they could not relate to them or if the performances contradicted their beliefs about human nature or about femininity and masculinity.

In her analysis of the settings of melodramas from 1800 to 1830, Marie-Pierre Le Hir found a change over time that supports the view that attitudes toward women and their roles were in transition in postrevolutionary France. In the mid-1820s, a shift occurred from a tendency toward outdoor scenes and *pièces historiques* to plays that took place in one room of a home, usually the salon.[47] These new *drames bourgeois,* which presented women in domestic surroundings, replaced the more outrageous scenes in caves and forests prominent in the earlier period. Le Hir views this trend as supporting arguments that the ideology of separate spheres was gaining ground in the 1820s. Although convincing, Le Hir's interpretation needs to be supplemented by a complementary explanation, because the plays may have changed for reasons other than a transition in such attitudes. Work on censorship shows that stricter controls under Napoleon had limited the choice of settings for plays to places and times distant from contemporary France, whereas under the Restoration, playwrights could return to portraying quotidian scenes from French society.[48] In addition, focusing on domestic bliss might have been seen as bolstering the image of the king as rightful father of his people.

The transition to a new form of melodrama can be seen in theater reviews from the 1820s, which reveal constant experimentation in order to suit the changing desires of spectators. First was an effort to make use of more prestigious and well-known heroes. "The peuple have a great need for novelty. Disgusted with the brigands who caused delight during melodrama's early days, the peuple are now only interested in bloody undertakings that receive rank and importance from the grandeur of the characters involved. . . . They [the peuple] want to shed their tears for great victims and no longer for the subaltern victims who only have the merit of being *innocent, unhappy, and persecuted.*"[49] According to this 1821 review, high-ranking heroes were drawing the biggest crowds to Boulevard theaters that year, replacing the lowly characters of early melodramas. Less than eighteen months later, the same newspaper included a review that insisted that "important people" had lost their appeal, while ordinary and realistic heroes had taken their place once again. Arguing that "a great revolution had taken place on the Boulevard," the reviewer concluded that "*innocent, unhappy, and persecuted* princesses . . . no longer inspire pity. . . . [Now] the heroes we want to see on stage are an old soldier honorably mutilated, a businessman who enriches his country with his useful enterprise, a cultivator who fertilizes the ground."[50] Here we also see a transition toward male heroes as opposed to the female heroes of "classic melodrama," a shift paralleled in French literature of the period more generally.[51] Constantly evolving to suit the desires of their consumers, melodramatic theater thus provides information on audience preferences, which appear to have been changing rapidly, especially in the 1820s. Such fluctuations reflect developing attitudes about the larger society that audiences brought with them into the theater.

## Audiences and Their Reactions: Popular Theater and Social Hierarchy

By 1800, when melodrama took its place as a genre that appealed to both the "illiterate masses" for whom it was purportedly written as well as their assumed social superiors, the egalitarian aims of the Revolution had been abandoned in all but rhetoric. Because the "democratic" nature of the theater placed individuals from virtually all social strata in close proximity to one another, it allowed spectators to observe firsthand how they differed from others of lesser or greater status. This section treats the issue of spectators as spectacle: who reacted how to these plays, and the significance of audience members' similar or dissimilar behavior as they observed each other inside theaters. This "visibility" in the mixed social space created by Boulevard theaters shaped spectators' notions of social distinctions as well as their sense of their own identities and roles within postrevolutionary society.

In many ways, the interiors of the theaters underlined class distinctions. The engraving *Theatrical Observations: The Crying Spectators* (Figure 3.2) depicts a clear-cut social and seating hierarchy. The poorest members of the audience crowded together in the parterre or pit, the benches nearest the stage. Shopkeepers and well-off artisans sat above them, in the balcony or *galeries.* Finally, at the top of the architectural hierarchy were the loges or boxes, which were beyond the means of any but fairly wealthy people. Images such as these highlight the hierarchical orientation of the physical space within theaters. Such engravings demonstrate how popular theater may have reinforced social hierarchies by emphasizing the huge distinctions between audience members: those in the parterre appear crude, dirty, and unintelligent compared with those in the loges above.[52] An image dating from 1837 when such "physiognomies" were all the rage, the engraving depicts the enormous differences visible among audience members so as to highlight the diversity of those found in theaters.[53] On the one hand, the hierarchy of seats and their differing degrees of crowding make a strong case for the class-stratifying capabilities of the theater even as all groups sat in one audience. On the other hand, however, such images portray diverse people reacting similarly and sharing in a common experience, which could be interpreted as dismantling such hierarchies.

The close proximity of individuals from such a wide spectrum of society would have made comparison of these different groups a simple task, allowing audience members to observe and construct the social hierarchies on display around them. This aspect of attending melodramas may have functioned as "cultural capital," a concept used by sociologist Pierre Bourdieu to emphasize the ways familiarity with cultural norms can be an important component of class distinctions. Bourdieu's work is helpful in that it brings attention to mechanisms that allow the ruling classes to reproduce

**Figure 3.2.** Clément Pruche, *Observations théâtrales: Les spectateurs pleurant* (Theatrical Observations: The Crying Spectators; 1837). The original French caption translates as follows: "We wipe our noses, we cry. . . . The poor innocent girl! And to think that she will be sacrificed, with her faded green dress and her hat with its pink pompom, before the unhappy eyes of her white-haired father! (Tears stream down everyone's faces. We have never seen anything so sad!)" Photo courtesy of the Bibliothèque Nationale de France, Paris.

themselves through educational institutions and cultural practices.[54] Though an important and influential discussion of culture and class in contemporary democracies, Bourdieu's analysis does little to show how cultural practices can also subvert social hierarchies, depending on the context. In postrevolutionary France, the issue at stake was not how to reinforce existing structures but rather how to rebuild (or construct new) forms of social hierarchy. Theaters on the Boulevard helped to clarify the meaning and significance of such distinctions. The overall experience at Boulevard theaters did not necessarily convince audience members of their superiority or inferiority, but it did help them gain a sense of how the new, postrevolutionary

social order would function, thanks to the opportunity it provided to observe others around them.

The theater represented an occasion for lower-class spectators to leave
their ordinary lives and concerns behind as they immersed themselves in another world.[55] Although the specific features of plays could determine their
level of success, plots and messages mattered less than the overall experience
of attending the theater. Audiences went to see how a well-known story
would be performed—not to learn about morals, even if playwrights de-
fended the genre as teaching them. They wanted an entertaining night out,
and if melodramatic theater functioned simply as escapism, that makes the
genre no less significant than other forms of literature or drama. In fact, one
could argue that melodrama's ability to encourage this feeling of experienc-
ing another world largely explains its success. The whole point of attending
these plays was to experience intense emotional responses to frightening and
thrilling situations that often caused audience members to shriek, and even to
faint. The success of La femme à deux maris seemed assured by the fact that
the "play was received with the unanimous applause and the continuous tears
of the spectators."[56] The obtrusive nature of audience responses meant that
theaters were often filled not only with the noise of thunder and gunshots
from the stage but also the laughter, whistles, applause, and screams of spectators. The multifaceted nature of the event—watching the play, watching
others, and being watched—only intensified the effect. As spectators became
part of the spectacle, French society itself was on display.

Recounting her visit to Paris in 1815, the Irish novelist Lady Morgan emphasized the popularity of the Boulevard across the socioeconomic spectrum
as well as the expansion of the "spectacle" beyond the performance itself.

> The Théatres [sic] des Boulevards ... divide among them drams [sic],
> melodramas, pantomime, dancing, and petites piéces [sic] of every de-
> scription. And though it is a sort of ton for persons of fashion to go in large
> parties to these most amusing of theaters two or three times in a season,
> yet the audience generally speaking appeared to me to be extremely coarse
> and so loud and vivacious in their disapprobation, or applause, and so cu-
> rious and varied in their costume and appearance, as to form almost as en-
> tertaining a part of the spectacle as the representations on stage.[57]

Lady Morgan's commentary, as well as other sources of information on audiences, leaves no doubt that wealthier spectators relished the opportunity
to observe those literally and figuratively below them. At first glance, it would

seem that the ability of the upper rows of seats to watch the lower rows with ease meant that the upper classes attended the theater in part to observe the lower orders of society, and perhaps to ridicule their behavior, whereas the working classes attended melodramas to watch the plays. However, one cannot simply assume that this one-directional observation was always the case. The peuple could watch more than the play itself, and those in the more expensive seats could become as engrossed by a melodrama as anyone else. Although the plays were ostensibly written for the "masses," for "those who cannot read," and the cost of tickets enabled quite poor people to attend, melodrama apparently appealed to everyone across the social spectrum.[58] One scholar has argued that "this period's theater can be described as 'popular,' not with regard to what was written but in thinking of the public which frequented these theaters regularly, [even] daily, and who, proletarians and bourgeois, cried and laughed together."[59] Regardless of who sat in these theaters, melodrama was defined as "popular" culture. As attending Boulevard theater represented a form of "slumming" for the upper classes, they interpreted the experience in a different manner than less wealthy theatergoers.

Nonetheless, early in the period, discussions of audiences underline their common motivations, expectations, and reactions, depicting elite spectators—especially female ones—as enjoying the plays as wholeheartedly as those in the parterre. In an 1809 poem about melodrama purportedly written for provincials to help them understand Parisian culture, Armand Charlemagne portrayed the typical spectator as a wealthy *mère de famille*. While in her loge, she puts herself on display as much as those in the parterre, and she insists on silence so as not to miss a moment of the performance.

> Radieuse de luxe, et belle de parure,
> Hortense, après dîner, demande sa voiture.
>
> . . . . . . . . . . . . . . .
>
> Madame aux boulevards, va, dans toute sa gloire,
> Voir le Pied de Mouton, ou bien la Forêt Noire.
>     Elle arrive, et prend place en loge d'apparat.
> Tous les yeux sont fixés sur elle, et son éclat,
>
> . . . . . . . . . . . . . . .
>
>     Hortense est reposée: elle a déjà reçu
> De quelques survenants un hommage impromptu,
> Ce sont des amis, idolâtres, comme elle,

Des beaux traits espérés de la pièce nouvelle,
Tous gens d'un très bon ton, comme elle, aux boulevards,
Amenés par l'affiche et le goût des beaux arts.

. . . . . . . . . . . . . .

Le signal est donné: noblesse et populace,
Honnêtes gens, faquins, tout le monde est en place.
Hortense se recueille au bruit des instruments,
Qui sont les précurseurs de ses ravissements.
Mais la toile se lève, et la pièce commence,
Madame à ses voisins a commandé silence.
Elle écoute . . . elle écoute avec attention,
Et rien ne peut troubler sa contemplation.[60]

[Radiant with luxury and beautifully dressed,
Hortense, after dinner, asks for her carriage.

. . . . . . . . . . . . . .

Madame is going to the boulevards in all her glory,
To see the Sheep's Foot or the Black Forest.
She arrives and takes her place in her loge.
All eyes are fixed on her and her luster,

. . . . . . . . . . . . . .

Hortense is relaxed; she has already received
From several chance-comers an impromptu homage,
These are friends, admirers like herself,
Of the beautiful features expected of the new play,
All fashionable people like her, at the boulevards,
Drawn by the poster and their taste for the arts.

. . . . . . . . . . . . . .

The signal is given: nobility and populace,
Honest people, rascals, everyone is in place.
Hortense sits back at the sound of the instruments,
Which are the precursors of her delight.
But the curtain rises, and the play begins,
Madame demands silence of her neighbors.
She listens . . . she listens with attention,
And nothing can trouble her contemplation.]

Despite the satirical nature of this piece, the author's decision to use an upper-class woman as his stereotypical spectator is significant. As other examples will show, women emerged as the imagined primary consumers of melodrama. This poem also raises doubts about the frequent assumption that the lower classes went to these theaters to watch the plays whereas their social superiors went to mock the other spectators and to ridicule the performances. This woman listened attentively to every word spoken in the play, as did the "nobility and populace, honest people [and] rascals" seated around her. Being literate and having money did not preclude one from enjoying culture created for "those who cannot read." An 1813 account of French theater life also drew attention to female spectators at melodramas, noting that "our ladies have developed a strong passion for melodrama: they prefer being frightened to being only weakly moved."[61] Upper-class female spectators could become spectacles as easily as others, as well. The Boilly painting *The Effect of Melodrama* (Figure 3.3) portrays a woman sitting in the most expensive area of seats who has found the play to be so moving that she has fainted dramatically into the arms of her companions. Though we cannot accept

**Figure 3.3.** Louis-Léopold Boilly, *L'effet du mélodrame* (The Effect of Melodrama; 1830). Photo courtesy of the Bibliothèque Nationale de France, Paris.

such images as unproblematic representations of social reality, their emphasis on female consumers of melodrama and their heightened sensitivity makes clear that this was an issue that attracted enormous attention. In these examples, it was upper-class women who were most moved by melodrama.

Contemporary theater critics and moralists expended great effort to explain and track the fascination with melodrama. Reviews from the first decade of the nineteenth century emphasized the novelty of the genre and the unbelievably strong attraction toward it among those who should have known better.[62] In 1806, for example, the *Gazette de France* argued that when it came to theater, "everyone seems equally rich, uses the same language, and pays attention to the same things." The writer continued with a more general discussion of Parisian life. "We no longer laugh in Paris: at the promenades, we yawn; in the salons, we play; at the theater we scream; while in the city, we pretend to prefer the country; while in the country, we transfer the activities of the city. *Everyone wants to change his condition. (Chacun veut changer d'état.)*"[63] Based on the array of activities listed, the author was clearly not referring to the working classes when he mentioned "everyone," as they were not among the people who had city and country residences. Yet he tried to suggest that all social groups enjoyed the same experiences at the theater. What implications were read into these common interests? Elites' enthusiasm for "popular" culture certainly struck many contemporaries as worthy of concern. Nonetheless, the overall point was that for better or worse, rich and poor were sharing a common experience: receiving the same messages, laughing and crying at the same moments. The resulting conclusion is that all were there because they were attracted to the same thing—men, women, children, servants, shop owners, respectable bourgeois, and even nobles enjoyed the emotional thrill of a good melodrama.

Over time, references to distinctions among spectators at melodramas became more pronounced and apparently more meaningful. Whether a real change had taken place in the composition and reactions of audiences is difficult to determine, but an acutely class-conscious sense of both emerged during the Restoration. Throughout the period, a more "popular" crowd attended melodramas on Sundays and Mondays, the days when workers were free from their jobs.[64] In a text published in 1814, a well-known playwright described this "other" set of spectators.

Sundays, the theaters of the peuple are filled with an altogether different class of individuals. . . . [We no longer find] workers . . . spending immoderately and [upper-class] misanthropes . . . bored with all pleasures

coming to yawn at a melodrama. . . . [Instead we find] modest shop owners *(commerçants)* or manufacturers *(fabricants),* hard-working artisans
who remain at home on working days, hoping to entertain their large
families with inexpensive amusement. In fact, the observer notices on this
day that the audience has a different composition: it is full of respectable
old men, interested mothers, young girls *( jeunes demoiselles)* and adoles-
cent boys.[65]

Depending on the day, then, the seating hierarchy may have represented
subtler distinctions among a narrower segment of the population than one
might expect based on depictions found in "physiognomies" (Figure 3.2).

Reviews from the early 1820s reveal a different emphasis: although audiences continued to represent a wide range of French society, critics chose to
emphasize the differing responses of various groups. From the first scene of
the melodrama *Les mogols,* which premiered in 1821, the reviewer struggled
to understand the dialogue because of the "sardonic laughter" and nearly
constant whistles with which it was received. He was able, however, to hear
the last lines of the final scene. The villain, Defresne, was addressing the
woman responsible for his capture as a usurper to the throne: " 'So, implacable woman, what do you want?' Mme Dorval responded to him
wickedly, 'your death.' Defrense, . . . presenting a sword to the implacable
woman [says,] 'Here . . . strike, ascend [the throne], and reign.' In response
to these magnanimous words, the audience in the parterre applauded, those
in the loges shrugged their shoulders, the spectators in the *galeries* whistled,
and the curtain fell."[66] Those in the cheapest seats responded enthusiastically to the "usurper" being brought down by this woman, while the more
well-off spectators were less impressed. Exactly what this distinction means
about either popular attitudes toward the monarchy or the journalist's political views is difficult to say. What matters for our purposes is the strong
contrast between reviewers writing in the first decades of the nineteenth
century who made no effort to depict the differing responses of various
groups within the theater and these later reviewers who went out of their
way to do so.

Dissimilar responses among the various groups within audiences are logical given that the significance of attending the theater must have been different for each group. Wealthier theatergoers could have easily attended the
theater several times a week. For poorer members of the audience, their experience at the theater represented a significant expense (in part because it

required a great deal of time) and a chance to step out of their day-to-day routines. The theaters of the Boulevard that included melodramas in their repertoires—the Théâtre de la Gaîté, the Ambigu-Comique, and the Porte Saint-Martin—staged two or three plays at a time. Preceding or following the typical three-act melodramas came one or two short comedies or vaude-villes, usually in one act. Spectators expected about four hours of entertainment, and they would queue up for hours to buy tickets.[67] The spectacle could begin even before entering the theater as people conversed and watched passersby. Of course, the crowds outside the theaters presented yet another opportunity for various forms of disorder. The Boilly painting *Free Performance at the Ambigu-Comique* (Figure 2.2) depicts an unruly crowd of mostly men in working-class attire climbing over each other as they try to reach the theater entrance for a free performance. Nearby, a well-dressed man and woman look on, wishing perhaps that they had chosen another night to attend this particular theater.

The architecture of the theaters accentuated the "elevated" form of entertainment the spectators had chosen and further highlighted the feeling of leaving one's ordinary life.[68] Through imitation of the elite theaters, the highly decorated facades of Boulevard theaters suggested luxury. As part of his discussion of what he termed "modern churches," critic Hyppolyte Auger described one of them with venom: "The façade . . . of the Ambigu-Comique theater is pretentious and ridiculous for its position *(situation)*, with its three rows of super-imposed columns and its statues."[69] Clearly, these perceptions cannot be taken at face value as the writer was ridiculing the pretensions of the working people who attended melodrama. Nonetheless, the architectural designs demonstrate a belief in (if not the existence of ) a desire for grandeur among the spectators (Figure 3.1). Like the later development of ready-made clothing that allowed shop girls to wear cheap imitations of wealthy women's attire, the theaters of the Boulevard replicated "true" theaters. The working classes' ability to emulate more upper-class forms of cultural consumption was a cause for concern, as indicated in the prize-winning essay by Jean-Baptiste-Louis Camel about the influence of secondary theaters on the peuple (see the Introduction to this book).

Attending melodramatic theater provided members of the working classes with a means to learn more about bourgeois behavior, and if they so desired, to imitate it. The plays they watched may have underlined seemingly unavoidable "natural" differences based on birth, but their attendance at the theater in itself indicated a desire to live like *les grands* to some extent. Also, regardless of their obviously differing "physiognomies," spectators could see that they were all in one place enjoying the same form of entertainment and thus had similar tastes regardless of class. Once in these theaters, the working classes simply needed to turn their heads to watch the more well-to-do members of the audience.[70] Audience members could then use their observations to develop an understanding of what signified higher class status, to learn to read the new markers of social position that were emerging and evolving during the Napoleonic and Restoration periods, and to emulate the behavior of both the characters on stage and the spectators around them.

In both melodramatic plays and in representations of audiences, the primary form of "cultural capital" being circulated within theaters was heightened sensitivity among women. Female *sensibilité* was a common trope in postrevolutionary literary representations of women. In her study of early nineteenth-century French novels, Margaret Cohen found a "pervasive gendering of sentimentality as feminine."[71] Constance de Salm, a staunch defender of women's right to participate in public life and one of the most prominent female writers and intellectuals of the Empire and the Restoration, depicted women as inherently more sentimental than men.[72] She explored female sensitivity in a short novel entitled *Vingt-quatres heures d'une femme sensible,* composed of letters written by a distraught woman who believes she has been betrayed by her lover. In the introduction to the novel, Salm stated, "Women have in their souls a multitude of feelings that [even] the most tender lover can barely understand: to him they may seem to be a form of delirium."[73] At melodramatic theaters, spaces in which both actors and spectators displayed their emotions, women's behavior attracted more attention than men's, suggesting that class distinctions relied more on women's comportment than men's.[74] Though women and men of all classes may have shared these spaces, their differing behavior and responses encouraged cross-class comparison and emulation. This dynamic may provide a partial explanation of how notions of women's sensitivity emerged and spread down the social spectrum.[75] By the time of the 1837 engraving discussed earlier (Figure 3.2), lower-class women appear most visibly distraught.

Theatergoers in the various sections of the audience experienced the plays and the space in which they watched them in different ways. On the one hand, those in the upper tier of seats were more shielded from view, as they could sit back in their boxes to avoid being seen, whereas women and men crowded together in the cheaper seats did not have an opportunity to hide from sight. Considering the implications of *femmes publiques* and the dubious reputations of actresses, this positioning may have helped to reinforce notions of upper-class women's greater respectability. As the women in the theater who were least on display, they were also least like the public women on stage.[76] On the other hand, women in the loges did go to the theater to be seen as well. As in more elite theaters, friends and admirers greeted them upon their arrival. They certainly appeared in public when they attended the theater, though having a loge meant that they could create a sense of their own private space. Women sitting in the parterre had no such opportunity to minimize the "publicness" of their presence and hence to maximize their sense of respectability.

Two ramifications of the experience of melodrama vis-à-vis gender and class arise from the complex and often contradictory images of women as characters in plays and as spectators in audiences during this period. First, notions of proper female behavior emerged through expectations of female spectators' responses, a component of the experience that was reinforced by representations of women on stage. Second, the various groups attending the theater helped spread class-specific notions about women's "nature" from bourgeois women to those of the working classes. Women were expected to cry, to shriek, and even to faint while watching these plays. Failure to behave in such a way indicated a lack of delicacy. However, overly obtrusive reactions to plays also indicated lower-class origins. "Proper" behavior in a public place like the theater functioned as cultural capital. The various classes were expected (and expected themselves) to behave in different ways. Within the audience, spectators made use of this form of cultural capital as a test (and proof ) of social skill and status.

The extent to which nearly everyone in French society seemed to enjoy melodrama during the very early nineteenth century was perhaps the most commented-upon aspect of the genre at the time. However, the widespread interest in this shared experience proved to be rather short-lived. In the introduction to his complete works, Pixérécourt reminisced about the days when his plays were at their peak of popularity. He complained that unlike his own work, the plays of the 1830s were too scandalous for mothers to allow their young daughters to attend. Instead, "good society has little by little retired from public places, it has created other private customs. . . . For more than thirty years, I saw all of France flock to multiple performances of my work. Men, women, children, rich and poor, everyone came to laugh and to cry at the well-made melodrama. Alas! those times are over."[77] The first lines of this quotation are especially meaningful in the context of historiographical debates about women's public and private roles: as the nineteenth century wore on, "good society," especially its women and children, reduced its participation in public forms of recreation like melodrama. In his history of theater publics, Maurice Descotes argued that after 1820, "melodrama returned to being a purely popular genre; the evolution of society and of social norms *(mœurs)* brought good society back . . . to the official theaters . . . to find other authors who better expressed their aspirations. . . . The fusion of publics that had been established around 1800–1810 was only a memory."[78] Boulevard theaters continued to draw crowds throughout the July Monarchy, but they became more purely popular in terms of their audiences as more-elite audience members chose to attend theaters in other neighborhoods. In the first decades of the nineteenth century, however, melodramatic spectatorship provided an opportunity for men and women of all classes and all ages to participate regularly in a shared experience in the "public sphere."

Social mixing played a vital role in the formation and articulation of new conceptions of gender and class in the postrevolutionary period. It helped men and women develop a sense of how these forms of identity would function. Examination of the plays themselves reveals that these concepts were still in flux but were becoming increasingly well defined as the century wore on. More important, however, consideration of the shared experience of melodrama shows how the theater shaped audience members' views of their own identities as well as the characteristics of the new social order. Exaggerated emotional responses on the part of female spectators reinforced the view that women were more "sentimental" than men and permitted such attitudes to spread across classes, thus encouraging a uniform sense of "femininity," even if many working-class women could not live up to these emerging norms of female behavior.

As social spaces in which so many different people interacted with their culture and their society, Boulevard theaters permitted individuals to observe markers of status, many of which were highly gendered. Melodramas incorporated characters of various social backgrounds, and the disparate identities of audience members—rich and poor, male and female, young and old—enabled the groups represented among the spectators to observe and categorize behavioral peculiarities that characterized each group. Interpretations of the makeup of audiences and their differing reactions changed over time. Before 1820, emphasis was on the equivalent appeal of melodrama among all social classes; later it shifted to the ways in which those classes differed in their reactions to the plays. Finally, during the later 1820s, it seems that elites became less interested in melodramatic theater and increasingly separated themselves from this form of "popular" culture.[79] Until then, however, these plays appealed to a broad mix of Parisians and visitors to the city.

After 1830, Boulevard theaters appear to have attracted mostly lowbrow spectators. According to one account, one no longer saw the upper classes *(la bonne compagnie)* in the loges of Boulevard theaters in 1830. One visitor to Paris in 1830 remarked: "The ladies who occupy the first balconies *(les premières galeries)* appeared to be successful shop owners *(bonnes grosses marchandes)*, laughing at the top of their voices while fanning themselves with fans that can be purchased at the theater for six *sous*."[80] He did not mention any bourgeoises fainting into the arms of their companions. In his recent history of French actresses, Lenard Berlanstein came to similar conclusions. "The declining allure of the boulevard du Temple for the upper classes in the 1830s—one sign among many of deepening class divisions—marked the onset of a new era in the social history of the French theater.[81] After 1830, the upper classes tended to frequent theaters in neighborhoods that catered specifically to them, and if workers occasionally attended, they did so on the terms of the more bourgeois spectators who dominated the audiences. Once postrevolutionary social structures had solidified, the function of melodramatic spectatorship as an expression of new social norms was finished, and melodrama became a more purely working-class, "low-cultured" leisure activity. Melodramatic themes and techniques appeared in the work of Romantic writers like Victor Hugo and Alexandre de Dumas, but the Boulevard theaters in which melodrama was born no longer appealed to upper- and middle-class theatergoers.[82] Separate from the tumultuous world of the boulevard du Temple, which would be destroyed during Hausmannization in 1862, bourgeois women and men were free to allow their fears of the "dangerous classes" to grow to previously unimagined heights.[83] Earlier in the century, Boulevard theaters appealed to a broad range of the population, giving their varied clientele a chance to laugh and cry together in highly visible, public ways. As the following chapter shows, provincial theaters also permitted diverse groups to mingle and observe each other, but in a more highly charged atmosphere in which social, political, and sexual tensions were more on the surface than in the theaters of the capital.

# — 4 —

# Sex and Politics in
# Provincial Theaters

In December 1811, Lyon's commissioner general of the police wrote to the prefect about an incident that had taken place in the theater. "Audiences whistle before the curtain is raised, and they whistle on and off throughout the performances." Although he viewed the public's expression of its displeasure as a right that came with the purchase of a ticket, he insisted there were proper and improper ways to convey discontent: "Thus the parterre or the loges should only be permitted to express their views on an actor or a play at the end of an act." He then explained why such limitations needed to be enforced. "We should prohibit audience members from hissing and whistling . . . not only because these are noises which any good police force should prevent, but also because they inconvenience the majority of spectators, especially the women, who are the most beautiful ornaments at any gathering. . . . You are familiar . . . with public sentiment *(l'esprit public)* in Lyon. In this town especially, it only takes a spark, even one word, to ignite a fire [that] can reanimate the parties."[1] From the perspective of this official, women's presence inside theaters added a desirable facet to the experience, but politics was a far less sought-after addition.

This single letter about theatrical controls brings together many issues of significance in the early nineteenth century. It epitomizes the ways that concerns about policing, politics, sex, and gender norms found expression and overlapped in spaces designed for entertainment. It also draws attention to the fact that middle- and upper-class women in early nineteenth-century provincial theaters were part of the spectacle, just as eighteenth-century Parisian *grandes dames* had put themselves on display at the Théâtre Français and Opéra and many others made spectacles of themselves at Boulevard theaters once melodrama became the rage. Theaters became sites of male

103

privilege and heterosexual pleasure, which required women's presence (on the stage and off) even as their atmospheres seemed increasingly threatening to female spectators and actresses. Theaters risked losing these "ornaments," however, when audience members created havoc for one reason or another.

This chapter makes use of archival records that exist as a result of such disruptions to consider the makeup of provincial theater audiences, the significance of the experience of attending the theater, and the political and gender implications of such attendance. Because so little is known about provincial urban life during these years, the chapter also sketches out some details on theater management and attendance: cost, seating, types of performances and performers, and other matters that seem necessary to develop an understanding of the impact of theater attendance on these cities' inhabitants. As spaces that put the new social, political, and sexual order on display, provincial theaters played a vital role in allowing people to work through, and eventually contest, this new order. More than a cultural event, theaters provided one of the few venues in which people could voice political opposition during both the Empire and the Restoration. The frequently disorderly atmosphere, often with political and sexual undertones, had repercussions on women's attendance, and women's presence in turn had an impact on the disorders as well as on how authorities dealt with them. Not generally participants in these tumultuous events, female spectators functioned as justification for quick and strict enforcement of laws governing the acceptable behavior of theater audiences. The theater had to be kept peaceful for the sake of the "ladies" in the audience, whose presence was a necessary element of theatrical "success," as directors and municipal officials assumed that if women stayed away from theaters, men would too. When efforts to maintain order failed and disruptions took place, women found themselves in the midst of politicized, sometimes violent episodes. Like the *tricoteuses* who did needlework as they sat in the galleries of the National Assembly observing the political events of the Revolution, these women found themselves in the postrevolutionary period's nearest equivalent, a public space where men (especially young men) could express their political views and their sexual desires.[2] In the process, the entire audience participated in putting the new postrevolutionary social and political order on display as their actions and reactions shaped perceptions of emerging class and gender norms. As ordinary people voiced their views on acceptable and unacceptable behavior for different groups, they created social norms and expectations about how society would operate.

Politics dominated theatrical experiences during the Empire, and it continued to do so even more during the Restoration when Napoleonic restrictions on theaters eased. Both regimes exercised strict censorship and policing to limit the opportunities theaters provided to criticize government policies, but neither could go so far as to shut down theaters because they were not explicitly political like a newspaper or club, and because abolishing them outright would never have been acceptable to either the populace or the government. The large numbers of people at theaters gave political opponents a space in which to make known their opinions, and they could do so with relative immunity if they kept their critiques subtle. Often though, as with the rash of incidents revolving around Molière's play *Tartuffe* early in the reign of Charles X, their attacks became more explicit, and the government reacted by intensifying the policing of theaters and making arrests when necessary.[3] By the mid-1820s, the theater—a space that relied upon the presence of diverse groups of men and women for its very existence—had become *the* venue in which to express criticism of the Bourbon regime. This would end after the Revolution of 1830, when political discussions could take place more openly and explicitly. One scholar concluded a chapter on "politics and the pit" with the statement that "under the July Monarchy and increasingly so later in the century, audiences were quieter than they had been."[4] They had other opportunities to express political discontent.

## The Place of the Theater in City Life

In his study of nineteenth-century cities, William Cohen describes the theater as "the center of municipal cultural concerns." Spending large sums of money on theaters—both the buildings themselves and on financial subsidies to keep them running—"cities subsidized theater productions before they had established a municipal school system, a corps of firemen, garbage collection, or a regular police service."[5] One of the clearest examples of this dedication to theatrical productions comes from Lyon. In the 1820s, authorities decided to tear down the theater, which had been designed by Jacques Soufflot in 1756 and had been considered one of the most beautiful theaters in Europe. They spent 4 million francs on a new building, money deemed worth spending before the construction of a water system (in the 1840s) or the establishment of public schools (in the 1870s).[6] Lyon needed a primary theater worthy of its position as France's "second city." As one theater director explained in 1810, the city's "glory" depended on it being able "to present to visitors brought there on business or for simple curiosity, a spectacle worthy of its distinguished rank in the Empire."[7]

In Nantes, too, authorities viewed the presence of a quality theater as bringing honor to the city. Phrases like *un théâtre digne de son nom* (a theater worthy of its name) appear repeatedly in official correspondence. In 1807, the mayor complained that if Nantes were unable to support two theaters, it would lose status. "Nantes has the honor of being counted among the first order *(rang)* of cities in the Empire and this would in a certain manner be lost if it reduces the number of its theaters to only one."[8] As in Lyon, authorities in Nantes were willing to spend large amounts on a losing proposition in order to ensure the continuation of the city's theatrical life. The writer Stendhal was suitably impressed when he visited the city in the early 1830s, commenting on the beauty of the theater and the large square on which it was located, the place Graslin. "Five or six streets meet at this pretty square which would be remarkable even in Paris."[9] Inspiring admiration among visitors and creating a space in which Nantais and Nantaises could display themselves and their city to others, the theater and its surrounding neighborhood seemed worthy of financial sacrifice.

During most of the period at hand, Lyon housed two theaters: one defined as the "primary" theater, the Grand Théâtre (today the Opera house), which seated eight hundred, and the other as a "secondary" theater, the Théâtre des Célestins, which seated four hundred. Imperial legislation, which remained in effect during the Restoration, defined the genres to be performed at each: tragedies, comedies, and operas—the classics of the French stage—were to be performed at the Grand Théâtre; whereas dramas, melodramas, vaudevilles, and pantomimes constituted the repertory of the Célestins.[10] Located across the street from the Hôtel de Ville and near the place des Terreaux, Lyon's Grand Théâtre was in a neighborhood known for its bourgeois cafés and reading rooms. The neighborhood surrounding Lyon's second theater is harder to characterize than the one in which the Grand Théâtre was located. The Célestins was not far from the place Bellecour, Lyon's "aristocratic" neighborhood, which contained many *hôtels particuliers* constructed in the late seventeenth and early eighteenth centuries (Map 1; note that place Bellecour is shown on the map as place de Louis le Grand). However, the streets in the immediate vicinity of the theater were known for prostitution, and the cabarets and cafés nearby also attracted less-than-reputable men and women.[11] In 1823, the *Journal du commerce* referred to the place des Célestins as the neighborhood par excellence of the city "because it offered seven or eight reading rooms, four or five restaurants, a dozen cafés, and a theater."[12] The presence of the theater offered unparalleled economic stimulation to the neighborhood, providing employment to large numbers of workers and ensuring the success of countless businesses.[13] It appears that men and women from nearly the entire social spectrum could be found in the neighborhood and its theater.

The history of Nantes' theaters is more complicated than Lyon's. Nantes too had a Grand Théâtre, a building now known as the Théâtre Graslin, after the financier who donated the land and oversaw the construction as part of a larger land development scheme involving the entire neighborhood (Map 2).[14] First opened in 1786, the theater was severely damaged by fire ten years later, and was reopened in 1813. For nearly the entire Napoleonic period, two other theaters filled the gap created by this closure, both known by their locations on streets near the place Graslin: the rue Rubens and the rue du Chapeau Rouge. For much of the period, they alternated the seasons in which they performed plays: the larger rue Rubens theater operated in winter when people attended in greater numbers, and the smaller Chapeau Rouge operated in summer.[15] Despite Napoleonic legislation defining the repertories of theaters, the genre of plays performed as well as the makeup of audiences remained ill-defined in Nantes. Until the Grand Théâtre reopened in 1813, a single repertory listed all the plays that could be performed at both theaters. Afterward, the Grand Théâtre's repertory included vaudevilles and melodramas.[16] This blurring of genres occurred in Marseille, too, where melodramas appeared at the Grand Théâtre.[17] Smaller audiences forced even "primary" theaters to stage melodramas in order to ensure a good turnout. In contrast to Paris, where theatrical controls were strictly enforced, provincial theaters had greater autonomy in selecting plays. Although less efficient control mechanisms partly explain this difference, financial realities also encouraged theater managers to flout the rules.

Constant financial problems plagued the management of most provincial theaters. A Montpellier journalist writing in 1820 found that his city was better off than most: "In Marseille the management is in disorder; in Lyon the theater can no longer maintain itself."[18] Such problems were even more evident in Nantes, where one director after another blamed diverse conditions for his or her difficulties. Writing to the prefect in June 1806, the theater directors contrasted their experiences to that of their eighteenth-century predecessors. Before the Revolution, successful commerce and numerous visitors from the colonies and elsewhere in Europe allowed the two theaters to coexist without any difficulty, "but due to the interruption of commerce caused by the ruin of the colonies, the city, without having diminished in population, presents fewer resources to the theaters than many cities of the second and third class."[19] Despite assistance, running Nantes' theater was a losing proposition. The Grand Théâtre was owned by the city; once it was rebuilt, the director rented it for free and received a small salary, though he or she was expected to be able to live from the profits made on the performances.[20] Small turnouts and high operating costs invariably led to financial difficulties, if not outright bankruptcy. Long before the end of his or her five-year contract, Nantes' theater director was generally forced to leave the job in financial ruin. In 1827, the theater even closed temporarily because the manager could not afford to keep it running.[21]

Lyon's theater directors faced similar difficulties. During the Empire, the Célestins made a profit, but the Grand Théâtre consistently lost money, again despite generous financial support from the city. The latter was forced to close in 1808 and again in 1812 due to financial problems, a situation that inspired angry commentaries. One irate theater buff quoted the minister of the interior to make his argument: "I have been informed of the closing of the Grand Théâtre . . . while, in another neighborhood, one sees a prosperous secondary theater, which performs only plays lacking any taste. . . . It is necessary that the Lyonnais . . . find in their walls entertainment worthy of them."[22] An essay on theater life in France written during the early Restoration also represented the Célestins as reaping greater success than the Grand Théâtre. "The *petit théâtre* des Célestins always attracts crowds; melodramas and vaudevilles are performed there with great success. The Grand Théâtre can only attract the public by varying its repertory: opera alone, no matter how well executed, cannot suffice."[23] In 1808, the shareholders of the Grand Théâtre produced a report arguing that competition from the Célestins made it necessary to hire one manager for both theaters in order to ensure the continued operation of the more elite theater. From 1809 to 1811, a man named Delisle managed both theaters in Lyon. Having successfully directed the Célestins for many years, putting away substantial amounts of money, he took over the Grand Théâtre as well when city officials forced him to run both or neither. Delisle quickly found that the larger theater was a losing proposition, and he wrote to the mayor to complain. He compared his situation to that of a predecessor, Madame Lobreau, who was able to run a successful business thanks to the financial support of the city. He required similar support, or, as he put it, a "millionaire would not last ten years."[24] The problems continued into the Restoration. Describing the late 1820s, a local historian found that "despite its small size, [the Célestins] was a gold mine for the director who ran it; and it was through the profits it procured for him that habitual deficits faced by the management of the Grand Théâtre could be covered."[25] The more lowbrow genres of the Lyon's secondary theater, as well as the lower ticket prices, attracted larger numbers of spectators than the elite experience of the Grand Théâtre.

Although melodramas and vaudevilles apparently drew larger crowds than the classics of the French stage, authorities did all they could to defend classic French theater. Responding to the financial difficulties of the Grand Théâtre, in 1811 the prefect produced a four-page document exploring possible solutions, even raising the possibility of shutting down the Célestins:

> Considering . . . on the one hand, that it is useful to offer to all types of spectators and all classes of citizens a diversion suitable to [their] tastes and in proportion to the education of most of them *(aux lumières de la plupart d'entre'eux)*; and on the other hand, that it is also necessary in an essentially manufacturing town, to avoid offering too many performances whose low price can distract workers, can encourage them to spend too much, and whose genres are not always favorable to morality.
>
> Considering that it would be wise for the authorities to restrict little by little, and if necessary to abolish completely the secondary theater, to maintain in the primary [one] performances of the great works of the French stage; to conserve for the Lyonnais, who have always distinguished themselves for their culture . . . a recreation worthy of them; to attract into their walls visitors, allowing them learn about the products of this famous city, and thus to use them more.[26]

Echoing the views expressed by moralists and theater critics on melodrama and other "popular" genres, the prefect felt it was worthwhile to end such performances if that could save Lyon's primary theater and the classics of the French stage. Though he recognized the value of entertaining workers, he seemed to believe that they might be better off without the Célestins' melodramas and vaudevilles. But the prefect was ignoring the fact that workers (and the members of other social groups as well) had many other options available to them, including circuses, touring companies, and various kinds of small-scale productions.

Seeing themselves in direct competition with these other forms of entertainment, theater directors attempted to convince authorities to forbid such performances at times when the theater was in operation. In 1819, Nantes' theater director complained about two forms of entertainment that, in his eyes, represented unfair competition and should not have been permitted to operate at times when the theater was open: inexpensively produced, open-air *spectacles* and *théâtres bourgeois*.[27] The theater director in Marseille made a similar complaint in 1816: "Since November, I have been the victim of lotto [an early form of bingo] in the cafés, which robs me of the custom of all the young men who would normally fill the pit; of a dance-hall which empties the 'gods' [the highest balconies in theaters] of sailors and their female companions. Amateur theatricals and private balls have reduced Sunday takings to nothing. It would be impossible for me to embark on another season under the same auspices and I implore your aid to relieve my miserable plight."[28] During the latter years of the Empire, the prefect received a letter arguing for the protection of Lyon's theaters, which "stimulated the economy and made the city more pleasant for visitors. . . . Originally theaters received precious and considerable support from the government. They benefited from an exclusive privilege that did not permit the absurd and ruinous competition that the Revolution brought into being and which has proven to be destructive to theaters."[29] The presence of numerous other venues for entertainment was making it increasingly difficult for provincial theaters to survive, despite the financial support they received.

Directors worried about their lowbrow competition because their audiences came from the same social milieu. While the privileged theaters wished to cater toward mostly bourgeois and aristocratic men and women, they also relied upon their appeal to working-class spectators for their financial survival. Similarly, the less sophisticated outdoor and amateur amusements no doubt drew fairly diverse crowds, not just those too poor to attend the established theater. According to Cohen, "The theater was a major social gathering place. The working classes occupied the pit, often coming equipped with bread, sausage, and wine for a long evening of amusement. In the loges occupied by the upper classes, all kinds of activities went on: from flirting to conducting business negotiations."[30] As on the Parisian Boulevard, the diverse crowds that filled these "social gathering places" provided an opportunity for people-watching, with postrevolutionary social hierarchies and behavioral norms acted out and in turn made visible by the spectators themselves. Authorities recognized the value of the theater as a site for teaching social norms as suggested by this excerpt from an 1802 report: "Theaters have too much influence on mores *(mœurs)*, on instruction, and on public sentiment *(esprit public)* not to receive government attention. It is necessary to give them useful direction and to make them work towards a return to morality and good taste."[31] The commonplace mixture of people in audiences enjoying a shared experience at the theater helped to reinforce and give meaning to new ideological constructions like class and gender norms, as well as the methods and mechanisms of the new social and political order.

Who actually attended provincial theaters and what were the costs involved? Many spectators purchased monthly or annual subscriptions to the theater, with women paying about half as much as men. In 1813, a yearly subscription to Lyon's Grand Théâtre cost 190 francs for men and 100 francs for women, and monthly ones were 36 and 18 francs respectively.[32] Based on tradition, this system of pricing was also a method for convincing more women to attend the theater. Such prices would have excluded workers; however, it was possible to purchase a ticket for one performance, which permitted less wealthy spectators to attend. Cohen concluded from his research into the makeup of provincial audiences that "the middle classes attended in large numbers and with considerable frequency, while a far smaller proportion of workers attended, and with less frequency."[33] The point of the theater was to have a central space in which elites could put themselves and their city on display, both for each other and for visitors to their city. Yet, to succeed as a business, theaters needed to attract less elite customers as well; there were not enough bourgeois and aristocratic theatergoers to keep them running.

Many sources confirm that workers attended provincial theaters and that authorities viewed their presence as useful for maintaining order. In his study of revolutionary Toulon, Malcolm Crook argues that the city's theater "flourish[ed] as never before" during the Napoleonic period despite "the regime's heavy-handed supervision." Authorities there encouraged theater attendance as a way to distract "persons who might otherwise be attracted to mischief."[34] In 1811, the owners of Nantes' theater argued that "*le spectacle* [was] for all classes . . . *laborieux et riches.*" The theater, they argued, was "the least pernicious amusement that one can choose. It is infinitely more agreeable to see young people, or even *pères de famille,* at the theater than at the cabaret."[35] It went without saying that cabarets were dangerous for young men, who frequently attended theaters, but older men, too, could benefit from spending more time in theaters and less time drinking wine in cabarets, which tended to be rowdy working-class spaces. In 1822, the

Marseille city council described theaters as the site for gathering "this crowd of foreigners, of idle people without family ties . . . who without honest distraction could compromise public tranquility."[36] In an 1827 report, the prefect in Nantes insisted on the need to devote financial resources to reopen the recently closed Grand Théâtre because "the theater occupies the leisure-time of a large number of young people, who, denied this distraction, would perhaps work themselves up [to stage] some reprehensible disorders."[37] Clearly, provincial theaters attracted more than just the city's elite residents. Both theater management and municipal officials encouraged working-class attendance, each for their own reasons.

Though it is difficult to trace these changes with precision, it appears that a growing "elitization" of provincial theaters took place during the Restoration. Most of the material focusing on the diversity of audiences dates from the Empire, whereas journalists during the Restoration emphasized the elite nature of theater audiences. This transition may be related to the explosion of lowbrow street performances (traveling circuses, acrobatic performances, and the like) during the Restoration, which drew many lower-class spectators away from established theaters, and perhaps more upper-class spectators as well.[38] According to a local historian, Lyon's Grand Théâtre appealed to "an assiduous and faithful" clientele who attended on a regular basis: "Bourgeois society frequented it willingly under the condition that they were noticed. 'Madame,' stated a satirical article from 1824 on *gens de grand ton*, 'must be seated in a reserved box, even if the lamps on stage blinded her; the essential was to be seen. Monsieur must find everything detestable.' "[39] Other anecdotal information from the Restoration confirms that the Grand Théâtre was viewed as an essentially elite space, as in this excerpt from an 1825 newspaper article: "By the status and the character of the people who frequent them, we have known for a long time that the first boxes (premières loges) at the Grand-Théâtre have been the refuge *(asile)* of tranquillity, of politeness and of good taste *(bon ton)*; it is here, especially, that ladies have always been assured of finding themselves surrounded in every regard with all the respect that the beautiful sex deserves."[40] The journalist went on to argue that the atmosphere had changed, however, because of the poor behavior of some medical school students, which guaranteed that much of the public would not be renewing their annual renting of boxes. It was in everyone's interest—spectators as well as directors—to ensure that women would continue to attend theaters and that they would use these spaces to display their charms, as this part of the spectacle drew men and women alike to theaters.

At Lyon's secondary theater, managers focused more on the plays than on the composition of audiences, though the two were related. Writing in 1807, the director of the Célestins explained that more than two-thirds of the spectators at the Célestins were *habitués;* in other words, they rented boxes on a permanent basis. "Only diversity can thus convince them to attend," he added.[41] The term "diversity" is an understatement: the theater's 1808 repertory listed over three hundred plays! It encompassed a mixture of "happy" plays, "somber" ones, and others described as "sentimental"; historical pieces were popular, as were *pièces féeries*—plays involving fairies and magic.[42] A literary study of the theater from 1817 expressed similar views: "In Paris . . . ones goes to the theater for the spectacle. In other large commercial towns, most of the public is composed of the same people, a crowd of *abonnés* who for ten, twenty, or more years go to the theater every evening, out of habit, curiosity, or laziness. . . . Without sufficient variety, their senses become worn out by over use."[43] The fact that such a large portion of the audience comprised people who rented boxes on an annual basis signifies first of all that most spectators were quite wealthy, because such rentals were expensive, and second that spectators grew to know or at least recognize the people around them. This lack of anonymity affected their experience at the theater, making it function almost like a club, albeit with greater openness and with the ability to observe other social groups occupying the same space.[44]

Of course, the actual performances mattered as well, with melodrama attracting attention because of its widespread appeal. In January 1824, the *Journal du commerce* commented on the fact that when posters announced "two great melodramas seasoned with vaudeville [at the Théâtre des Célestins], *fashionable theater lovers* amass[ed] in a great crowd before the door of the temple, and brave[d] the rigors of the season for two or three hours to dispute the paltry benefit of being among the first admitted."[45] Like many of his Parisian counterparts, this lyonnais theater critic looked upon the enthusiasm for melodrama with disdain. Later that year, an article in the same newspaper treated the genre with a bit more respect. After praising a visiting actor, Odry, whose presence drew large crowds to the Célestins on a Thursday evening in August, the journalist commented on the experience of a much smaller group of spectators who attended another play, *Le commissionaire:* "The melodrama lives up to the accolades that we have given it in advance, and that we do not squander on this spurious *(bâtard)* genre. . . . All the ladies were sobbing, . . . and if the men were not crying, they were no less moved."[46] The "ladies" who cried at this play were not members of the working classes. As in Paris, even elite women were moved by a genre supposedly created for "those who cannot read," and their highly visible sensitivity functioned as cultural capital, as proof of their class status.

In addition to the general atmosphere within theaters and types of plays performed, the presence of well-known actors drew spectators to the theater. When Parisian performers came to the provinces, it was a special event. A woman in Lyon remarked in 1801 that "for the past eight days, two actors from Paris have been performing at the Grand Théâtre . . . [and their presence] has brought abundant crowds despite the heat."[47] In letters written to her daughter in Paris, a bourgeois woman in Rouen, Catherine Arnaud-Tizon, who always purchased an annual subscription yet generally complained about the poor acting at her city's theater, expressed enthusiasm whenever a Parisian actor graced the provincial stage. When Talma spent a few days in Rouen in 1808, Arnaud-Tizon described his talent as "incomparable" and planned "not to miss a single performance." When Mademoiselle Duchesnois performed there in 1814, Arnaud-Tizon lauded the "force and nobility" that the actress brought to her characters.[48] For this woman, who frequently grumbled about the dearth of entertainment in her city compared to the capital, it was an event worthy of discussion to observe the impressive talents of these actors.

According to a nantais journalist who wrote an article about the theater in 1823, the combination of competition from other venues and the mediocre quality of the performances at the Grand Théâtre kept audiences small throughout the first half of the Restoration, except when visiting celebrities sparked their enthusiasm. Then things changed:

> What revolution has taken place in our theater? Where are the solitary benches on which the peaceful subscriber slept each evening in comfort, the balconies where one also saw officers from the garrison and a few fans looking bored and distracted? Everything has changed! The regular attendee stands stupefied as he searches vainly for a seat; crowds siege the ticket office; the prettiest women found the path to the temple of Thalia; one only notices beaming and joyous faces; one only hears long bursts of laughter, prolonged "bravos" . . . [and loud] applause.[49]

How did this journalist explain the radical transformation of the theater? He had a simple answer: a famous actor, Perlet, was in temporary residence at the theater and his talent inspired great enthusiasm. Spectators, especially female ones, were more likely to go to the theater when a "celebrity" was in their midst. The presence of "the prettiest women" had transformed the space of the theater as much as Perlet himself, encouraging all in attendance to consume the sights of these happy spectators while also enjoying the performance of the visiting actor. The journalist seemed to enjoy their "beaming faces" as much as anything happening on stage, and he hoped that Perlet's influence would continue even after the actor left, although that seemed doubtful because of the questionable talent of the regular actors. Of course, few other options existed for the leisured classes to amuse themselves while residing in the city. Theater management could thus rely on at least some spectators to attend despite the poor quality performances, but something extraordinary was required to draw large crowds.

Despite their weaknesses, provincial theaters played an important role in defining a city's status and in the self-definition of its more elite inhabitants, accomplishing this classifying function in the presence of working-class residents, and even relying on the presence of these people for their existence. Viewed as an essential component of the experience of attending the theater, women put themselves on display as much as, if not more so than, the men in the audience. Their beauty and charms helped turn theaters into spaces where men could "exercise their gaze" on women of all sorts: actresses, prostitutes, and "respectable" women of the different classes all became "ornaments," despite their divergent social and sexual positions, in this public arena. Women's behavior in turn played an integral role in the identity-formation function of the theater. As diverse crowds filled theaters, bringing different expectations with them, authorities had to grapple not only with the inherent danger of large crowds but also with the particular desires and behaviors of specific groups within audiences.

## Policing the Public: Politics and Class, Gender and Sexuality

Early nineteenth-century provincial theaters were alive with social, sexual, and political tensions. Audience members disrupted performances in countless ways, forcing municipal authorities to keep a careful eye on theaters and theatergoers and placing actors and spectators under constant surveillance. In the battle for control over the theater, the government certainly had the upper hand with its censors, strict regulations, and police force. However, on a local level, inside these buildings with real people gathered to share an experience that may or may not have been directly related to the play being performed, authorities' control was far from assured. Frequent outbursts, most often staged by male youths, expressed a variety of social, political, and sexual tensions. A journalist in Montpellier described disruptive audiences as a constant problem: "In the pit, in the loges, [and] in the parquet there is a constant deafening buzz, a confusing roar that covers the voice of the actors. Should we be surprised? The pit is truly a market; the first balconies are the meeting place of our pleasant dandies *(petits maîtres)*, the parquet the meeting place of another species. . . . Below, noisy youth compete with the racket. Settled near the orchestra, their sudden uproars drown out the sound of the instruments."[50] Theaters were spaces that brought people together for reasons beyond simply enjoying the entertainment on stage. Specific social groups—noisy youth, respectable businessmen, prostitutes, and so on—occupied different parts of the audience, and they behaved differently depending on their motives and desires.

Seating arrangements help to explain the disorderly atmosphere in theaters. To assist in controlling the interiors of theaters, one box was reserved for municipal officials, but even this system caused problems. In 1801, Nantes' police chief pointed out that "for a long time, the public has noticed and complained about the fact . . . that many ladies fill the box designated for local authorities."[51] We cannot know who these "ladies" were, but they certainly were not municipal officials. Other boxes could be rented by the month, the season, or the year. Such a rental did not reserve a particular spot in the theater, however, because all seats and boxes were unnumbered.[52] Rather *abonnés* (the term used for those who rented these loges) had the right to a box within a certain area of the theater. This practice meant that the women employed as ushers *(ouvreuses)* could earn good incomes, as tips largely determined the quality of the seat within a given price range. Single-seat tickets worked similarly: they guaranteed a place within a certain part of the theater, not a specific seat. No doubt some confusion must have resulted from this arrangement as spectators wished to position themselves in particular places.

Excerpts from police regulations, which the mayor's office reprinted on large posters at the beginning of each new theatrical season, suggest that concerns about seating were of less interest than the audience members' ability to affect what happened on stage. The issues most commonly brought up on these *affiches* were those pertaining to control of the actual performance, such as audience members interrupting performances by shouting and making demands of actors, or the possibility of having unsuitable material read from stage.[53] Such tumultuous behavior appears to have been more common in provincial theaters than in Paris. In her work on eighteenth-century theater, Martine de Rougemont explains that despite the lack of anonymity in the provinces, as most people inside theaters would have known each other, spectators were not more reserved than those in Paris. In fact "what emerges from all the witnesses of the eighteenth century is a violence, an immediacy of reaction stronger than in Paris."[54] Cohen, too, contrasts provincial audiences, whose "inattention and noise were great," with their Parisian counterparts, who seem to have been better behaved.[55] According to a literary and theatrical guidebook published in 1817, "In Bordeaux, as in Lyon and Marseille, we find everywhere *abonnés* [who are] blasé toward the performance: each loge forms a noisy committee; the stage is just another space *(cadre)* for these circular chats."[56] Provincial theatergoers had not been affected by the supposed "silencing" of audiences scholars have observed in eighteenth-century Paris.[57]

At the heart of many disruptions was a battle between spectators and police over who would control the theater. In Nantes in 1804, for example, officials learned that "several young men in parterre, [were] planning to disrupt the performance, either by calling out for the director or by whistling at the actors." The police officer in charge of the theater placed four gendarmes near the troublemakers. As he returned to his box, he noticed that a man had "lifted the end of his cane where he had attached a large piece of paper on which he had written in large letters THE PIT ORDERS *(LE PARTERRE ORDONNE)*." When the gendarmes and police officer tried to bring order to the theater, "young men in the first balconies, the parquet, and the parterre rose en masse against them." The policeman concluded that the real motive behind their behavior was to insult the gendarmes, not to attack the performers or the director.[58]

Policing theaters required delicacy: officers needed to stop disorderly behavior without worsening the situation. As Jeffrey Ravel found for the eighteenth century, "Local and royal officials, uneasy with the potentially disruptive forces at play any time an audience gathered in a playhouse, often fueled civil disruption through their confused intervention."[59] The Marseillaise Julie Pellizzone, whose journal includes many rich details on life in that city from 1787 to 1824, went so far as to blame the police for disturbances: "Thursday evening, November 11 [1819], there was a big uproar at the theater, fruit of the good police who have been reigning for a long time

and who oblige honest people to withdraw themselves [from the theater]."
During a performance of *Françoise de Foix,* some spectators began to shout,
"On your knees!" whenever the actor playing François I appeared on stage.
They made so much noise that the play had to be stopped. Pellizzone believed that this event was perpetrated by "a few disorderly individuals . . .
[who wished] to have the sweet satisfaction of seeing a king of France on his
knees."[60] Pellizzone's royalist sympathies may have contributed to her interpretation of the event, but she was surely not alone in reading politics into
these disturbances. This politicization of theatrical performances was exactly what authorities were working to avoid.

Social tensions also entered these tumultuous spaces as spectators expressed their opinions of the performances and of each other. One evening
in Nantes in 1808, for example, the noises being made by one section of the
audience threatened to bring a halt to the performance. In response, "some
people seated in the first boxes addressed the workers in parterre . . . and
threatened to stop furnishing them with work if they kept the play from being performed." The prefect asked the mayor to verify the details of this incident "which could have great significance for the maintenance of public
tranquility in this large city."[61] Having workers and bourgeois together in
the same theater did not seem unusual, but an exchange of threats and in-
sults between the two groups was not to be permitted. Workers caused
problems in Lyon's Grand Théâtre as well, where for example, the parterre
fell into disorder in May 1818 as spectators whistled and shouted at an actress. One of the men involved, the son of a baker, replied to a policeman's
order for calm: "Why peace? This is not your concern, withdraw right
away!"[62] Observations made two days later again suggest that class conflict
played a role in the problems. A man being dragged out of the theater
shouted, "if I were bourgeois you wouldn't be taking me [to prison]!" A police report blames the problems on liberals, but this outburst puts that
analysis into question.[63]

Age mattered as much as class in these disruptions. Twice in November
1810, police officers forced some youths to leave Lyon's Théâtre des Célestins
because they were causing commotion in the parterre by "shouting indecent
comments," presumably at the actresses.[64] Youthful disregard for behavioral
norms appears to have been anticipated, even accepted, in these contexts. In
1824, the troublemakers involved in some problems at Nantes' Grand
Théâtre included an *ouvrier horloger* (watchmaker's assistant) and a *commis
négociant* (clerk). Those listed without their professions were referred to as

*fils* (son).[65] These were young artisans and petty bourgeois. Others appear to have been wealthier, including a medical student designated as the instigator of a *tumulte* in June 1822. He managed to interrupt a performance by shouting continually whenever a particular actress appeared on stage.[66] Similarly, an actress received "a very large number of whistles" from the parterre upon entering the scene in May 1822. A visible police presence and the requests of other spectators finally silenced the troublemakers, but as soon as another actress came on stage, the parterre broke out into whistles once again.[67] In this case, students, in other words young bourgeois men, were the perpetrators.

Class and age may have contributed to these disorders, but sexual tensions played a role as well. Seating for spectators in the pit or parterre of provincial theaters remained absent for many more years than for those in Parisian theaters, where seats appeared in the 1780s. In Montpellier, for example, benches were only installed in 1829, reducing the number of spectators who could fit into that part of the theater from about eight hundred to four hundred.[68] In eighteenth-century Paris, a standing, masculine parterre encouraged a reaction of violence that would diminish when the spectators in the parterre were seated and included women.[69] For most of the period examined here, the provincial standing parterre was a highly masculine space, and the outbursts of the mostly young men who filled it affected all audience members. Sexually aggressive young men grew to dominate the atmosphere within theaters. "Cabals" of young men regularly shouted particular women off the stage, bringing attention both to the actresses and to the men's ability to shape performances. In May 1806, the minister of the interior received a letter accusing the youth of Nantes of causing problems everywhere they went: "at the theater, in brothels *(chez les filles)*, in cafés, and even in the streets and other places where the public gathers."[70] Later that year, "a group of young men formed a cabal against Madame Nej who was playing the role of the *mère coupable*."[71] Several troublemakers were arrested. During the ensuing trial, the young men used their age as justification for their behavior, which they described "an involuntary movement of youth which they [now] disavow."[72] According to a recent history of French actresses, "The public [of this period] expected that theater women would enflame men's senses."[73] Stories arise with regularity about actresses running offstage in tears after young men had interrupted their performances by whistling from the parterre.[74] It is possible that some of these disturbances were planned when an actress refused to associate herself with one of these *jeunes gens* (youths). As women who chose to put themselves on display, actresses seemed deserving of such treatment.

As the examples cited thus far indicate, going to the theater in this period entailed anything but sitting passively and enjoying sophisticated entertainment. These were decidedly contentious spaces in which people expressed their wishes and views, often to the displeasure of other spectators around them. Negative responses to plays would frequently become so intense that performances ground to a halt midway through a scene. In Nantes in 1818, for example, at the beginning of a play called the *Château de Palazzi,* "the spectators seated in parterre suddenly declared unanimously that they did not want to see this play."[75] In another disruption in Nantes a few years later, audience members whose discontent was discernable from the first act brought to a halt the performance of a play called "The Black Forest." "During the second act, noise *(tapage)* could be heard, and finally the third act was completely drowned out by numerous whistles. The curtain was drawn [and] the spectators were invited, in the name of the law, to evacuate the theater. . . . It appears that most of these disturbances come out of a cabal formed against the director."[76] The underlying question was who had the right or duty to control theaters: the management, the police, the government, or the spectators, that is, the public. Audiences saw themselves as engaged in active struggle to determine who would have the right to claim they were the "public."[77] Of course, the next question is who constituted the public.

Clearly women numbered among spectators; it seems logical that they were seen and saw themselves as part of this active theater public as well. Occasionally, direct evidence exists to prove that women participated in theatrical disturbances. In January 1819, for example, a group of bourgeois men and one woman—Madame Mellinet-Mallassis, publisher of the *Journal de Nantes*—set off several small explosions in the theater, using small bombs called *dragées,* which caused a disagreeable odor to spread throughout the room.[78] Although it is not clear what exactly they were trying to accomplish with this behavior, the age and status of the perpetrators suggest that this was not simply a childish prank. Mellinet-Mallassis and her co-conspirators were part of the liberal opposition; in all likelihood political motives inspired their actions.

Despite the frequent disturbances in Nantes' theaters during the Empire, no one seemed concerned about women's presence or absence, or with the impact of disorders on women's attendance, in marked contrast to Lyon, where the effects of disorders upon women received frequent commentary. Yet an 1813 letter suggests that women were frequently the victims of disruptions. A spectator from Nantes used the fact that women were *not* mistreated during a particular disorder as evidence that the disturbance was not as serious as it might have been: "The audience found itself in darkness; yet despite the fact that the theater was full, no woman was insulted."[79] That comment implies that women were, in fact, often "insulted" during tumultuous moments at the theater. However, no one seemed concerned about women's discomfort; it was not deemed worthy of comment by police or journalists in Nantes.

According to Pellizzone, female spectators often became the targets of rowdy young men. In 1816, she commented on the jeunes gens at Marseille's theater whose behavior, she argued, had worsened since the Revolution:

> Earlier, it was only among the lower classes that we found what we call bad subjects *(mauvais sujets);* now it is the youth of the best families that amuse themselves by being insolent troublemakers. It is the height of fashion. *(C'est le sublime bon ton.)* They go to the theater in groups of ten or twelve to scream louder than the actors. . . . They permit themselves to behave indecently with the prostitutes *(filles)* they find among the audience and sometimes take honest women for prostitutes and insult them. . . . Since the police cannot or do not want to control them, we cannot attend the theater without risking insult. . . . Most [ladies] have already chosen to leave *(avait déjà pris le chemin de la porte).*[80]

Pellizzone saw this disruptive behavior as a postrevolutionary phenomenon, a reflection of the social ambiguities of the period. Earlier controls had been lifted, and new ones had not yet emerged to replace them. She commented with regularity on the poor behavior of these *jeunes gens des meilleurs familles* (male youth of the best families). One passage dating from early 1821 also merits quotation:

> It is impossible to imagine their boastfulness *(jactance)*, their rudeness *(malhonnêteté)*, [and] even their incivility *(grossièreté)*, without having been witness to their behavior every evening as I am. Their manner of dress *(mise)* is ridiculous, their remarks indecent, their countenance insolent; they speak to each other more loudly than the actors and prevent honest people from hearing the play. If we ask for silence, they respond with foolishness *(sottise)*, if we threaten them, they sneer and that's it. If we ignore

them, they whistle without reason at the best actors, they insult the other [actors] and sometimes the well-disposed *(bénévoles)* spectators, especially the women, whom they fear less than the men. One evening, they permitted themselves to pose a crown made of thick blue paper on the head of a lady who did not have the luck to be attractive to them. . . . And the police permit all of this because they are the children of nouveaux riches families.[81]

This account helps to explain why contemporaries feared that disorderly behavior might have convinced many women to avoid the theater, though Pellizzone herself (and no doubt many others like her) kept going "every evening." Men and women alike associated the theater with the disruptive behavior of these youth, but women were most often their victims.

With the Restoration, both female spectators and actresses received more attention from authorities than they had under the Empire. In 1826, the prefect wrote to the mayor of Nantes to instruct him on the issue of actresses' positions in the theater when they were not on stage. Rather than allow them to sit where they wished during a play in which they did not have a part, the prefect argued that actresses needed to have a specially designated box. He was concerned that when actresses mixed with audience members their presence would "lead to disorders among the young men who ordinarily flock around these actresses; plus it [would] expose young ladies to hearing many ill-placed proposals and would force mothers to forbid [their daughters from going to] the theater."[82] By the later 1820s, concerns about morality and women's experiences at the theater were expressed with regularity in ways they were not earlier. Women as a group—ordinary spectators, actresses, and prostitutes—all became objects of increasing surveillance and control.

The increased attention to women's presence in the theater is evident in new efforts to limit the circulation of prostitutes in the theater. Early in the period, prostitutes were largely left to their own devices when in the theater, often drawing attention to themselves to attract customers. In his 1807 annual report, the director of the Célestins, suggested that one area of the audience be reserved for *"femmes publiques. . . . It is painful to see disseminated in the first balconies and everywhere else femmes prostitutées."* He hoped to thus "encourage the attendance of reputable women *(personnes honnêtes)."*[83] Maintaining an atmosphere that would be acceptable to women was a primary goal of theater management as female spectators were essential to the theater's success. In 1809, the mayor of Lyon established that *filles publiques* (prostitutes) could only sit in the parquet—the floor seats nearest the stage—at the Célestins, a rule that had already been in effect at the Grand Théâtre with "beneficial results."[84] Similar legislation passed in Nantes 1816 established a separate section of the theater for "*filles publiques* or [women] with such a reputation" in the third row of boxes. Women who were reputed to be prostitutes were seen as equally threatening as actual prostitutes. Authorities introduced this new regulation because of their realization that "prostitutes were sitting all over the third row of boxes, a [situation that was causing] honest women and their families who normally sat in that area to absent themselves from these boxes."[85] Nonetheless, prostitutes remained omnipresent in public life; and their presence in turn affected other women. The trend on a national level was toward the separation of prostitutes from everyday life, but this was a slow transition that was only beginning to take effect during the last years of the Restoration.[86]

Despite such laws, some spectators remained dissatisfied with the prominence of prostitutes within theaters. One man wrote to the director of Nantes' Grand Théâtre in 1821 to complain that he and his wife had been insulted by the "immoderate laughter" of a "*femme publique* sitting in the first row of seats below them" (and not in the third tier of boxes where she belonged). He had learned that "this nasty woman created trouble and disorder wherever she went" and argued that it was in the interests of the director to ensure that the "beings who are destined to be ornaments at the theater are no longer dirtied by [the presence of] women deserving of public scorn."[87] Reiterating the language of the letter that opened this chapter, this spectator viewed women as "ornaments": their presence made men's experience at the theater more enjoyable. It was thus in everyone's interest to create an atmosphere in theaters that would encourage women to flock to the theater. By the 1820s, this effort included separating prostitutes from "respectable" women, legislation that put all women under greater surveillance. However, laws could not stop real social, political, and sexual issues from entering urban spaces like theaters.

With the return of the Bourbons, politics took center stage in theaters around France. In October 1814, authorities in Lyon forbade the director from staging a play entitled *Eduourd en Ecosse* because it was inspiring "inappropriate applause," despite the fact that certain provocative passages had been cut.[88] In July 1815, a poster published by the Prefecture in Lyon warned of severe repercussions for those causing problems at the theater and referred to "outrageous provocations" toward men in uniform.[89] In December 1815, a series of disruptions took place inspired by the presence of some decorative eagles, Napoleonic symbols that hung in Nantes' theater. In a letter to the mayor, the commissioner of police explained that someone had placed white cockades on them, "which only made them more obvious; I know that it has been proposed to smear them with cooked pears today, all of which seems to me as more likely to excite uproar than to produce a good effect." Despite such an apparent understatement, the officer took the dangers of these eagles seriously. Knowing that it had already been decided that it would be too expensive to remove them, he asked the mayor whether it might be possible to use "some drapery to hide these emblems that could inspire an incident."[90] Another event in Lille makes clear how easily politics could enter the theater. When the well-known actor, Talma, first appeared in Lille in 1816, a brawl broke out between his supporters and detractors. According to theater historian F. W. J. Hemmings, "The reason was purely political: the royalist officers belonging to a regiment quartered in the town objected to the applause given to an actor suspected of Bonapartist sympathies, and tried to enforce their opinions at sabre-point."[91] Theaters and politics went hand in hand; these were spaces that permitted urban dwellers to express and absorb diverse viewpoints.

The continuous nature of the theatrical disruptions during the Restoration reveal the extent to which the theater had become the principal site used by the regime's opponents to make known their frustration with the returned monarchy. The resulting atmosphere must have been quite tense, as disorders could surface at any moment. Among many others was an incident that took place at Nantes' Grand Théâtre in November 1817 when a group of troublemakers supposedly demonstrated "conspicuous irreverence toward his Royal Highness the duc d'Angoulême who was honoring the theater with his presence that night." Included among the occupations of the twenty-seven men listed by the authorities as involved in the incident were notaries and a notary's clerk, a lawyer, a teacher, and a journalist. The latter, Victor Mangin, was still quite young, as were many on the list as they were referred to as "fils." Mangin would go on to be a prominent liberal in the later 1820s and during the July Monarchy.[92] Few other venues existed in which to express political views.

An incident that took place in Lyon in June 1820 had similar political undertones, but this one ended humorously. During a performance of the tragedy *Marie Stuard* at the Grand Théâtre, "the spectators, who were quite numerous, responded to diverse passages with abrupt expressions of approval, making allusions to certain contemporary political circumstances. . . . Cries of 'vive la charte, vive le roi!' were made in the parterre. The noise was brought to an end when a spectator shouted, 'let's go, everyone go to bed, you are boring me!" which made everyone laugh. No further noise was heard as the people left the theater."[93] In this case, a spectator who was unhappy with non-dramatic aspects of theater attendance brought an end to the tension-filled moment. But the shouting easily could have evolved into an incident like others that took place in the theater when audience members chose this location as the site in which to voice their political views.

In the mid-1820s, politics entered the theater even more forcefully as young men chose it as the venue in which to express their growing frustration with Charles X's recalcitrant policies. Beginning in Rouen, and then spreading around the country, audiences demanded that Molière's *Tartuffe* be performed, shouting down performers as they tried to stage other plays. The plot of *Tartuffe* revolves around a confidence man (Tartuffe) who, pretending to be a pious ascetic, enters into a wealthy Parisian family. By duping the father, Orgon, Tartuffe nearly manages to swindle his way into a marriage with the daughter of the family and to convince Orgon to sign over all his wealth to him, even as the rest of the family tries to make Orgon understand that Tartuffe is a hypocrite and a swindler. In the end, the king saves the day by sending an official who exposes Tartuffe for the sham that he is.

In her study of Restoration political culture, Sheryl Kroen interprets "Tartufferie," the incidents revolving around demands for *Tartuffe,* as a manner of criticizing the regime's growing clericalism and its support of internal missionary projects around France. In addition to studying the incidents themselves, Kroen examined placards, broadsheets, and songs, as well as the prefaces to cheaply produced editions of Molière's play from this period, all of which encouraged readers to "oppose the Tartuffe of the stage with the Tartuffes of the world."[94] In her examination of these events on a national level—and Tartufferie hit nearly all of France's larger and some smaller cities between 1825 and 1829—Kroen found that "what was significant was the fact that people all over France were acting in concert, using the same means to criticize local manifestations of the regime's increasingly unpopular clericalism."[95] It is difficult to say with precision who staged these events. Authorities blamed "liberals" based on scanty evidence that liberal bourgeois were paying workers to attend the theater and cause problems. In his January 1826 report on the situation in Nantes, the prefect insisted that the men involved in political intrigues were also at the root of troubles in theaters, whereas the peuple, most of whom were indifferent toward politics, were "busy *(occupés)* and peaceful, poor but religious."[96] In other cases, notes with many spelling errors forced officials to recognize the "popular" nature of the movement. Kroen argues that "participation was broad, including members of all parts of the social and political spectrum."[97]

Newspaper coverage of Tartufferie in Lyon gives insight into who was involved and why, as well as evidence of the broader impact of these events. According to a local newspaper, cries of "le Tartuffe!" along with "Down with the missionaries! Down with the Jesuits!" were heard in Lyon's Célestins for the third night in a row on 30 October 1826. Someone threw a copy of Molière's play onto the stage (an illegal act in itself), and with that came demands for it to be read. In reaction to all of this, an official announced, as he had the two previous days, that as *Tartuffe* was not in the repertory of a secondary theater, it could not be performed at the Célestins. "This response was received by the instigators with the same signs of impatience and disapproval that they had displayed at the two previous performances. The tumult continued, and the authorities gave the order to evacuate the theater." Once outside, the troublemakers continued their "vociferations, in such an insolent manner, that it was necessary to employ force to disperse the crowd." Five people who appeared to be leaders of the group were arrested.[98]

In another article on the same page, a journalist drew an explicit connection between the demands for *Tartuffe* and the perceived hypocrisy of the missionaries touring around France at the time. Though he seemed sympathetic to the views of the troublemakers, he disapproved of their manner of voicing an opinion. "We share with these religious men who demand *Tartuffe* their indignation towards the hypocrites; but it seems to us, that to deplore excess virtue, it is necessary to have some of one's own. . . . That virtuous men raise up with force against the tartuffes, nothing is better; but that people . . . protest abuses . . . with voices hoarse with wine, to demand that we turn false devout people into laughing stocks of the populace . . . this is going too far." Though he believed the motives of these youthful troublemakers may have been just, the journalist felt that the disruptions were causing more harm than good. Just below this article, the newspaper printed a letter in which the mayor pleaded with "fathers, businessmen, [and] work-shop supervisors (*pères de famille, négociants,* [and] *chefs d'ateliers*) . . . to use [their] influence over [their] subordinates so that order and tranquility [can] continue to reign in our town."[99] In discussing similar incidents in Nantes, authorities focused their attention on "jeunes gens" as well.[100] Young men all over the country were caught up in this national expression of dis-satisfaction, all of which occurred in and around theaters. This generational cohort and identity carried with it potent political force.

The theater is a perfect example of the complexity of the issue of public and private: it was a public space, but the interiors of boxes could take on some characteristics of a more intimate, private gathering.[101] At issue is not whether the theater brought women of the upper classes into the "public sphere," but rather the extent to which the space inhabited by audiences came to be particularly gendered. The increasingly politicized nature of theater attendance transformed the space from one that was gender neutral, or even feminine, to a more masculine one during the Restoration. This "masculine" atmosphere did not mean that women stopped attending the theater. If anything, it meant that their presence was more noticeable and more sought out than had been the case when the space inside theaters seemed more "feminine." As sexually aggressive youth came to dominate theaters, women felt under attack. Yet they kept on going. In fact, regardless of such disturbances, "respectable" female spectators not only attended provincial theaters, but they even went unaccompanied by men. The bour-geoise from Rouen whose views on actors were mentioned earlier went to the theater accompanied only by another woman.[102] However, their pres-ence was threatened by the proximity of prostitutes and by disorderly erup-tions. Like the women who participated in other forms of culture and pub-lic life, female theatergoers received greater attention during the Restoration than they had under the Empire. Frequent disorderly outbursts caused journalists and police to comment on women's discomfort at the theater. Still, women went to the theater and they were an integral part of the over-all experience as they watched and responded to plays and put themselves on display in the process.

In the course of providing entertainment, theaters furnished urban dwellers with an excuse to gather in public. The makeup and experiences of these di-verse crowds gave spectators an opportunity to comprehend, shape, and contest the new postrevolutionary social order as it was solidifying. Through its police forces and censors, the state worked to control the space but had limited success. Rowdy young men increasingly claimed these spaces as their own, bringing into theaters sexual, political, and social tensions that shaped the experience for all in attendance. Under the restrictive conditions of the Empire and Restoration, theaters and other "cultural" gatherings were the only places available to express oppositional political views. This situation brought an ambiguity that permitted women to have access to one of the few spaces in which politics could be discussed, albeit indirectly. This window of opportunity would soon close as politics moved to male-only political organizations during the less restrictive July Monarchy. The very characteristics that made women "attractive" as theatergoers—their sensitivity, delicacy, and beauty—could also eventually serve to exclude them from the rough-and-ready "masculine" world of politics.[103] During the Empire and the Restoration, however, politics operated in "liminal" spaces, ones that brought men and women together. Normative restrictions of women's public behavior in such contexts help to explain women's exclusion from men's organizations during the July Monarchy and later, as well.

# — III —

# Social Life

# — 5 —

## Building Solidarity

### Cercles, *Salons, and Charities*

In 1801, a nantais journalist complained that the men and women of his city were not spending enough time together: "The two sexes [which are] meant to socialize together are often too isolated here. The overly numerous reading rooms [and] *cercles* (clubs) have become warehouses of men, whom nature did not destine to live as though in a convent."[1] It appeared that men's opportunities to gather in spaces outside the home were multiplying, whereas women's were shrinking, at least relative to those available to men. From the perspective of this commentator, such trends went against "nature": men and women were made to share their time together, not to live as though they had taken vows of chastity. Although the two sexes continued to spend their leisure time in shared activities in the postrevolutionary period, such gatherings seemed to be losing ground to purely male clubs and associations. The journalist saw a solution, however: a professor of physics planned to offer classes and demonstrations that the journalist hoped would attract both sexes. In addition to providing an opportunity for men and women to mingle, these lectures would give women greater knowledge, which would improve their relationships with their husbands: "When our ladies are better educated, [we] will find them more worthy of us. We will be happy to spend more time with them even at home." It was important to this journalist that the city orchestrate events that would encourage women's involvement. Men and women enjoying moments of leisure together would add to the experience itself, while also improving the participants' home life and, presumably, the larger society as well. Such activities would give women access to public spaces for discussion and amusement. However, the terms of this appeal for women's inclusion in social activities were implicitly heteronormative, as they were based on a model of gender complementarity that accommodated women only in certain terms, above all as the attractive and stimulating companions of men.

Associations geared toward entertaining and enlightening members and allowing them to work together to reach common goals tended to attract more homogeneous and like-minded participants than other kinds of urban amusements. Rather than providing opportunities for observation of diverse people sharing similar experiences, these gatherings encouraged particular social groups to develop a sense of shared concerns. Salons brought wealthy men and women together to discuss literature, philosophy, and politics well into the nineteenth century; cercles and reading societies appealed to more middling men interested in nurturing business relationships and keeping up to date with political developments; and charities brought elite women and men together while bringing them into contact with the "deserving poor" in a highly controlled and limited context.[2]

Organizations that brought people together for conversation and socializing evolved in both their range and their form during the postrevolutionary period. Although eighteenth-century corporate outlooks were slowly evolving into new kinds of groupings that divided people along lines suitable to the new order, these new social structures were not immediately comprehensible, and their emergence was a slow process.[3] By the end of the 1820s, social spaces were becoming more clearly defined based on the class and gender identities of those who filled them. How did this happen? Aristocratic lifestyles encouraged shared male/female spaces, whereas bourgeois society largely relied upon more purely male institutions. As bourgeois modes of behavior grew to dominate, the mixing of the genders in public became a mark of working-class behavior. As workers and the locations in which they gathered grew to be defined as "dangerous" by social observers and officials, the middle classes chose to separate themselves from urban public spaces, particularly those that appealed to these threatening groups. Gender and class norms thus reinforced each other. All classes participated in socializing that included both sexes, but the terms of that mixing relied upon and solidified gender norms.[4] In the process, gender (and, as Chapter 6 shows more clearly, sexuality) became a defining feature of class sensibilities as emerging ideas about the social order built on perceptions of male and female "natures."

In Lyon we can see an evolution toward women having less control over these social spaces and, to some extent, becoming less involved in urban public life by the 1820s; however, Nantes' associational life presents a contrasting trajectory. There, where religion played a more prominent role in organizing social life, associations that permitted women to be involved, and even to direct them, remained quite numerous. Male-dominated cercles existed in numbers roughly equal to those in Lyon, but religious charities and other organizations that encouraged both sexes to participate flourished. Regardless of whether men and women shared these spaces and practices, or if they tended to be segregated by sex, ideas about gender shaped the activities and the experiences of those who participated. Over time, women were more likely to fill roles in these associations that corresponded to their supposedly more "nurturing" tendencies, whereas men filled the positions that required decision-making and administrative skills. Women may have continued to participate in these forms of public life, but their activities grew increasingly limited.

## Cercles versus Salons: The Politics of Gender and Class

In 1803, the proto-fashion magazine *Le journal des dames et des modes*, published a letter purportedly from a reader that depicted men and women gathering to hear the latest issue read out loud and to discuss its contents. Monsieur Rienar, a bachelor from Avallon (a town in Burgundy) who defined himself as the thirty-second subscriber in his town, explained that each issue of the publication was

> read publicly at the society for the instruction of those who, not being well-to-do enough, are not included in the subscription, and for the pleasure of the subscribers, among whom several like to reread it. The fashion article is commented upon, interpreted, explained, and the next day, the young women of the town dress themselves exactly as your engraving indicates. Moreover, women are not the only ones who like your journal; some young men also benefit from it. I have even seen older men *(pères de famille)* smile at certain articles where you have had the candor to ridicule certain fashions that deserved such treatment.[5]

The letter depicts the *Journal des dames* as appealing to everyone in the town, across class and gender boundaries. Of course, the idea that women who could not afford to subscribe to the journal, even on a shared basis, had enough money to buy or make a new dress every five days pushes the limits of credulity, and it is likely that the letter was entirely fictional. Yet, it is of value in suggesting the plausibility of a mixed-sex "society for instruction."

For most histories of clubs during this period assume that associational life was for men and only men. The letter also depicts a multifarious readership gathered together to learn from the fashion journal. Again, it is unlikely that poor women and men concerned themselves with fashion, but the letter begs the question of how common mixed-sex and cross-class gatherings may have been during the postrevolutionary period.

The best known form of middle-class sociability in France during the early nineteenth century was the cercle, an institution Maurice Agulhon has defined as "an association of men organized to practice together a non-lucrative activity, or even to share time of non-activity or leisure." The cercle was also a provincial phenomenon. In Paris, bourgeois men had "beautiful, clean, and comfortable cafés" available to them, but in smaller provincial cities, where the café was "a sordid and noisy inn and where the rare *hôtels particuliers* only received in their salons those of immaculate monarchism, bourgeois men had two reasons to try to gather amongst themselves."[6] Authorities, too, had reason to allow such venues to exist. The Napoleonic regime tolerated both cercles and salons because it could use them to listen in on conversations. Ordinary police kept cercles under surveillance, and a system of upper-class spies kept track of salon activities.[7] In the most complete study of cercles, Agulhon argues that the cercle defined itself against the salon: bourgeois as opposed to aristocratic, a new practice as opposed to a traditional one, a supposedly imported practice (presumably from England) as opposed to a supposedly national one. And their "most striking [feature] perhaps: *the cercle defined itself against the salon as a purely masculine [form of] sociability versus [one that] included men and women.*"[8] However, these were not always purely male or purely bourgeois gatherings, at least not in their earliest forms; and they seem to have pre-dated the Revolution.

Lyon's Cercle de Bellecour, which reopened in 1801 after shutting down in 1793, included among its members a broad array of the city's elite male and female residents. Contradicting the findings of Agulhon, Louis Trénard emphasized the fact that "in contrast to cercles of the second half of the nineteenth century, women were not excluded. . . . Bourgeois and *rentiers* (wealthy propery owners) mingled, and mothers brought their daughters in the hope of finding suitable future sons-in-law."[9] Documents held in lyonnais archives confirm Trénard's argument: the first words of the bylaws stated, "The Cercle will be comprised of 100 ladies and 100 men." In 1811, however, when the national government initiated an investigation into groups that brought together more than twenty people on a regular basis, only nineteen women and forty-four men appeared on membership lists. Many had names beginning with the particle "de," denoting their aristocratic background. Members included Camille Jordan as well as many high-ranking officials.[10] The prefect noted that the members of the Cercle de Bellecour were "almost entirely composed of former nobles who searched in their meetings [for some] social recreation." For Agulhon, the Cercle de Bellecour was "an exception to the rule," an example of aristocrats "for economic reasons, perhaps" imitating the bourgeoisie but holding on to their own practices, "galente à la française."[11] Certainly the cost of an annual membership, seventy-two francs, made it out of reach for anyone but the city's wealthiest residents. One local historian described the Cercle de Bellecour as a place where "mothers brought their daughters. It was the rendezvous of nobles and rich bourgeois *rentiers.*"[12] Although the Cercle de Bellecour seems reminiscent of Old Regime forms of aristocratic sociability, as a club with an annual membership fee, it differed in essence from the salon.

Proscriptions and prescriptions announced by the direction of the Cercle de Bellecour give a sense of the goals of the group. The cercle made reading material, mostly political and literary journals, available to members for consultation on the premises. In addition to reading, card playing figured prominently, but gambling was strictly forbidden. Article 10 of the bylaws warned that members who disobeyed the rule against it would lose their subscription.[13] To enter the cercle, one had to be an official member, with one exception: mothers could bring unmarried daughters with them without paying any additional fee.[14] Sons of members apparently had to pay the full subscription rate in order to attend. This unequal treatment may have been part of an effort to encourage more female attendance, as nearly twice as many men as women subscribed. Although they were outnumbered, women took prominent roles in the club, even participating in its direction. In 1811, the administrative council consisted of six men and four women, one of whom was the comtesse de Fargues, the wife of Lyon's first mayor during the Restoration. The activities and membership of the Cercle de Bellecour suggest that it represented an intermediary stage between the older institution, the salon, and the newer male cercles. Salons continued to exist throughout the nineteenth century, and they continued to be organized by women, but cercles evolved into purely male institutions.[15]

In addition to the evidence based on the social positions of its members, the name "Cercle de Bellecour" by itself made clear the organization's elite status and furthered its similarity to salons. Upper-class gatherings of the eighteenth century were typically "salons de Bellecour" and the most elegant ladies were "dames de Bellecour." Bellecour was (and is) a large public square located at the heart of Lyon (Map 1). A wealthy neighborhood, it was also (not coincidentally) the location at which the fire of 1793 was set as part of the Committee of Public Safety's decision to punish the city, which was renamed "Commune Affranchie" (Emancipated Commune), for having overthrown a Jacobin-dominated municipal government. The buildings along two sides of the square were burnt to the ground before the representative on mission, Georges Couthon, decided to take no further the threatened destruction of all wealthy people's homes.[16]

Thus, the Cercle de Bellecour, one of the few cercles for which there is unquestionable evidence of women's participation and even leadership, functioned as an aristocratic space, although some wealthy bourgeois participated as well. Its disappearance under the Restoration and the composition of its membership while it was in existence lead to the conclusion that it was a veiled monarchist organization. Its likely raison d'être—covert political opposition to the Empire—disappeared with the return of the Bourbons. A similar association exists in fictional form in Balzac's novel *Le contrat du mariage,* in which the main character, Paul, returns to Bordeaux in 1810 to live with his elderly father. Paul's father drags him to "a royalist society comprised of the debris of the *noblesse parlementaire* and the *noblesse d' épée.* [The two groups had] united since the Revolution to resist the Empire."[17] The Cercle de Bellecour probably resembled the organization described by Balzac. Historian Louis Trénard made a similar comment that some cercles existed to "defend the values of the Old Regime."[18] Members may very well have read and played games, but in all probability they discussed politics, too. With the prominence of women as members and organizers, the Cercle de Bellecour provides evidence for elite women's continued involvement in political discussions during the Napoleonic period.[19] As we saw in the example of political festivals, these women were more likely to oppose Napoleon than to support him.

Though ostensibly for men, intellectual associations also brought together both sexes to discuss ideas, and perhaps politics. In 1801, the wife of a notary received a letter from a female friend recounting what had taken place at a public meeting of the Athenée de Lyon: "The director, M. Martin, a surgeon, read a report on the semester's activities; M. Laurencin [read] a poem about his mother's death, which was received with loud applause; and M. Petit [read] the second part of his epistle in verse on medicine, which was as tasteful as the first."[20] The letter writer frequented these meetings regularly, and her friend was at least interested in the event, if not a regular participant herself. The Cercle des Dames had both male and female participants, too, when it was founded in 1807. Members, who seem to have joined as couples, came from Lyon's most elite circles: their names appear on lists of those invited to a ball at the prefecture in 1807. In 1812, the club was renamed the Cercle du Midi, and its membership lists contain only men's names from that point on.[21] Agulhon's and others' assumptions that cercles were evolving into male institutions seem correct.

Although cercles were becoming more uniformly male, literary sources suggest that mixed-sex gatherings were not uncommon. *Le conteur des dames, ou les soirées parisiennes,* a collection of stories, some in prose some in verse, that were supposedly created for a *petit cercle littéraire* at which men and women gathered once a week, was marketed as a useful publication, one that would improve readers' morality. The title page even included the statement that "mothers will permit their daughters to read this" *(la mère en permettra la lecture à sa fille).*[22] Its marketing efforts appear to have succeeded: the book was reprinted several times in the early 1820s. Developing assumptions about gender and sexual norms set the tone for such imagined mixed-sex gatherings: addressing men, the introduction reminded them "that women take part in your meetings, and that good morals [and] decency" are thus necessary.[23] The collection brought together pieces written for such gatherings, mostly simple love stories with surprising but happy endings. The decision to print the book speaks to contemporary assumptions about French sociability bringing both sexes together. French publications of the period often compared French and British ways of life, with the assumption that men and women led separate lives in England, whereas they shared much of their time in France. Like the nantais journalist who encouraged women to attend the physics demonstrations in his city, Germaine de Staël praised the French way: if French women became more like English women, she argued, men would lose the intellectual companionship they had grown accustomed to in their wives and the other women in their families. Then they would seek fulfillment elsewhere.[24] Although men and women appeared together in these venues, they did not necessarily participate in equivalent manners. Mixed-sex sociability could reinforce gender norms as much as, if not more than, practices based on the notion of "separate spheres." Ideas about gender complementarity could force women into roles that were as narrowly defined as those put forth in domestic ideology, even if they did not find themselves relegated into a purely "private," "domestic" existence. In addition, other kinds of clubs did exclude women, making it clear they were not welcome in all contexts.

In contrast to the more elite gatherings discussed thus far, middle-class cercles appear to have limited their membership to men from the beginning. One such association in existence in Lyon during the Napoleonic period was the Cercle Littéraire. More than a reading society, this organization, which was founded in 1806, offered members an opportunity to publish their own writings. Held in a print shop, the meetings attracted professors and writers who were required to submit original work on a regular basis for the members to read and discuss.[25] In comparison with the Cercle de Bellecour, where people read and socialized, the Cercle Littéraire defined itself as an organization for professional writers, those who actually created literature, and women were presumed ineligible. Like the Cercle de Bellecour, however, members' politics appear to have been quite conservative, as a poem published in their first proceedings indicates. Mourning recent changes, the poem attacked the entire revolutionary project. Each stanza has two sections that compare previous, in other words prerevolutionary, mentalities with current ones.

> *Jadis* une amante infidèle
> Coûtait la mort à son amant:
> Certes, se noyer pour sa belle,
> Ce n'est pas aimer foiblement!
> *Aujourd'hui* dès qu'une maîtresse
> A couronné tous nos désirs,
> On doit la gagner de vitesse,
> Rompre, et chercher d'autres plaisirs.
>
> . . . . . . . . . . . . . .
>
> *Jadis* on avait des scrupules . . .
> Les bonnes gens que nos ayeux!
> Nous rions de leurs ridicules . . .
> Ils étaient simples & pieux.
> *Aujourd'hui* tout devient problème;
> L'honneur, la vertu sont des mots:
> On détrônerait Dieu lui même,
> S'il n'en fallait un pour les sots.[26]

[*Formerly* an unfaithful mistress
Brought death to her lover:
Surely, drowning oneself for a woman,
That is not loving weakly!
*Today* as soon as a mistress
Has rewarded all our desires
We must win her speedily,
Leave her, and find other pleasures.

. . . . . . . . . . . . . .

*Formerly* we had scruples . . .
The good people who [were] our ancestors!
We laugh at their ridiculous behavior . . .
They were simple and pious.
*Today* everything is difficult;
Honor and virtue are only words:
We would even dethrone God himself,
If it wasn't necessary to have one for fools.]

Explicitly celebrating the Old Regime, the poem criticized the new order's immorality in matters of love and lack of religious conviction, and it complained of corruption in the judicial system, the lack of talent among playwrights, and the silliness of fashions. After being published in the *Journal de Lyon,* the second stanza cited here, along with another about judges accepting bribes and deemed "injurious to the current *magistrature,*" drew attention from government censors, who then revoked the paper's license.[27] The sentiments expressed suggest that the Cercle Littéraire was another cover for right-wing political opposition to Napoleon. Because of the formidable surveillance apparatus of the Empire, political opponents met under the guise of literary, intellectual, and social organizations, forms of association to which women, in some cases at least, had access, unlike later more explicitly political groups that were defined as male only. As we saw in the example of provincial theater, the repression of the First Empire created spaces that opened doors to women's inconspicuous involvement in venues for political debate. The greater openness of later regimes would render such involvement more difficult and less frequent as women found themselves excluded from explicitly male forms of political activity during the July Monarchy and throughout the nineteenth century.

Two other clubs existed in Lyon during the Empire, the Cercle de Commerce and the Cercle de Terreaux, both of which attracted middle-class men.[28] A local historian described their members as "gros négociants" (big businessmen) and "petits commerçants" (shop owners), respectively.[29] These clubs correspond better to the typical representation of the cercle: their meetings took place in cafés, women were not admitted, and their members tended to be bourgeois and liberal as opposed to aristocratic and monarchist.[30] As these institutions evolved, they organized along class (and gender) lines, with specific clubs for specific social groups and political viewpoints. Although theaters and some other venues continued to draw diverse groups, these associations epitomized the trend toward greater social segregation. As postrevolutionary social structures solidified, specific amusements also evolved to suit these different groups. The trend in Lyon was for purely male, middle-class gatherings to become more frequent and more highly politicized, even as older kinds of more heterogeneous socializing continued.

Like Lyon, Nantes had a lively associational life, though less information exists about it because the results of the 1811 investigation have disappeared for that part of France.[31] In an 1808 police report, cercles and reading rooms *(chambres de lecture)* are listed together, further confirming that cercles had evolved from the latter. The main business district of the city housed five clubs, two of which were called "cercles": the Cercle du Port-au-Vin and the Cercle de la rue Jean-Jacques. Most of the chambres and cercles listed continued to exist well into the Restoration. Their names appear in reports from 1819 and 1820.[32] According to the 1820 report, both the Cercle du Port-au-Vin and the Cercle de la rue Jean-Jacques came into existence in 1780 and had operated continuously ever since, except in 1793. Two other cercles, one known just by its location on the quai Brancas and the other called the Cercle du Soleil, had existed for over fifty years in 1820. Only one cercle on the 1820 list, the Cercle des Amis du Roi, was new, having been established in 1815. This information from Nantes casts doubt on the assumption that cercles were a postrevolutionary phenomenon. They may have existed earlier, along with but not replacing salons; or it may be that clubs which had been known as *chambres littéraires* in the eighteenth century took on the name "cercle" as that term became more common. Whatever the case, they appear to have been purely male institutions; even those listed as "*chambres*" were directed by men; whereas in Lyon, many *cabinets littéraires* were run by women, even if their members were men.[33] Perhaps the nantais journalist cited at the opening of this chapter was correct in his assessment of Nantes' associational life: it encouraged men to gather in the absence of women.

As in Lyon, political discussions took place in these clubs on a regular basis. Under Napoleon, authorities expressed concern that cercles existed as covers for royalist organizations, whereas those in operation under the Restoration were presumed liberal. In Nantes in 1817, the prefect ruled that the Cercle de l'Union was to be closed because of the "indecent behavior that the members had manifested during the visit of the prince." Six weeks later, the cercle was allowed to reopen.[34] Such lenience suggests that Restoration authorities did not see the cercle as a significant threat to the regime, despite the political leanings of its members. Lyonnais officials assumed that cercles and reading rooms were gathering places for the liberal opposition, as well. In an 1820 report on the reading material sought after at these clubs, the prefect commented on members' political views: "Most of the cercles and *cabinets* are frequented by liberals; this circumstance explains why works favorable to this opinion are especially sought after in these establishments."[35] The 1820s would bring an ever more clearly articulated sense of bourgeois political identity, a transition that is visible in many contexts, including the growing numbers of cercles and reading rooms, as well as an explosion of newspapers that spoke to middle-class interests.[36]

The political nature of these bourgeois organizations may help to explain the exclusion of women as members. However women often appeared in these spaces, as owner-operators or as employees. A journalistic account suggests that reading material was not the only draw of reading rooms. "The amiability of the lady charged with doing the honors at the *cabinet,* is . . . the only magnet capable of attracting the largest number of readers. It is so pleasant, for example, when you have tortured yourself over the enigmas in prose of *Le pandore,* to cast a furtive glance toward the lady at the counter! . . . When by chance my eyes meet those of the amiable lady, I find in this look enough strength to read an article in the *Gazette universelle de Lyon.*"[37] As we will see with cafés, which are discussed in the next chapter, the presence of female workers enhanced the experience of male customers in these increasingly politicized spaces. The possibility of making eye contact with the "amiable lady" running the reading room could serve as a greater attraction than the newspapers available there. The *Gazette universelle* was a right-wing paper, and the reference to needing strength to read it would have been a transparent political comment to readers of the *Journal du commerce.*[38]

The political bent of reading rooms and clubs was not always liberal. Aristocrats had their own version of such gatherings: a "société de la noblesse" called *du Cours* (of the court) existed in Nantes during the Restoration. As elite families spent eight months of the year at their country homes, this club only met during the winter months when nobles resided in the city. The club had its own *chambre littéraire,* which subscribed to the anti-opposition newspapers, leading the prefect to announce in an 1826 report: "love and respect for the king are the sentiments that fill all the hearts of Royalists, Bretons or Vendéans." He contrasted these views with those of the businessmen *(commerçants)* who had their own "société" known as "de la Fosse," after the street on which it was located. According to the prefect, the two groups, nobles and bourgeois, rarely mingled, except at occasional festivities held by public officials.[39] Each had its own meeting places, with the perhaps "bourgeois" system of male-only socializing slowly replacing the aristocratic mixed-sex gatherings in private homes. However, aristocratic life in the country remained much as it had been before the Revolution, with families socializing together on their estates.

The best-known form of elite sociability, salons, which were intellectual gatherings held by women, emerged in the seventeenth century, peaked in the eighteenth, and then evolved in form over the course of the nineteenth century.[40] Although we know quite a bit about Parisian salons and *salonnières* in the early nineteenth century, little research has been done on provincial salons. Lyon had a vibrant intellectual life under the Empire, with a handful of women running salons. A letter written to Juliette Récamier in 1812, when she was about to leave Paris under force and return to her husband's family in Lyon, gives a sense of the intellectual circles that existed in that city. A friend of the family, Monsieur Voght, wrote to say that he had just been to Lyon, and his letter depicts Lyon as a place that Récamier would find enjoyable.

> You will have in Lyon Mme de Semérsy [*sic*]. . . . Her circle of men is made to be yours. They include artists, literary men, and no politicians. Revoil, Artaud, [and] Richard are amiable, a Dr. Martin, M. Ballanche despite his awkwardness, another acquaintance of Camille [Jordan], a young man whom I saw at M. Delille's, the author of *Les Soirées provinciales*, etc. They could form a school, give lectures. And you will have Camille [and] Regny, and his family. He suggests that you spend some time in the country with Mme Monico; when your suffering has calmed, you will live in Camille's country home. There you will find all this—and rest and tranquility. That's definitely something.[41]

Life in the provinces lacked the glitter of Paris, but there an educated woman like Récamier was able to find intellectual stimulation and a more peaceful lifestyle than in the capital. Récamier resided at the Hôtel de l'Europe from June 1812 until the spring of the following year. She received numerous luminaries there, while keeping up links between Lyon's intellectual elite and those in Germany, Switzerland, and Italy.[42]

In addition to salons, various kinds of intellectual and scientific endeavors, including the development of libraries and the distribution of books to the poor, found support in provincial cities and provided opportunities for elite women and men to involve themselves in public life. During the Empire, a group of *négociants* (business owners) in Nantes worked with municipal officials to establish a library.[43] Later, with the Restoration, an association devoted to the propagation of "bon livres" came into existence. In his report to the minister of the interior, the prefect minimized the influence of "politically and morally dangerous books. . . . [But] good books distributed by an association based [in Nantes] have multiplied greatly. About 2000 volumes of good works of piety, morals, and literature, principally destined for the peuple were published in 1826."[44] Authorities apparently supported such efforts. In her study of scientific societies, Carol Harrison argues that these institutions emerged on the eve of the Revolution and then developed further in the early nineteenth century as "bourgeois men wrested science from aristocratic salons and made it their own."[45] Although these societies tended to attract middle-class men, there is evidence to suggest that women and aristocrats participated as well. Three women were elected to the Société Académique de la Loire-Inférieure during the period at hand: Eléonore de la Bouisse in 1806, Elisa Mercoeur in 1827, and Constance de Salm-Dyck the following year.[46] And even those who were not members could participate in particular events. In 1821, at the association's annual public meeting, which took place in the great room at Nantes' city hall, several women attended to hear the presentations. A journalist commented that he had "noticed with pleasure the ladies [who] embellished this meeting."[47] Although they apparently functioned as "embellishments," that is, as nonessential characters who made such gatherings more pleasant without contributing to their substance, women's presence shaped the makeup of these social spaces, which were neither purely male nor purely bourgeois.

Authorities paid little attention to these meetings, as long as participants remained focused on the narrow subject under discussion and did not stray into politics. But political topics were unavoidable, and political issues colored the experience of those in attendance at diverse kinds of gatherings. In an 1827 report to the minister of the interior, the prefect in Nantes expressed some concern about the political opposition, both republicans and Orléanists (supporters of another branch of the royal family, the Orléans). However, he insisted that whatever dissatisfaction may have existed, it remained below the surface, and no violent disorders with political causes had taken place in 1826. The "only" evidence of political leanings were in "animated discussions in salons and *chambres littéraires,* allusions made at the theater, meetings at the bourse, and the coldness and distrust that generally reigns in social relations."[48] The long list of public spaces and the reference to social relations in general suggest that if the dissatisfaction was below the surface, it was not far down. Politics entered into everyday life through these spaces, with middle- and upper-class women and men participating together in many of them.

## The Social Art of Benevolence

Charitable work brought elite women (and men) into the public arena in more visible ways than salons and academic societies. Secular or religious, national or local, providing help to indigent mothers or instruction for poor girls, a wide range of charities staffed by women came into existence during the first decades of the nineteenth century. Historians have devoted significant attention to these kinds of institutions, in France and elsewhere. For the French case, Parisian charities have been thoroughly explored, particularly in the massive work by Catherine Duprat on benevolence, a study that focuses on women's and men's organizations. On the provinces, Christine Adams has published an article on the Bordeaux branch of the Société de la Charité Maternelle, and she is engaged in a national study of the group. In addition, a large body of work addressing the topic of women's charitable activities in the Anglo-Saxon world has emerged over the past few decades.[49] In all this research, regardless of geographical or chronological focus, two key debates stand out: first, the extent to which charities should be viewed as institutions of control, as a method of forcing bourgeois norms onto working-class households; and second, the capacity for these institutions to enable women to assert themselves in the public world without contradicting prevailing domestic ideology.

In the examples discussed here, similar issues emerge. Female charities certainly did represent an opportunity for emerging middle-class values to be pushed onto lower-class households as well as a chance for women of the upper classes to take active roles in public life. However, this section's goal is not to replay these debates. Rather, it puts charitable work into a broader context—presenting it as one among many options for women to involve themselves in urban life. Charities also represented an opportunity to build a sense of class solidarity among the elite women who ran them, and in bringing together nobles and bourgeois, they helped to construct a sense of what it meant to be a female *notable,* just as the government (Napoleonic or Bourbon) helped to build a male class of notables to work at both the national and local levels in various kinds of official capacities. Finally, these institutions show how the process of "secularization" was far from straightforward, as religiously based charitable projects staffed by both laywomen and nuns grew in influence during these years.

The best-known charity run by women was the Société de la Charité Maternelle. Initially founded in 1788, with Marie Antoinette serving as its first president, it reappeared in 1810 with the empress at its head.[50] Run out of Paris, the association had a chapter in each city of the Empire. The number of members on local administrative boards varied depending on the population size of the city. Lyon, with a population of greater than eighty thousand, was to have twelve.[51] The organization was operated entirely by and for women, with the exception of a male treasurer, often a banker or other person whose skills made him suitable for this role. The board members donated five hundred francs to the organization, a huge sum of money. Other residents donated smaller sums.[52] Like the Cercle de Bellecour, this organization represented a continuation of aristocratic lifestyles. The women involved practiced a form of "paternalism" (so to speak) toward women clearly defined as inferior to them. They also had extensive power, as their decisions about who would receive assistance could be a matter of life or death. A form of "good work," the experience must have solidified these women's already strong sense of superiority. In contrast to older forms of charitable activities, however, this group took its orders directly from the capital and functioned as a national organization with local chapters all operating similarly.[53] The goal of the organization was to give assistance to impoverished pregnant women and mothers whom the members deemed "worthy" of such help. To be eligible for aid, women needed to be married, and they had to submit a certificate of moral uprightness. A woman assisted by the Société de la Charité Maternelle received medical care during her delivery and a monthly stipend to allow her to feed and care for her child. In addition, the members of the society supervised the women they assisted to ensure that infants received proper care. One of their biggest concerns was that women should breastfeed their children.[54]

The women who participated in the Lyon chapter of the Société de la Charité Maternelle were proud of their accomplishments and spelled them out in their 1813 annual report. Having assisted 171 women with 17,496 francs, the members underscored that this was "many more than we should have been able to [take care of] with such a sum." They managed to economize in part because several of the mothers came to them having recently given birth, which meant that the organization paid for neither the doctor nor the "layette." All the women they helped received six francs per month for fourteen months. In a further note of pride, the letter mentioned that "of the 137 children adopted by the *société maternelle* of Lyon in the course of 1812, 125" were still alive.[55] Helping members to create a meaningful existence for themselves as they worked to assist the "worthy poor," the Société de la Charité Maternelle also gave elite women a chance to exercise administrative and organizational skills. Like they did in the Cercle de Bellecour, women participated in all aspects of this organization. Unlike that other group, however, the Société de la Charité was part of a national network and was defined as a specifically female association.

A second charity run and staffed by women came into existence in Lyon during the early years of the Restoration: the Société des Jeunes Econonomes (Association of Young Thrifty Housekeepers). Young, unmarried women filled every position in the administration and operation of the association, from president, to secretary, and even to treasurer, all the way down to *visiteuses* (female visitors). The charity provides an example of the provinces leading Paris: an organization by the same name was founded in Paris in 1823, five years after one was established in Lyon. The Parisian members of the Société des Jeunes Econonomes, also all women, visited poor families to determine their needs and to teach them how to live economically.[56] The eight-year-old girls they "adopted" received trousseaus, lessons in reading and writing, and the costs of an apprenticeship. The lyonnais organization focused on running a free boarding school for girls aged nine to twelve. They paid careful attention to how the children would be selected: "We will only take children whose parents have [demonstrated] irreproachable conduct, the goal of this association being not only to alleviate misery, but also to reward virtue."[57] Morality counted more than neediness. Once admitted, the girls were only to leave the school with their teachers "and under no pretext with their parents, with the exception of New Year's Day."[58] Following further rules about the children who would be admitted, the association's bylaws delineated the organizational structure, explaining in a precise manner what responsibilities came with each position. The "demoiselles" who were members of the organization would meet every six months to learn about the girls' progress, whereas those holding offices would meet once a month. The women involved took their project seriously, as suggested by the fact that they went to the effort of having their bylaws printed. It appears that the Jeunes Economes were a younger version of the Société de la Charité Maternelle, with similar goals and views though a different focus.

Such private, female-operated charitable organizations were joined in their efforts to alleviate poverty by municipal institutions that also relied on women as sponsors: the city ran its own Bureau de Bienfaisance and some hospitals for the poor. Created in 1802, the Hospices Civils de Lyon oversaw two institutions: the Hôtel-Dieu, the city's public hospital, which had nearly eleven hundred beds for sick men and women, and the Hôpital Général de la Charité, which took in the elderly, pregnant women, orphans, and abandoned children. Local donations were crucial to the continuation of these institutions and constituted the majority of their budgets.[59] During the economic crisis of 1807, the prefect lauded the efforts of the Bureau de Bienfaisance, whose assistance, "augmented by donations from individuals, greatly alleviated" workers' difficulties.[60] The Bureau de Bienfaisance raised money through a variety of means, including benefit performances at the theater. Women attended these *spectacles* and concerts and also performed in them, and men handled the planning and organization.[61] Nonetheless, women were involved in the daily operation and money-raising activities of these charitable efforts. Donating their time and money allowed them to demonstrate in public and among their peers their generosity as well as their administrative capacities. These charitable institutions—the Société Maternelle, the Benevolent Committee, and the Hospices Civils—reflect the strengths and weaknesses, the successes and failures, of Napoleonic centralization efforts. Controlled to a large extent by Parisian directives, despite being technically run under local auspices, charities attempted to address social problems but could go no further than to assuage some of the worst effects of intense poverty.

Religious institutions that fulfilled charitable functions also proliferated. After being dismantled during the Revolution, several convents reemerged in Lyon following the signing of the Concordat, as the pragmatic Napoleon recognized their utility for promoting obedience to his regime. According to a recent history of teaching orders, a group of bourgeois women in Lyon formed an association in 1804 to support the Sœurs de Saint-Charles. "These well-off ladies published books and pious images for congregational pupils, distributed prizes, bought ornaments for the convent chapel, paid for heating, and subsidized the pensions of one or two novices as well as the salaries for nuns who visited the poor and sick."[62] Both the Sœurs de Saint-Charles and the Frères de la Doctrine Chrétienne offered free instruction, while promoting military service and the virtues of the Napoleonic state. Along with the fundamentals of reading and writing, the congregational schools taught their pupils the Catechism of the Empire, which included the statement, "We owe in particular to Napoleon, our emperor, love, respect, obedience, fidelity, military service, . . . and the defense of the Empire and his throne."[63] As seen in other contexts, like festivals, Napoleon strove to use religion to reinforce his reign.

More of these religious orders opened their doors in the period after the Hundred Days. Some acted as refuges for rich women who chose to separate themselves from society; these places existed thanks to the donations of women who entered. Others were less wealthy and relied upon the work of the women in the convent to survive financially. Still nursing their wounds from the revolutionary period, nuns avoided attracting attention. In response to an 1817 request for information about their goals and functions, an Ursaline nun in Lyon expressed suspicion: "Considering that the nation once threw us out of our homes . . . and that it is still using those locations . . . who can assure us that any information gathered now will not be used against us in the future?"[64] The Dames Ursalines, along with other congregations such as the Dames Sainte Elisabeth, provided instruction to children whose families could afford to pay and to indigent children whom they taught to read and to sew.[65] Convinced that these women performed valuable functions, Restoration authorities encouraged the expansion of these church-run schools, which grew in number during the 1820s.[66]

The greater openness toward and reliance on religion during the Restoration is particularly evident in Nantes where the cooperation between religious and state-run charities went further than elsewhere. On 21 January 1821, the anniversary of the death of Louis XVI, two collections were made at mass: one for the poor by the Dames de Charité and the second for the support of institutions that the Association Paternelle des chevaliers de

Saint-Louis created to help widows and orphans. All of this took place in Nantes' cathedral.[67] These practices contrast with those of the Empire, when, despite the existence of locally run charities, the discourse of charity made the state into the key agent in distributing aid and alleviating the sufferings of the poor. After the emperor's visit to Nantes in 1808, the mayor's office published a poster to inform the populace of Napoleon's response to their warm welcome:

> You honored the *Nation Bretonne,* you celebrated suitably the presence of your Emperor; his heart took part in your festivities, he appreciated the sincerity of your homage, he noticed the unanimity, and the glorious confidence that he demonstrated in mingling among you, is the most flattering prize. . . .
>
> Numerous benefits have been promised for your city. . . . Large sums have been accorded to the indigent class, even more to your ill-fated industry, more to your institutions of public assistance.[68]

The Restoration replaced this impersonal, passive-voice version of charity that kept the emperor in the spotlight with one that made local religious and secular institutions the key sponsors of benevolent deeds.

The Restoration government encouraged Nantes' religious orders to expand their influence, particularly in education. Female congregations focused on the basics of writing and some practical, vocational skills. Nantes' Sisters of Providence "taught reading to those girls who demonstrated an inclination; the goal of the institution being to board *(traiter)* these children, and not to instruct them, the sisters limited themselves to teaching the Catechism to those who learned with difficulty. They trained young girls to work as much as their age and their health permitted."[69] A letter from the mother superior of the Dames du Refuge justified the order's plan to buy a larger building than the one it had been using, so as to "allow a larger number of indigent children to benefit from instruction and especially from a religious education, the only type that forms good morals." Emphasizing the value of the order's efforts, she insisted that these girls would in turn "exert the influence they necessarily have in the family to form good citizens for the state and faithful subjects for the king."[70] The mixing of the language of citizens and subjects is an interesting twist with similarities to Napoleonic discourse.[71] Despite the self-serving nature of such rhetoric, the important role taken on by religious women to educate poor girls cannot be questioned. Prior to the Revolution, few women's religious orders had devoted themselves to such efforts.[72] Although such activities would continue through-out the nineteenth century, they would become less significant as larger numbers of lay primary schools came into existence.

Though benevolent efforts during the Restoration increasingly functioned under the rubric of religious institutions, secular efforts continued as well. In 1819, a charity concert was held in Nantes to raise money for the poor. According to a newspaper article, "The mayor hoped that bureaucrats, citizens, and especially ladies, whom we always see associated with good deeds, would like to participate . . . in this soirée that furnishes an opportunity for both pleasure and benevolence." A similar event held in Lyon in 1824 drew a "large crowd of elegantly dressed ladies."[73] Attending such events was another way for women to see and be seen in public performing roles as elite *dames patronesses*, even if they did not have the means to pay the excessive dues of the Société Maternelle. Newspaper coverage only made such participation more "public." Describing the Bureau de Bienfaisance in 1829, the *Etrennes mignonnes lyonnaises* specified that each arrondissement had its own auxiliary committee that distributed food and other necessities to the poor. Men staffed these committees and were "aided in their efforts by *des sociétés des dames*, commendable for their virtue [and] their charity, who act concurrently with them and second their zeal by giving abundantly."[74] Exemplifying the model of gender complementarity, men directed the work, and women contributed their "natural" traits of charitable behavior. Here was another organization that continued to bring men and women together, although in contrast to earlier examples like the Cercle de Bellecour, women did not participate in its direction. Such gatherings denote a broader transition: over time women were becoming less likely to control the spaces in which they gathered with men in public. Unlike salons and some of the examples discussed earlier, female attendees at these later events observed what went on and may have participated in discussions, but they did not lead or direct the gatherings.

In the conclusion to his detailed study of eighteenth-century Lyon, Maurice Garden emphasized the importance of associations, calling them the first law in the social life of cities. In fact, he asserted, individuals only participated in urban society through their associations and other organizations that united people by their trade, neighborhood, or parish.[75] Although the Revolution officially abolished many of these forms of social connection—some forever, like guilds, some temporarily, like religious institutions—associations continued to structure urban social life in the postrevolutionary period. As members gathered to amuse themselves, to advance their careers, to discuss politics, or to organize charitable efforts, they created social spaces in which to act out and construct behavioral norms—to perform the social roles they had accepted for themselves. Some of these spaces grew to be gendered male, whereas others welcomed both sexes and others only women. Regardless of the nantais journalist's concerns about "warehouses of men" in his city, men and women still found countless opportunities to socialize together. However, it is important to remember that even those spaces that did not separate men and women were nonetheless organized by ideas about gender: women's and men's presumed roles in clubs, salons, and charities reflected notions of their "natures."

The social spaces analyzed in this chapter fostered a sense of class solidarity, at times with both sexes present, at others among only men or women. Despite an apparent trend toward growing separation of the sexes, women of the various classes participated in many of the activities examined in this chapter. Salons and charitable associations continued to be dominated by women; and women also participated in intellectual gatherings like the physics lecture described by the nantais journalist whose views opened this chapter. This female presence continued to be the case throughout the Napoleonic and Restoration periods, even as male organizations grew to dominate urban culture over the period. Still, an evolution toward women having more limited control in setting the tone and making the decisions that shaped these spaces is visible. Even in mixed-sexed clubs and charities, women became less likely to hold positions of power. Associational life grew increasingly masculine and bourgeois by the 1820s. However, workers and women contested this domination and did so with greater intensity as the characteristics and functioning of the new social order became more visible and thus better understood. In helping to construct behavioral norms for different groups, associational life and the social spaces in which such gatherings took place made people aware of their differing degrees of access to urban space and the varying limitations placed upon their activities. This education prepared the way for contestation once true workers' and feminist movements came into existence. Both socialism and feminism emerged as vocal political movements around 1830, with utopian socialism becoming visible by the mid-1820s. These movements gathered strength through newspapers founded after the Revolution of 1830.[76] The frustrations of the 1820s helped to lay the groundwork for these movements that took shape once the political terrain made them possible.

Associational life in these cities fostered the development of postrevolutionary conceptions of gender and class by providing social spaces for specific groups to recognize their shared concerns and values. Salons and cercles welcomed only very narrow segments of society, and charitable associations brought together the urban elite as members worked to help the "needy poor." In some cases, women participated in these groups; in other cases, women's pronounced absence shaped the tenor of the spaces and the experiences of the men who filled them. With or without the presence of women, gender norms played themselves out in these spaces, as did conceptions of class as the new notables of postrevolutionary France mingled and reinforced their connections. Although most clubs and charities brought together only narrow segments of society, and often people with the same political views, more public spaces for amusement, like cafés and dance halls, theoretically permitted greater mixing of diverse people. However, as the next chapter demonstrates, most businesses that encouraged crowds to assemble for the sake of amusement and discussion catered to equally homogeneous clientele and thus also created spaces for specific groups to gather and to develop notions of group identity among themselves.

# — 6 —

# Drinking, Dancing,
# and the Moral Order

In 1801, the *Journal des dames et des modes* included a story told from the perspective of a young man trying to flirt with a bourgeoise he saw on the streets of Paris. "Sundays, the boulevards are crowded with a thousand groups that cross and succeed each other; amidst them I noted a young bourgeoise at least as fresh as my *grisette,* but more modest and sweet; I followed her from afar, watching her, and occasionally catching her eye on me. I swore that I would follow her until the end of her promenade. We entered a dance hall *(guinguette),* and needless to say, my young lady was not alone; her papa and mama were at her sides."[1] The bourgeoise in this story was not forced to lead a domestic existence, safe from potential admirers other than ones brought to her by her parents. Like the working-class mistress the author referred to as his "grisette," she was able to go to these public places without causing a stir, enjoying the music, dancing, and crowds, while no doubt recognizing that she was putting herself on display at the same time as watching others around her. It was titillating for this male observer to see her there, but it did not surprise him and it did not seem dangerous for her to be there. However, as the last sentence in the quotation makes clear, a class marker was immediately visible: the close proximity of her parents distinguished the "bourgeoise" from the "grisette"; bourgeois girls would not roam the streets without a chaperone. Despite such obvious class differences, in the early years of the nineteenth century, women and men from across the social spectrum amused themselves while interacting in various urban spaces. Drinking and dancing were two of the most common activities that people enjoyed together in public spaces like cafés, cabarets, and dance halls.

Although these kinds of public venues had the potential to bring more diverse groups together than associations did, most provincial establishments catered to relatively narrow segments of society, in apparent contrast to Parisian spaces for drinking and dancing. Provincial cafés were largely middle-class spaces, whereas cabarets attracted workers and soldiers. In addition, women were not typically among the customers, though many occupied these spaces as servers and owners. Some cafés went so far as to hire "exotic" female workers, creating a sexual atmosphere that kept "respectable" women from appearing in such spaces. Cafés may have permitted some social (and sexual) mixing, but only under specific circumstances. In contrast, elite men and women would never have set foot in the more lowbrow cabarets situated on the outskirts of cities. Dance halls necessarily attracted both sexes, but most appear to have catered to specific social groups as well.

Drinking establishments, dance halls, and more formal balls permitted the relatively homogeneous groups gathered in these spaces to observe others they viewed as like themselves. These experiences aided in building group solidarity. But drinking and dancing also had potentially dangerous outcomes: drunken disorderliness was one, and the supposed debauchery encouraged by dancing concerned both religious and secular authorities, particularly with the Restoration. Evolving out of age-old traditions of village festivals that drew on carnival traditions of mocking social superiors, popular festivals and dances were mostly staged by relative newcomers to urban life and had many of the same undertones.[2] Authorities recognized this fact, but they also knew that it was in their interest to allow some youthful blowing off of steam to take place. Of course, the postrevolutionary context differed from the Old Regime in that overthrowing the current political and social order now appeared as a real option. The events of 1789 to 1799, whether interpreted positively or negatively, shaped the significance read into all social gatherings of the postrevolutionary period.

Official treatment of such gathering places changed during the period under examination here. Under Napoleon, a pragmatic approach underlay official treatment of working-class amusements. Napoleonic officials seemed confident that they could maintain control over the "common people": as long as workers showed up ready for work at the appropriate time, they could more or less do as they wished. In contrast, moral issues came to the forefront with the Restoration as officials and elites more generally were unsure of their ability to keep the "masses" under control. Working-class amusements came under greater surveillance as both church and state officials saw them as sites of disorder and as competition with more "accept-

able" kinds of behavior. One of the first laws proclaimed by Restoration officials concerned the hours of operation for drinking establishments and
dance halls, particularly on Sundays and festival days. The law, which was
reprinted on large posters, ordered all wine shops, cafés, billiard halls, and
cabarets to close their doors on these days during the time when church services were held, from 8 A.M. to noon, or risk a three hundred franc fine. The
poster also stipulated that on Sundays, performers (acrobats, *maîtres de curiosités,* musicians, and so on) could not "exercise their métier" in theaters
or on the street until 5 P.M., and that no dances or musical performances
could take place until the same time, at the risk of a five hundred franc fine.[3]
Building the postrevolutionary moral order required that opportunities for
"debauchery" be limited as much as possible. Of course, the limitations in-
stituted out of supposed "moral" concerns also helped to minimize the political potential of these gatherings. The frequent and vocal expressions of
concern about "morality" uttered by Restoration officials paralleled larger
social and political transformations. Concerns about "debauchery" reinforced emerging middle-class attitudes toward the "dangerous" classes. Another result was that "respectable" middle-class women avoided the spaces
in which "disorderly" workers amused themselves. The organization and
regulation of sexuality helped to constitute class itself as the working classes
seemed in need of moral and sexual enforcement as much as other kinds of
control.

## "Parliaments for the People": Cafés and Cabarets

Balzac titled one of the chapters in his novel *Les paysans,* "Comme quoi le
cabaret est la salle de conseil du peuple" (Showing that the Cabaret Is the
Parliament of the People).[4] As he so often did, Balzac put into words widely
held views and assumptions: in this case that by bringing people together,
cabarets provided venues for discussion and debate. Lowbrow establishments located in small towns and on the outskirts of large cities (to avoid
the taxes placed on wine brought into cities), cabarets sold refreshments to
locals and travelers. Cafés, in contrast, tended to be situated in the heart of
fashionable commercial districts. They were geared toward wealthier clientele, and in addition to serving food and drink, they often provided reading
material like newspapers. Little study has been done on provincial cafés and
cabarets. However, it is clear that cafés and cabarets functioned as locations
for discussion of current events and politics, and both spaces, in apparent

contrast to those in Paris, tended to attract mostly men, with the exception of female owners and servers, and perhaps prostitutes.[5] By the last years of the Restoration, Lyon housed dozens of cafés, and as the establishments grew in number, café owners sought new ways to attract customers, attracting the attention of the local press.

Relatively little information exists on provincial cafés during the Empire, partly because they were fewer in number than would be the case later and partly due to the nature of Napoleonic policing. One example from Nantes in 1813 arose when a particularly tumultuous occurrence took place in Nantes' theater. In investigating the incident, officials assumed that the perpetrators had made their plans in a café. According to a local newspaper, the trouble began when "some apparently drunken young men in parterre interrupted the actors and cried out for the director. . . . The police refused to give in to the troublemakers *(tapageurs)*. Then the situation worsened. . . . The troublemakers broke some benches and stools, and continued their stupid cries. Not wanting to create a bloody scene in a place of amusement, the police did not have soldiers enter the theater. Later in the night, the people who had planned this vile behavior *(ignoble sottise)* in a café or cabaret were arrested and will be punished."[6] The article then warned others who might be planning similar behavior in "places consecrated to the pleasures of the spirit" in the future that they would be punished severely. Already under Napoleon, officials and journalists equated cafés and cabarets with disorderliness, violence, and political disruptions.

More information exists about Restoration cafés, particularly after 1820. The early 1820s brought good economic tidings to Lyon, and that in turn led to an explosion in the number of cafés in operation in the city.[7] Some were located in the aristocratic neighborhood around the place Bellecour or the nearby Théâtre des Célestins, but the best-known cafés were on or near the place des Terreaux, the square in front of the Hôtel de Ville, a location that confirms official views on the social makeup and political leaning of their clientele. The police assumed that cafés attracted "liberals" and businessmen who gathered to talk and read newspapers. In his history of eighteenth-century Lyon, Maurice Garden argues that on the eve of the Revolution, cafés at the place des Terreaux brought people together to read gazettes, play cards, recite poems, and discuss politics.[8] The neighborhood housed the homes and businesses of Lyon's *négociants* (large-scale business owners), and the drinking establishments there catered to them after 1789 as well. With the Grand Théâtre nearby, these cafés also attracted the clientele of the theater who would refresh themselves before and after performances.

Although "bourgeois liberals" mostly filled cafés, officials believed that workers also visited them. In his October 1822 report to the minister of the interior, the head of the Gendarmerie Royale in Lyon insisted that the peuple frequented cafés, where they found liberal newspapers and absorbed dangerous ideas. "The commercial and manufacturing class seems to delight in the anti-monarchical myths of the so-called liberals; the dangerous journals produced by these enemies of order do the greatest evil to the *peuple lyonnais* who frequent a great deal the cafés where these *feuilles* can be found. The *chefs de commerce* generally blame the government for the current economic stagnation, and this liberal wickedness only supports the bad spirit of the working classes."[9] The belief was thus that cafés aided in the spread of bourgeois liberalism to workers, a group that was generally described as politically apathetic. Though officials' paranoia about "liberalism" may have led to exaggeration, at least a grain of truth existed on which to base these claims. They arose from more than just irrational fears: "liberal" and "Bonapartist" uprisings, including people marching with tricolor flags, had taken place in Lyon in 1817 and 1820. In her work on associations, Carol Harrison found that the presence of potentially dangerous, that is, working-class, elements in cafés motivated bourgeois men to create cercles so that they could socialize and hold discussions among men of their own class.[10] "Middle-class" cafés were not purely for the middle classes.

Contemporaries associated cafés with political discussion and the spreading of "dangerous" ideas, in part because they made newspapers available to their customers. It was common even for newspapers to be read out loud.[11] An 1822 police report provides a typical portrayal, in this case of Lyon's café Le Grand, on the place des Terreaux: "[F]requented by old Jacobins . . . people express the most scandalous opinions there and communicate ill-disposed information."[12] The police viewed Le Grand as one of the most offensive, but the other cafés nearby, including the Colonne, Minerve, Apollo, and Commerce, stimulated concern, too. In part because of the neighborhood in which they were located, authorities assumed that "bourgeois liberals" would patronize these places and circulate their dangerous views to others who happened to be there. Such assumptions support Sarah Maza's recent argument that "Restoration politics gave birth to bourgeois identity."[13] The experience of being united in the political opposition to the Restoration helped give this diverse group its sense of collective identity, and cafés appear to have been the group's favored gathering spots. Cafés thus represented one of the prime spaces in which to cement this identity.

Incidents from around the country underscore the potential politicization of gatherings in cafés. When two priests were arrested in Lyon in 1818, causing much discussion throughout the region, a lawyer criticized several government ministers in a Villefranche café until authorities forced him to leave.[14] In January of that year, the police investigated a report that a customer at Lyon's café Cérès had proclaimed that he would have preferred to attend the funeral service of Louis XVIII instead of the one taking place to honor Louis XVI.[15] An 1820 police report from Toulouse expressed concern about "agitation" among the "ultra libéraux subalternes" in that city spreading rumors about liberals being under attack in Lyon. The letter closed with the comment that "the seizure of the ultraliberal brochures caused a lot of discussion in the cafés." A postscript added that "we no longer see these brochures in the cafés; they circulate from hand to hand among the partisans."[16] In May 1821, some people who had been causing disruptions in a café began singing "La Marseillaise" through the streets of Rouen; and in December 1828, another group in the Côte d'Or left a café and began shouting "Vive Napoléon!" as they walked by some statues of Napoleon.[17] In 1823, a group of "ultraliberals" (the preferred language of local officials) marched through Lyon in masks to draw attention to themselves and their movement. They began their trek, which attracted large numbers of spectators, some of whom joined them, at a café located near the Pont Morand in Brotteaux (then a *faubourg*—or suburb—of Lyon) called the café de la Perle.[18] Examples like these help to explain the perception that cafés were venues for the discussion of politics, and particularly of the political opposition during the Restoration. As they catered primarily to men, cafés also reinforced views that politics was masculine terrain.

Although these were largely male spaces, many of these establishments welcomed certain women and in fact relied upon their presence to attract male customers. Women regularly ran *cabinets littéraires* and bookshops, and they were often proprietors as well as servers in cafés.[19] Female servers enhanced the male nature of these places as they positioned themselves as objects on display, making cafés into social spaces in which men of various social positions, but predominantly bourgeois men, mingled with working-class women who were there not to amuse themselves but to earn a living. By providing spaces in which to act out (whether in real life or in the realm of fantasy) cross-class sexual dynamics, cafés helped to constitute the postrevolutionary social and *sexual* order. The presumption of working-class women's sexual availability was an integral part of emerging social identities.[20]

Writing in January 1824 about the beautiful decor at Lyon's newest café, a journalist underscored the appeal of its female employees: "The enchanting sight offered by the café Parisien is not the only attraction that will draw crowds. Four young girls, of about the same age, who one would say were formed in the same mold, and wearing the same elegant dress, are there to obey the slightest gesture you make at them." In the course of hypothesizing on the perspective of these waitresses, the writer reflected on their everyday experiences: "obligated to respond to a thousand and one daily *galanteries,* they must at the same time carefully close their young hearts against any emotions capable of bringing them to a moment of weakness." A week later, in response to negative correspondence his article had inspired, the writer apologized for his comments regarding the *demoiselles du café Parisien.*[21] Nonetheless, sexually tinged interchanges, and probably outright sexual advances, must have taken place regularly between customers and café workers.

The successes of the café Parisien inspired the owners of other cafés to imitate the strategy, and in their effort to outdo their rivals, they found some "special" women. In 1824, the café de l'Europe at the place Bellecour announced plans to launch a new theme and a new name for the café—Ourika (a reference to the Madame de Duras novel about an African girl in France)—and hired two "African beauties" as servers. A local journalist waxed poetic about these women and their effect on the café's clientele: "A red scarf draws out the ebony of their skin; and without braving the heat of the tropics or the dangers of the desert, the shy Lyonnais finds himself in *Nigritie.* Celebrated, complemented, our two *Africaines* need not lament the slave trade *(n'ont pas à gémir de la traite des nègres).*"[22] Their presence inspired the following commentary in a subsequent article in the *Journal du commerce:* "Served by their ebony hands, sugar seems whiter and perhaps sweeter, mocha more suave, beer more foamy and liquors more intoxicating. . . . Hasten then, *Messieurs les amateurs:* the most exquisite products of our colonies will be offered and served to you by *les naturels du pays.*"[23] It is quite possible that these really were women of color, though we cannot know with any certainty where they came from. Sufficient numbers of black men and women lived in France during the period to justify Napoleonic legislation creating a special surveillance apparatus for them.[24]

In addition to confirming the widespread enthusiasm for the novel and its main character, the café Ourika's choice of employees demonstrates the prevalence of "orientalism," as men rushed to enjoy the experience of being served by such exotic women.[25] An engraving published in the 1826 edition of the novel (Figure 6.1), gives an idea of how Ourika was imagined. The whiteness of her attire accentuated the blackness of her skin; the armband and headpiece drew attention to her different culture. The real women hired to work in the café may have been dressed similarly. A journalist's discussion

**Figure 6.1.** Jean-Jaques-Marie-Achille Devéria, *Ourika derrière le paravent* (Ourika behind the screen). From Claire de Duras, *Ourika* (Paris, 1826), opposite page 42. Copyright © University of Kentucky, all rights reserved. Special Collections and Digital Programs, University of Kentucky Libraries.

of the café's employees demonstrates further this interest in the exotic: "While waiting for the theaters to procure us the pleasure of being moved by the difficulties of the sensitive Ourika, this *personnage à la mode* is being exploited in an altogether different manner. . . . Two charming Ourika[s], who have nothing black about them but their skin, work in concert with a male Ourika at this establishment. . . . [B]y simply having a few glasses of punch in your head, it will be easy to persuade yourself that you are in the New World, even though you have not left the place des Jacobins."[26] The fact that the character Ourika was from Africa, not the New World, did not seem to have an effect on this reviewer's ability to imagine himself on the other side of the Atlantic.

The coverage of these cafés suggests that women of color (and in this case, a man as well) performed a dual role: they allowed men to fantasize about far-off places most French people would probably never visit; and they functioned as highly sexualized, exotic beings about whom the men could also fantasize. The presence of these servers precluded bourgeois women's participation even further and turned these venues into highly masculine social spaces. The sexual and social order was constructed through the experiences of the men and women in such places. As bourgeois men went to these establishments to amuse themselves separately from their wives and their families, cafés evolved into highly male, highly politicized spaces.

Just as cafés drew a largely male clientele, cabarets catered mostly to men, typically of the lower ranks of society; however, there is some indication that women may have been regular customers as well. Discussing "la vie populaire" in Lyon at the end of the Old Regime, Maurice Garden lists "the cabaret, the guinguette of Brotteaux, [and] the *bal populaire,* despite certain religious interdictions," as "the only distractions offered to city dwellers."[27] The same can be said for the period after the Revolution, when all these establishments grew even more numerous. Whereas dance halls necessarily catered to both sexes, cabarets were more rowdy, masculine spaces, although women worked in them, often running them with their husbands. In 1818, for example, a *cabaretière* was nearly stabbed by a drunken soldier when she told him that the bottle she had sold him was the biggest she had.[28] Workers and soldiers constituted much of the clientele, and as a result cabarets did their best business on Sundays and holidays. Of course, both groups were known for their disorderliness. One frequent occurrence during the Restoration was that of drunken men in cabarets shouting "Vive

l'Empereur!" attracting the attention of other patrons, and sometimes causing fights.[29]

The treatment of cabarets changed over time. Under Napoleon they were
allowed to remain open until 10 or 11 P.M.[30] During the Restoration, officials increasingly viewed working-class drinking establishments with concern and trepidation, limiting their hours of operation more and more. In
1819, authorities in Nantes required that guinguettes and cabarets in the
Ville-en-Bois, Nantes' western faubourg, close at 5 P.M., a restriction that
would have caused the ruin of these businesses had it been enforced: they
would have only been open during times when the majority of their customers were working.[31] Whereas Napoleon permitted workers to amuse
themselves as they wished, so long as they did not cause problems or miss
work, Restoration policies were geared toward limiting opportunities for
drunken disorderliness, as though any gathering of workers would auto-
matically devolve into unacceptable scenes.

Working-class drinking establishments tended to be located on the outskirts of cities, in the faubourgs. Most of these "suburbs" have since been incorporated into the larger towns they bordered. In the early nineteenth-
century, however, they were separate municipalities, and their businesses
drew customers because they were not required to pay the taxes charged on
alcoholic beverages that crossed into the city limits. Lyon's faubourg with
the largest number of drinking establishments was La Guillotière. Beginning during the first years of the Empire, and continuing throughout the
Restoration, growing numbers of dance halls, cabarets, and other such venues opened there, and it became known as Lyon's prime location for
working-class amusements. Two bridges, the Pont de la Guillotière and the
Pont Morand, connected the faubourg on the left bank of the Rhône to the
Presqu'île, the central part of the city located between the city's two rivers
(Map 1). In comparison with the tall buildings and densely crowded streets
of the area between Bellecour and Terreaux as well as the right bank of the
Saône, La Guillotière had an almost rural feel to it, with one-story buildings
and broader streets. It made the neighborhood amenable to Sunday strolls,
not just for workers who lived there and elsewhere in the city, but also for
bourgeois families wishing to find some fresh air.[32] Spacious areas to stroll,
grassy lawns, and shade trees created an atmosphere that appealed to men
and women across classes, though many of the business establishments in
the neighborhood catered more to the "popular" classes.

Brotteaux, a neighborhood that was technically part of La Guillotière but was often treated like a separate community, housed the majority of these diverse amusements. Brotteaux was directly across the river from the place des Terreaux, where both the Hôtel de Ville and the Grand Théâtre were located, as well as a large number of cafés. With the Pont Morand connecting the two towns, the neighborhood was within easy reach for Lyon's inhabitants. According to a history of these suburbs, "On Sundays and holidays as many as thirty thousand people crossed the Rhône bridges to amuse themselves in Brotteaux, a northern district of La Guillotière, with its many guinguettes, theaters, and other kinds of amusements."[33] In an 1809 letter to the minister of the interior, the mayor of Lyon described the neighborhood's attractions:

> The faubourgs, and principally les Brotteaux, are places where three-quarters of the working-class population of the city flock on holidays; even on ordinary days there exists in Brotteaux very numerous gatherings because it is here that race courses, public games, dance halls, cafés, inns, and guinguettes of every variety can be found: how then can we suppose that municipal authority can spread its surveillance there, especially when we consider that these separate communities do not have the means to execute [such surveillance]?[34]

Primarily concerned with control and surveillance, the mayor also emphasized the great draw among workers of the diverse attractions in Brotteaux.

In language reminiscent of the guidebooks' accounts of the Parisian Boulevard, the *Journal du commerce* described the multifarious pleasures available to the people who packed the streets of Brotteaux during the carnival season of 1824. The neighborhood was filled with "almost the entire population of the city. . . . What crowds! They had so much to see!" As masked celebrators mingled with professional performers, all could enjoy a spectacle that included "harlequins, clowns, apothecaries, buffoons, puppets, doctors, swordsmen, noblemen, companies of actors, horse troops, mamelukes, strongmen, paladins, troubadours, amazons, and magicians."[35] The continuation of carnival traditions involving masked balls and revelry permitted all the inhabitants of the city to enjoy a break from day-to-day routines. As this description appeared in a bourgeois paper, it suggests that workers were not the only ones to enjoy this type of amusement, which involved display and observation as much as Parisian attractions did. In fact, the article made clear that wealthy Lyonnais attended: "Everywhere [one saw] elegant equipages and brilliant carriages dropping off their treasures."

Carnival season in Brotteaux apparently attracted the "Tout Lyon." The very diversity of the sights and of the crowds themselves explained that appeal.

Policing issues again, as well as the fact that Lyon's inhabitants constituted the majority of the people who went to Brotteaux, convinced local officials that Brotteaux needed to be annexed to Lyon, though that would not happen until 1852. In 1810, the mayor described the neighborhood as a "very vast terrain planted with trees and surrounded by guinguettes frequented regularly by workers, principally on Sundays." In these guinguettes situated near the Pont Morand, he added, "turbulent workers assembled."[36] In 1813, the prefect repeated concerns about maintaining order in the faubourgs where "the inhabitants of Lyon, above all workers, went for promenades on Sundays and holidays to refresh themselves after the workweek." Policing was a particularly pressing issue in La Guillotière, "where the number of cafés, cabarets, [and] meeting places of all genres augment daily."[37] Rather than try to shut down all these places, adequate surveillance seemed sufficient to the prefect, as to the mayors of Lyon and La Guillotière.

Similar issues arose in Nantes, where that city's version of La Guillotière, Chantenay, and more specifically a neighborhood known as the Ville-en-Bois because of the wooden barracks that lined its streets, also attracted many workers from the city. Bordering the western edge of Nantes, the faubourg housed numerous venues for cheap entertainment (Map 2). Offering billiards, dancing, gardens, and cheap wine, these businesses attracted clientele both from Chantenay itself and from Nantes. In 1821, Nantes' mayor successfully convinced the prefect to allow him to exercise greater control over the neighborhood, whose businesses, he argued, had become "the home of disorder. . . . That is where all the vagabonds . . . [and] bad subjects of the city meet. . . . That is where fathers, . . . expecting to spend a half an hour to drink half a bottle of wine finish by getting drunk and losing an entire day."[38] A royal ordinance of 30 March 1826 officially extended the jurisdiction of Nantes' police force to the commune of Chantenay.[39] The growing number of working-class amusements, along with growing concern about the undesirables who filled these spaces, led to this decision.

Popular venues for drinking and carousing in Lyon's faubourgs raised similar policing issues. In 1818, the prefect wrote to the mayor of La Guillotière regarding frequent problems at "several dance halls *(danses publiques)* in Brotteaux at which soldiers gathered and which were not receiving sufficient police surveillance."[40] Soldiers were also at the heart of disorders at "an isolated guinguette in Brotteaux . . . known as Saphos" in 1819.[41] As young men without local ties, soldiers were deemed a particularly disorderly group. Throughout the 1820s, cabarets and dance halls also served as meeting halls for workers' associations. These assemblages occasionally caused problems because quarrels would ensue when the space was reserved for one particular group and people who were not members of that group would try to enter the establishment.[42] As in Nantes, the number of these businesses increased significantly throughout the Restoration, and concerns about their effect on social order intensified. Historians have argued that "fear came to dominate bourgeois discourse" during this period.[43] Responding to this fear, the mayor of La Guillotière created four new posts in 1829, two in La Guillotière and two in Brotteaux, for police officers whose sole duties would be surveillance of "dance halls and [other] establishments that . . . bring people together for diversion."[44] Official discussions of the neighborhood and the businesses there portray them as catering only to the "dangerous classes": workers, soldiers, and prostitutes appear as their primary clientele.

In 1819, the liberal nantais newspaper *L'ami de la Charte* depicted the Ville-en-Bois as a neighborhood that attracted purely working-class revelers:

> We know how much artisans and workers work all week so as to be able to relax on Sundays and sometimes even on Mondays. Rich people do not take such pleasure from the distractions that their occupations allow them with as much abandon and joy as this interesting class of society [when] profiting from the moments of pleasure that its work-life permits. Their salaries, often very minimal, naturally require them to economize. There exists in Nantes . . . a collection of small wooden shacks that form a sort of small city known as the Ville-en-Bois; several guinguettes built with a certain elegance are nearby; one of the oldest is called the Rossignol. The diverse businesses, situated outside the city limits, sell wine at a much lower price than in the city, where exorbitant taxes greatly raise the price of this liquor. It should certainly be permissible to those who live weekly with privations to find the means to compensate for [such behavior] one day out of seven. The existence of the Ville-en-Bois is well known, since on holidays a considerable crowd gathers there.[45]

Workers found the low prices charged by drinking establishments in the Ville-en-Bois attractive, but the middle classes disdained these cabarets for exactly the same reason. When they gathered to talk over a drink, workers and bourgeois inhabited separate spaces, both physically and mentally. They may have been an "interesting class of society," but workers' outlooks were so different from those of the middle and upper classes that they appeared to be virtually another species. The growth in the number of cafés and cabarets encouraged these separate outlooks as businesses catered to increasingly narrow groups. This separation then helped to foster mutual incomprehension and distrust.

Aside from those who worked in them, "honest" women appear to have avoided cabarets, but women who were thought to be prostitutes were a common feature. One such woman of questionable morals ("*mœurs au moins très équivoques*") found herself at the center of a scandal when two events were collapsed into one, her mistreatment in a cabaret in Saint Just (a faubourg on the hill overlooking Lyon) and the suicide by drowning of a young woman. Officials' attention subsided when they realized that the woman who was raped was a prostitute, and that the cabaret's habitués had no connection to a "respectable" woman drowning herself.[46] Authorities viewed violence toward prostitutes as part of the normal course of events. In 1810, a prostitute named Catherine Verga was abused *(maltraitée)* under the Guillotière Bridge. She had spent the day in a cabaret in La Guillotière with a man and was strolling by herself in the evening when eight or nine people attacked her. The mayor was involved with the ensuing investigation, which ended with the arrest of the man with whom Verga had spent the day.[47] The impression given by the police reports, admittedly a very one-sided perspective, is that cabarets attracted violent troublemakers and prostitutes.

One anecdote from Nantes, which appears in a police report from 1823, provides telling information about cabaret customers, proprietors, and the potential for sexual encounters to take place in these spaces. One winter night at 11:30, "demoiselle" Emma Désirée Noble appeared at the guardhouse attached to an entrance to the city, the Porte au Vin, near her establishment, which was sometimes referred to as a cabaret and at other times as an *auberge*, or inn. She came to ask for armed men to help her remove a man from her business. The man had lain down in her bed and was refusing to leave. After some insistence, she succeeded in convincing the officer to send some of his men. Then the officer decided to go himself, since her *auberge* was close by: "I found the corporal and the two soldiers working on getting this man, who was lying in the bed of the said demoiselle, to leave. When I asked him why he did not want to go, he responded vulgarly (*grossièrement*) that I probably had the intention of replacing him in the bed. So I forced him to get out of the bed and had him brought to the guardhouse."[48] As the "demoiselle" ran a drinking establishment, the customer apparently believed she was willing to serve him more than a glass of wine. Such assumptions on the part of cabaret customers would have made daily life harrowing for the women who worked in these businesses.

Some men tried to put themselves in the shoes of these female servers. In *Les cabarets de Paris,* J.-P.-R. Cuisin, a writer of many borderline pornographic or at least quite licentious publications about Parisian life, includes an anecdote about a barmaid who was a voracious reader. Cuisin's wish to provide humorous anecdotes about life in Paris no doubt inspired this story. Despite its dubious veracity, the passage merits quotation as it provides a rare portrayal of a woman who worked in a cabaret. After describing her "voluminous chest" and "enormous derriere," Cuisin devoted attention to her reading habits:

> She is a girl with a lot of spirit; subscribed at 1 fr. 50 per month to a *cabinet de lecture,* she . . . says curiously, without effort, that madame de Staël is unintelligible . . . and above all she prefers the literature of the Pont-Neuf, about which she revels: "How I love this passage," . . . while showing you a chapter from *l'Enfant du Mystère,* "one cannot stop oneself from crying." But at the moment when she reads the sentimental excerpt to you, in the style of the declamation of the boulevards, the waiter cries: "a half a liter at 16 and five glasses!" It is thus necessary for the sensitive priestess of the altars of Bacchus to rush down to the cellar iron candlestick in hand.[49]

She may have been a "sensitive priestess" thanks to her reading practices, but this woman had a job to do. This chronicler of Parisian cabaret life clearly believed that his readers, presumably middle-class men, enjoyed an opportunity to see into this woman's heart and mind. How actual cabaret customers might have treated real-life servers we can only imagine, but there is no doubt that the women who worked in cabarets and cafés were subjects of male curiosity and fantasy, and often they were subject to more than that.

Whoever they were and whatever their views and behavior, there were enough customers in these cities to support an extraordinary number of cabarets. Nearly two hundred of them appear on lists drawn up in Nantes in 1831. The greater number of cabarets in Nantes than in Lyon may have been due to the presence of sailors in the port city. It seems likely that most of these establishments were small, perhaps only a few chairs and a table, with one person running the whole place. Selling a few drinks a day may have been a means to secure a small income, to avoid complete destitution, particularly for women on their own. The humble nature of such venues comes across in an example from Montpellier dating from the late 1820s. In a letter to the mayor requesting that her café be allowed to remain open despite recent disturbances there, a woman explained that her husband was in the military and she was running the café as her only resource. "Her café is too simple *(trop peu de choses)* to be the meeting place of people who had received a sophisticated education *(une éducation soignée);* she only receives and can only receive workers *(gens de travail)* and soldiers, and cannot be held responsible for fights that might take place between them outside of her café."[50] This was a typical story of small-scale business owners trying to stay on the good side of the authorities. Simple and inexpensive venues for drinking (and other activities that went along with it) such as this one no doubt existed in cities all over France; larger, slightly more upscale cabarets offered billiard tables and other attractions.[51]

Cabarets and cafés were social spaces that attracted men who wanted to amuse themselves; women mostly appeared in them as workers. Defined as middle-class spaces, regardless of the actual makeup of the clientele, cafés permitted discussion of politics among like-minded men. Cabarets similarly brought together workers and soldiers to drink and talk on their days off. These were highly masculine spaces: politics, sexuality, and violence often entered, creating atmospheres that made "respectable" women less likely to participate in them. Of course, who entered these spaces and what went on in them came to define both the spaces themselves and what female "respectability" meant in different contexts.

## Dancing across Society

In 1811, the mayor of Lyon wrote to the prefect to explain why he had denied a request to open a public dance hall, which the prefect had thought was a simple dance school. The mayor argued that these "places of assembly, one of the principal causes of the moral dissolution of the peuple, at the same time that they are the frequent occasion of fistfights, thefts, and other offenses . . . were rigorously prohibited . . . before the Revolution."[52] From the mayor's perspective, dance halls represented an example of revolutionary permissiveness, a view confirmed by historians. In his study of nineteenth-century Parisian dance halls, François Gasnault argues that the *bal public* came into existence because of the Revolution's effects on the "very idea of diversion: pleasures which under the Old Regime were reserved for certain select groups became public and ostensibly open to all."[53] A study of the internal missions in Restoration France refers to "dances in cabarets or in the open air during church services" as dating from the Revolution.[54] The mayor's reaction to dance halls suggests that he too saw them as a postrevolutionary phenomenon.

Dancing was *the* activity of choice for all classes when they wanted to celebrate something in particular or simply to amuse themselves. It stands out as one of the most prominent leisure-time practices at all levels of the social spectrum. Louis-Sébastien Mercier devoted an entire chapter of his 1799 account of Parisian life to dancing. According to Mercier, "Every class has its dancing society . . . from rich to poor, everyone dances; it's a furor, a universal inclination *(un goût universel)*." He then described all these different types of dances, from the aristocratic *bals d'hiver* to bourgeois balls where mothers put their unmarried daughters on display: "They dance with matrimonial intentions; they all wish to marry the richest man of the neighborhood." Finally, come balls for "water carriers and charcoal sellers. . . . In cellars, even at the end of alleyways, in dirty cabarets; to the sound of a vulgar *(grossier)* violin, or a raucous accordion *(une rauque musette)*, every Sunday and every *décade* (as the peuple takes off both days), often even in between" workers danced.[55] One scholar has argued that dancing exploded in popularity during and after the Revolution, before changing in tone with the Restoration: "Fans of the waltz and other fashionable dances invaded le Tivoli, le Marbeuf, . . . and the innumerable balls, bourgeois or popular. People also danced in the salons, where difficult dances were all the rage. [This was] a vogue that passed with the Restoration, when the ball returned to being an upper-class *(mondaine)* ceremony."[56]

As these quotations make clear, dancing could take many different forms. Each social group had its own kind of dance: upper-class men and women gathered at formal balls where mothers sought husbands for their daughters, whereas workers spent Sundays dancing outdoors to the sound of a violin. Even the hours during which dances took place varied. Masked balls held in theaters began after the performance, around 11 P.M., and could continue until 5 A.M.[57] The more lowbrow dances usually ended by the time elite balls began. Another distinction was their price. Balls were expensive: the Wauxhall d'hiver [Winter Ball] of 1815, which was held at Nantes'

Chapeau Rouge theater, cost one franc per person, or one franc and fifty centimes for a couple (*"un cavalier avec sa dame"*).[58] A masked ball held at the Grand Théâtre the same winter cost three francs per person.[59] This was more than any worker could afford. According to historian David Garrioch, Parisian "Waux-Halls" of the 1780s, were "indoor establishments . . . [that offered] mixed entertainments: fireworks, dancing, pantomime, gardens, cafés, and various sideshows."[60] In contrast to these relatively expensive forms of entertainment, guinguettes, the popular dance halls located on the outskirts of cities, cost only a few sous. The opening night ball at a new dance hall *(salle de danse)* in Brotteaux in 1810 cost fifty centimes for "un cavalier et une dame."[61]

Despite their technically being open to the public, balls that charged higher entrance fees did so in an attempt to limit admission to well-off, "respectable" dancers, but they were not always successful. In 1797, the owners of Nantes' "Bals de Wauxall" requested that prostitutes be forbidden from entering their establishments. Their intention, they insisted, was to provide amusement suitable for families and to "receive honest *Républicains et Républicaines.* But their hopes were dashed by the presence of vile women lacking morals . . . who caused some of these honest people" to stop attending the dances. For this reason, they sought permission to state on their posters that prostitutes were forbidden from entering the balls.[62] The entrepreneurs decided that in order to make their businesses successful, they needed to make them appear to be "respectable." Their goal was to create spaces in which "honest" young women and men could dance and amuse themselves, but people other than those intended sometimes managed to sneak in. One February night in 1804, a twenty-three-year-old domestic servant named Marie Faupin was arrested for using a counterfeit ticket to enter a ball. Around midnight, "having closed her master's apartment (a printer/bookstore) . . . [she] went to the ball with Monsieur Jean, another employee in the same print shop. Their plan was to obtain cheap tickets to enter the ball." The tickets were recognized as fake when they entered, and they were arrested. The two servants were not alone in their use of counterfeit tickets. The women who collected tickets at the entrance to the ball informed the police that several people had presented such tickets.[63] The elevated prices of the balls were meant to discourage those without sufficient means to attend these gatherings and thus to mark them as elite spaces.

Dancing also entertained more than just the dancers themselves. In August 1822, a fight between some local soldiers and the *regiment suisse en garrison* in Nantes led to two people being seriously injured, one of whom was a woman, Jeanne Panaud, *femme* Debesse, a porter. Around 9 P.M., she had gone to the dance being held at the place Royale to watch the dancers with a friend, *femme* Abel, who was the wife of a shoeblack. Panaud was injured during the confusion, which is why the story exists in the archives.[64] For our purposes, the anecdote is interesting in that it shows working-class women attending an open-air dance in the heart of Nantes' most elite neighborhood. Panaud specifically stated that they had attended the event not to dance themselves but to watch the other dancers. As on the Parisian Boulevard, participants were both spectators and spectacle—and often both at the same time—as they danced.

These upper-class gatherings drew particular attention to women as participants in urban amusements. Mercier commented on women's recognition of their being on display: "The women, whom we judge out loud, pass by repeatedly as though [they are] indifferent to these comments; but they miss nothing of what is being said about them."[65] Describing the dances *(redoutes)* held at Nantes' theater in December 1814, a journalist made a point of mentioning that "a large number of women have already subscribed." Commenting on the fact that the first dance drew small numbers but the second attracted a large crowd, he theorized that it was the concert held before the dance that contributed to the unexpected success of the second event. "In fact, it belongs to music to reinspire the lost habit of dancing as there exists between these two arts a close affinity. Monsieur Arnaud must be applauded for having found this ingenious means to encourage ladies to enjoy these pleasures, which are offered under their noses *(sous leurs pas)* [a pun in French: literally 'under their steps']."[66] The journalist went on to express hope that these events would continue to bring women out to partake in the pleasures of waltzing in public, as "Monsieur Arnaud . . . has found a way to engage our ladies." In 1825, a brilliant soirée was held by one of Lyon's richest bankers on the occasion of his daughter's marriage. More than two hundred people from the highest echelons of Lyon's banking and commerce sectors attended. "The most beautiful fashions enhanced the natural traits of ladies and *jeunes personnes*. Despite the sumptuous meal, the ladies hardly stopped dancing."[67] A "private" event such as this, which already existed outside of a narrowly defined "domestic" sphere, became even more public when it was covered as news by local papers, as in this case. Women put themselves on display in "public" at such moments, and they probably enjoyed reading about their activities the next day.

Dancing had its potential dangers, however, especially for women. In 1807, the *Journal de Paris* warned its readers of the possible side effects of the waltz: "For years, husbands, mothers, and all reasonable people have spoken against the waltz. . . . No other dance . . . is more suitable for making women's heads spin [and] exhausting their organs. . . . Last week, a woman sadly proved this. She left the child she was nursing to throw herself into the whirlwind of a waltz. The blood and milk went to her head; she barely had the time to say 'I don't feel well,' when she dropped dead in the arms of her dance partner."[68] In raising the specter of the nursing mother leaving her child to enjoy the pleasures of the waltz, this journalist collapsed moral and physical concerns so as to warn his readers of the dangerous practice of waltzing. Such exaggerated tales of the potential risks of dancing served as a warning to women of all classes, whose excessive passion for dance concerned many moralists of the period.

Open enjoyment of being on display could make women vulnerable to accusations of being "coquettes." According to a widely published doctor, Julien-Joseph Virey, women's "natures" made them likely to fall into this dangerous trap. "Nature, by an admirable economy, derived coquetry, this ancient need to please [that is] innate in woman, from the same fragility of organization that is the source of her other penchants."[69] Under the guise of scientific objectivity, Virey argued that coquetry evolved out of women's moral and physical natures. In her book instructing girls on how to run a household, *La petite ménagère*, Adélaïde Dufrénoy gave a more sympathetic explanation for women's tendency toward coquetry: "Girls are born with a violent desire to please; as they find all paths leading to glory and authority closed to them, they take another route . . . and misdirect their lives with embellishments *(les agréments)*. . . . Rise above this wish to please, or at least do not make it visible."[70] According to Dufrénoy, social restrictions on women's lives in part explained their leanings toward superficial accomplishments like drawing and piano, as opposed to less spectacular, but in the end more satisfying, pursuits that kept them out of the public eye. The fixation with the coquette was a reflection of postrevolutionary reactions against women's prominent visibility in public spaces. "Domestic ideology" was just that—an ideology, a set of prescriptions that had little impact on the level of actual practices. In fact, if women really were leading domestic existences, there would have been little reason to try to convince them to do so.[71]

Some vehemently misogynist publications focused their anger on the issue of women mingling too much in public amusements, including dancing.

A pamphlet published in Lyon in the 1820s called *Eve en France* makes use of exaggerated language and extreme examples to prove its point that women's bad behavior was bringing about the destruction of French society. The tone itself testifies to the intensity of male concerns, if not outright fears, about women's behavior. According to the anonymous author of this eight-page piece, Eve was personified in France by the woman who "separates herself from her husband, especially when she races about to theaters, balls, concerts, and all the fashionable gatherings *(sociétés mondaines)* where she dangerously can gain access and a welcome that may appear favorable but that always becomes perilous and fatal to her."[72] The text goes on to complain about the lack of control men had over women and how that would lead to women falling into temptation. Husbands, the author insisted, needed to take command of their wives, or they would be sorry; they would find themselves cuckolds. More than a coquette, this "Eve" was an adulteress. The pamphlet made explicit what many other texts of various sorts left implicit: it was vital to control women's sexuality. Coquetry seemed to lead directly to women's moral and sexual downfall and thus to the destruction of their families and of society as a whole.

Over time the "coquette" lost her appeal to a new literary "type": the grisette.[73] A grisette was a young, unmarried working-class woman whose social life depended on bourgeois admirers. Not prostitutes, grisettes nonetheless allowed these men to take them to theaters and restaurants and to buy them small gifts.[74] By the mid-1820s, the grisette had replaced the coquette as the obsession of the moment. Although a coquette could come from any class, she was typically a wealthy woman as only a woman of means could afford to live a life centered on pleasure and luxury. The transition from coquette to grisette suggests that fewer women of the upper classes seemed to be acting like coquettes or, at least if they were, that such behavior no longer seemed so worrisome. Working women, however, were becoming ever more available and interesting to bourgeois men, and the emergence of the grisette as an icon reflected this change. Auguste Ricard's successful 1827 novel simply entitled *La grisette* bears out the fascination with this archetypal figure.[75] Ricard's portrayal also draws attention to the potential dangers of reading: grisettes were working-class women whose romantic sensibilities had been stimulated, often by novels, as in the example of the cabaret server described by Cuisin. They preferred romance and excitement to a stable relationship. The typical public space in which grisettes and their lovers met was the popular dance hall or guinguette.

Beginning around 1800, guinguettes started to emerge on the outskirts of many French cities. Although research has been done on Parisian guinguettes, provincial ones have received little attention. The ones in the environs of Paris were open-air cabarets where families would spend Sunday afternoons and evenings eating, drinking, and dancing in a semirural setting. Representing an opportunity to escape the congestion and dirtiness of the city by getting out into the "country" for a day of relaxation and fun, Parisian guinguettes drew men and women of all ages and appear to have been defined as "family" entertainment.[76] In contrast to their Parisian equivalents, provincial guinguettes appear to have attracted mostly young, unmarried men and women, not families. As the police defined male youth (jeunes gens) as the most unruly segment of the population, officials tended to view these gatherings with suspicion. Despite officials' concerns about their encouragement of "debauchery," dance halls were springing up everywhere on the outskirts of French cities. In addition to shedding light on popular forms of amusement and recreation, discussions of guinguettes reveal tensions between local officials as prefects, big-city mayors, and mayors of smaller communities neighboring larger ones all struggled to define their areas of control.

Officials disagreed about the nature of these events and the extent to which they represented a danger to social order. Most viewed dancing itself as acceptable, but they worried that these gatherings could engender other, more worrisome behavior. In 1811 the mayor of Vaise, a faubourg bordering Lyon on the right bank of the Saône, informed the prefect in no uncertain terms of the dangerous nature of dances being held in another community, Tassin, which bordered Vaise:

[T]here exists in Tassin . . . a salle de danse [that is] infinitely dangerous, where all the girls and boys of the nearby communities gather. Since its existence, fathers and mothers, landlords (propriétaires) and cultivators can no longer control their children and domestics; they are perverted [at the dance] in a frightful manner; it is a location for the most extreme debauchery in every sense of the term; as soon as they set foot there, they are lost. . . . All the corrupt people of both sexes in Lyon and its faubourgs gather there regularly on Sundays and Mondays, and prolong their debauchery well into the night. This assembly simultaneously inspires horror and pity, while striking a fatal blow at agriculture. Domestics become worthless; there exists within them an arrogance and an insubordination beyond all expression. . . . The suppression of this salle de danse is the only means of remedying such an evil . . . [and thus] return agriculture to its vigor, and moral and physical tranquility to landowners.[77]

The prefect then wrote to the mayor of Tassin, explaining that he had been informed that the gathering was "an occasion for debauchery and corruption: all decency is forgotten; . . . the dancing goes on well into the night, and has even taken place on Mondays in defiance of police regulations. [This behavior] distresses inhabitants who have children or domestics because the salle de danse causes them to acquire the bad habits of laziness and insubordination."[78] In his response to the prefect's request for information on these dances, the mayor of Tassin minimized their dangers, arguing that this was not a dance hall at all. He insisted that the Sunday activities simply involved two violinists paid by the participants to play in the courtyard of a private building. In addition, he specified that the gathering took place only on Sunday afternoons and dissipated before evening.[79]

Despite the self-interest involved in each of these accounts, the correspondence sheds light on popular recreation and official attitudes toward it during the Empire. The particular issues the prefect chose to include in his letter out of the laundry list of improper behavior recounted by the mayor of Vaise give an indication of what components seemed most relevant, or most threatening, to this powerful person. Rather than deal with the issues of girls and boys mixing and the immorality of the dancers and of dancing in general, the prefect focused on the twin issues of the dancing going on until too late into the night and its taking place on Mondays as well as Sundays. What mattered to him was that workers be available to work. As long as order was maintained, and the participants appeared for their jobs on Monday, dancing was neither against the law nor particularly dangerous to the social and moral order. Correspondence from 1812 reflects the same pragmatic concerns about a dance, even one that attracted "men and women of the worst morals . . . who served as an extremely dangerous example to the youth attracted to the place." Rather than trying to shut it down altogether, the official simply reminded the mayor that danses publiques were not permitted on workdays.[80] Throughout the Empire, the biggest concern of authorities was for those who attended dances to continue to be reliable workers. So long as leisure pursuits did not interfere with their work lives, people could basically do as they wished.

This pragmatic approach to leisure changed with the Restoration, when moral concerns grew more pronounced. In 1817, the mayor of La Croix-Rousse, another faubourg of Lyon, expressed concerns about the corruption of morals caused by salles de danse when he wrote to the prefect to explain why he wished to stop the spread of these establishments in his community. He argued that dance halls were the sites of "frequent serious quarrels . . . scandalously offering to the youth [of the community] the means toward corruption [that led] to trouble and divisions within [their] families.[81] In 1823, the mayor of Vaise, contacted the prefect with a similar request for support in closing down a danse publique being held in a cabaret owned by a retired military officer whose political opinions were "very suspicious." He went on to complain that such venues caused disorder in families as they distracted children and domestic servants from their duties.[82] The mayors of most of Lyon's faubourgs condemned guinguettes, salles de danse, and danses publiques for causing disorder and immorality among the youth in their communities. Yet they never succeeded in shutting them down.

As they had no choice but to allow these events to take place, Restoration authorities worked to minimize the threat to social, political, and moral order represented by the popular festivities. So, for example, when the carpenters *(ouvriers menuisiers)* of Lyon celebrated the Fête de Sainte-Anne, their patron saint, in July 1819, officials went to great lengths to ensure that the potentially rowdy group of revelers did not get out of hand. A meal and a ball held in Brotteaux continued until 6 A.M. Afterward, the police congratulated themselves on maintaining order throughout.[83] The annual *fête baladoire* held in La Croix-Rousse came under greater control as well. Among a long list of rules and regulations printed on a large poster in 1829 was a stipulation that the dance held in the town's main square, the Grande-Place, could only last from 4 P.M. to 8 P.M., though the cafés and cabarets nearby were permitted to remain open until midnight.[84] Limiting hours and maintaining a heavy police presence were among the favorite tools of authorities to control the possible dangers of large crowds gathered to dance in public places.

Some of these *fêtes patronales* drew more than just the popular classes. This was the case for the largest annual festival and dance of the Lyon region, which took place on the Ile Barbe, an island in the Saône River a few kilometers north of the city. The police of neighboring communities cooperated "to ensure order among such large and diverse crowds."[85] Wealthy men and women traveled in carriages; poorer people walked along the riverbank to attend the event. Journalists took note of the visibility of women who stood out among the spectators: "A triple row of chairs on which the prettiest and most elegant ladies of this town could be seen; young men on horseback, strollers on foot, everyone in the most refined dress, made this promenade into a Longchamp lyonnais."[86] As on the Boulevard, these "elegant ladies" chose this venue to display their charms while observing everyone else around them. One of the rare events in Lyon that drew participants from across the social spectrum, the Fête de l'Ile Barbe nonetheless created separate physical and mental spaces for elites to inhabit while they were observing the diverse groups of revelers.

Celebrations called "vogues," popular festivals that were a particularly lyonnais institution, tended to draw fewer elite participants. Vogues emerged out of the tradition of village youth battling those of nearby villages.[87] By the nineteenth century, they had evolved into dances organized by villagers. Local inhabitants sponsored them, often without the explicit approval of authorities who distrusted such spontaneous expressions of local solidarity. Vogues tended to be a more rural than urban phenomenon: they were organized not in Lyon proper, but in the communities surrounding the city. An account of what happened at the vogue of the faubourg Sainte-Irénée, held for the first time in sixteen years in 1824, appeared in the *Journal du commerce*. The journalist began by praising municipal authorities for permitting the faubourg's youth to stage the event despite the views of "some mayors and priests, sworn enemies of dancing." In describing the vogue, he emphasized the "great tranquility" that reigned during the celebrations:

> The dance began only after church services. The jeunes gens of the vogue, all wearing hats topped with white feathers *(chapeaux à la française, surmontés de panaches blancs)* ran through the streets of the faubourg several times. . . . In the evening, these young people held a dance at an inn. . . . If only all the vogues of rural communities could follow this example, and could proceed with such calm and decency: the detractors of *danses champêtres* would not have the slightest pretext to inveigh against such innocent divertissement.[88]

Writing for a bourgeois newspaper, the journalist appreciated this event as an outsider. These were neither urban nor middle-class events, but the proximity of these faubourgs and villages made it simple for inhabitants of Lyon to attend them. The assumption on the part of officials was that such events only caused problems. In 1813, for example, soon after the vogue sponsored by the jeunes gens of Irigny, the married men of the community requested permission to stage their own vogue. For the previous ten years, however, only one vogue had been allowed annually. Holding a second vogue caused concern on the part of the mayor because local *propriétaires* (property owners) complained that vogues made their employees waste precious work time.[89] Another argument against granting such permission was that the dances were potential sites of disorder. Workers and domestics from neighboring villages and from Lyon attended these vogues to dance and presumably to drink, which could in turn lead to violent episodes.[90]

Requests to hold vogues and *fêtes patronales* usually came from the so-called jeunes gens of these communities, a phrase I have generally translated as "male youth." These outdoor dances were associated with youth, which in this context meant unmarried men. A song sung at village weddings included these lyrics:

> Vous n'irez plus au bal,
> Madame la mariée . . .
> Vous gard'rez la maison
> Tandis que nous irons.[91]
>
> [You will no longer go to balls
> Madame the bride . . .
> You will stay at home
> While we will go.]

The song suggested that only young, unmarried women and men organized and attended these dances. Sometimes these jeunes gens even wrote directly to the prefect. In most circumstances, the official response was that these festivities had to be permitted, or there would be too much discontent. To avoid disorder and immorality, however, they needed to be carefully supervised. In addition, vogues had to end at a reasonable hour so as not to interfere with work. Finally, they distressed religious authorities who saw them as dangerous to religion because they took attention away from regular church observances, despite the fact that these fêtes were supposedly held to celebrate local saints.

Who were these "jeunes gens"? "Jeunes gens" probably referred to young, unmarried men, as the phrase "jeunes personnes" seems to have been the preferred expression when dealing with young women. Although both "gens" (a masculine noun) and "personnes" (a feminine noun) can refer to people of either sex, in this period the gender of the nouns almost invariably corresponded to actual gender. Use of "personnes" to refer to young women probably resulted from the fact that the term "filles" carried a certain amount of ambiguity, as prostitutes—*filles publiques* or *filles de mauvaise vie*—were often simply called "filles," too. Most of the records that contain information about the participants in vogues mention boys as opposed to girls, though we can safely assume that girls were in attendance. In the early modern period, "the female sex was thought the disorderly one par excellence," according to historian Natalie Zemon Davis.[92] By the early nineteenth century, however, young men had come to replace women as the most troublesome group in society, evidenced by official views on the organizers of vogues, as well as the discussions of this group's behavior at provincial theaters.

Regardless of these perceptions, women and girls were more than peripherally involved in these events. When the young women of Chaponost, a village a few kilometers from Lyon, organized a dance there in 1816, the local curé wrote to the prefect to complain that it had occurred at "eight steps from the church" before the Sunday mass was over. After mass, the chairs from the church were brought out into the public square to seat spectators, and the dance continued until 9:00 at night, at which time the cabarets were "filled with this multitude of both sexes where they spent the entire night . . . with the permission of the authorities. There was so much noise that it was impossible for those nearby to get any rest all night long."[93] Not only had this event disrupted the religious services of the day and the needed repose of the towns' inhabitants at night, but also another vogue was being planned. Girls of thirteen to sixteen years of age had requested and received permission from the mayor to stage it, and they were searching all around the area for musicians. Their dance partners were "little boys of their age to whom were added all the older boys and girls [of the community]."[94] This time they were forced to hold the dance farther from the church, a change appreciated by the priest.

However, the priest continued to be concerned about the ramifications of these dances. As with the previous dance, the cabarets of the town were filled with customers all night long. To make his point stronger, the priest emphasized that these dances did not even correspond to the *vogue patronale* of the village, which took place in March. In other words, such merrymaking would have been acceptable, or at least understandable, if it came in conjunction with the annual celebration of the town's patron saint. But it seemed entirely unacceptable for events such as this to occur on a monthly basis. The priest hoped the prefect would demonstrate the government's attachment to "good morals and religious sentiment" by prohibiting future dances. This example was part of a general effort on the part of the Church to dissuade young people from dancing. One historian has found examples of missionaries trying to get girls "to swear that they would give up dancing," which infuriated young men. According to a recent study of Restoration political culture, the clergy "declare[d] war on popular festive culture . . . [including] dancing. They denounced all forms of non-religious entertainment as debauchery, attacking more private forms of leisure such as the reading of novels, as well as public pleasures enjoyed in cafés, cabarets, and theaters." One chapter of an older work on the internal missions of Restoration France is entitled "Guerre à la dance" (war on dance).[95]

As with dance halls, Restoration authorities focused more on moral issues in their treatment of vogues and other *fêtes champêtres* than Napoleonic officials had. In 1818, the curé of La Guillotière accused the mayor of allowing the town's vogue to overlap with the celebration of mass. The mayor responded that his ordinances required that the games stop during mass and that dancing could not begin until 3:30 in the afternoon, at which point the priest should have made sure to have finished all religious activities "so as not to mix the holy and the profane." Instead, church services continued until 6 P.M. The mayor then complained that the curé acted as though religion, for which the mayor underlined his great respect, was the only concern in the town. "Monsieur le curé sees only the church, but I must be able to see (while at all times respecting religion) the advantage that this community acquires during such a day when the concourse of twenty to thirty thousand souls pour ten or twelve thousand francs into consumption of all sorts."[96] In his enthusiasm for the moneymaking possibilities of such events, the mayor attempted to organize another vogue in Brotteaux only a month later, and the prefect informed him that it was not acceptable to permit these divertissements with such frequency. "The interests of the owners of wine shops must not be the only concern. The administration must also embrace general moral considerations affecting the entire population."[97] Thus under the Restoration, as during the Empire, merrymaking suited larger goals of maintaining order, but workers' leanings toward debauchery had to be kept on a tight rein. "Moral considerations" seemed more significant than they had under Napoleon, and one such "moral" concern was the behavior of women and girls, particularly when they appeared in these spaces for public amusement.

Despite the greater concerns expressed and stricter controls sought by religious and secular authorities of the Restoration, in both Lyon and Nantes there was a vibrant working-class culture, with cabarets, guinguettes, and other venues providing spaces for amusement and a chance to discuss matters of concern over a bottle of wine. Workers also organized their own festivities, like the lyonnais vogues or parties organized by *compagnons.* Authorities may have found this merrymaking all too disorderly, but they could not put a stop to, or even really control, the jovial, at times violent, gatherings of working-class men and women.

With some variation due to the political and social context in each city, venues that brought urban dwellers together for drinking and dancing indicate an evolution toward increasing separation of the classes and, to a lesser extent, the sexes. The growth in the number of cafés illustrates a trend in urban sociability in postrevolutionary France. Venues meant exclusively for men became more numerous, while venues meant to attract both sexes became less common. Elites also increasingly chose to separate themselves from "popular" amusements and, in the process, created more purely bourgeois spaces in which to converse and amuse themselves. These spaces also tended to be highly masculine, and the activities that went on in them— reading newspapers, discussing politics, drinking alcohol, and flirting with attractive serving women—all came to be viewed as male occupations. These practices strengthened the idea that middle-class women did not belong in public venues like cafés, where the topics of conversation and the overall atmosphere would have made them uncomfortable. In contrast, men and women of the lower classes continued to share activities like dancing and other merrymaking in public spaces.

Organizing and regulating women's sexuality was an integral part of the new class distinctions emerging in these years. The class-stratified society that would dominate the rest of the century was coming into being thanks in large part to the experiences of these urban dwellers who increasingly saw those in other classes as "others" thoroughly unlike themselves. The presence of working-class women in the "disorderly" crowds that gathered to enjoy a dance in a public square on Sundays only solidified emerging bourgeois views of the immoral and dangerous peuple. Literary obsessions with the upper-class coquette and the working-class grisette emerged out of the same set of concerns expressed by officials when they tried to put a stop to working-class debauchery. The social and moral order hinged on controlling women's behavior, especially their sexuality. Domestic ideology grew increasingly influential during these years in response to fears that women were out of control and needed to be reined in.

# Conclusion

The French Revolution of 1789 created great uncertainty about the significance and representation of social distinctions. It made evident the artificial nature of social norms that had seemed necessary and timeless during the Old Regime. After 1799, when a more stable political system took hold, a stable social system also started to emerge. Nonetheless, during both the Napoleonic period and the Bourbon Restoration, anxieties about how to read and interpret markers of social status remained. The ambiguities of the period created a widespread desire to see and be seen in public—to express one's sense of social position and to observe how others did so. In Paris, these trends are most visible on the Boulevard, a neighborhood where large and diverse crowds assembled to partake in various amusements, with a large part of the draw being the crowds themselves. In provincial cities, too, diverse groups often availed themselves of the pleasures and pastimes their cities offered, enjoying the experience of rubbing elbows with those around them. While in these spaces, participants were simultaneously on display and observing those around them. Their behavior marked their class and gender positions, and while they were laughing or crying, dancing or walking, they could observe and categorize all they saw around them. Urban social spaces were defined by the identities and behavior of the people who filled them. At the same time, these spaces played an important function in putting the social order on display. Participants developed a clearer sense of their own identities, as well the class and gender norms that were taking shape around them.

Where did the new social markers in operation in postrevolutionary society come from? They emerged as ordinary people observed the behavior of men and women of the various classes. Urban life, with the diverse crowds that circulated on city streets, in public squares, and in and around theaters and cafés, gave city dwellers innumerable opportunities to put themselves on display and to participate in people-watching at the same time. As they did so, participants created social spaces in which their comportment, dress, and language reverberated with meaning. Armand Charlemagne's poem, with its image of "Hortense" demanding silence so as to immerse herself in a good melodrama, reflected contemporary expectations about women of her class. When young men voiced their political views in theaters, they were creating a sense of self while making themselves visible (and audible) to those around them. A sense of who these troublesome "jeunes gens" were and why they behaved as they did, as expressed by Julie Pellizzone and many journalists, spread through society as people watched these "youth" and formed conclusions about them based on their dress, activities, and behavior. The spectatorial quality of urban life put French society as a whole on display, allowing participants to act out, observe, and even shape the postrevolutionary social order.

Other spaces allowed particular social groups to develop a sense of solidarity with others like themselves: workers as they drank in cabarets; middle-class men as they enjoyed the titillating experience of being served by an "African" waitress in a café; elite women as they demonstrated their organizational skills and self-sacrificing natures as they ran charities for the "deserving poor." In all these cases, the people who filled and created these spaces expressed their sense of who they were, where they fit into society, and what characteristics they possessed that determined their social positions. Then, as urban dwellers reemerged in the more heterogeneous crowds that filled other kinds of spaces, such as theaters or the political festivals that opened this study, they did so more certain of their identities and thus were better able to display and maneuver around the increasingly agreed-upon attributes that corresponded to a particular social position. They could also more successfully contest the social order that they had grown to understand through their observations.

As urban dwellers interacted with each other in these different spaces, they were in constant negotiation with larger forces at play. These forces include the state (most visible in festivals and in the policing of theaters and other public spaces), the Church (in charitable activities and in its attempt to enforce its view of "morality" regarding dancing and other activities), and finally the producers of the culture (playwrights, journalists, theater reviewers, and writers of prescriptive literature). In every case, these larger forces shaped the messages communicated to those involved, as well as the atmosphere of the spaces that brought people together. Cultural consumption always reflects this kind of dynamic interchange as powerful institutions and individuals try to direct and control the options available to ordinary people while consumers constantly shape and reinterpret those options based on their tastes and preferences. This book has emphasized the power of ordinary people in constructing and shaping social structures—the agency side of the dialectic of structure and agency.[1] However, we must not forget that this process was always one of negotiation between these "agents" and the larger "structural" forces at play in society.

Once the class and gender norms of postrevolutionary society became more stable and more widely understood, people became less interested in mingling with those who differed from themselves. They preferred more comfortable locations that brought them into contact with people like themselves. Beginning around 1820, venues and spaces that attracted specific social groups became more numerous while the appeal of those that catered to more diverse crowds seemed to be shrinking. But urban life never completely lost its ability to captivate through the spectacle of diverse groups interacting with each other. "Popular" neighborhoods like Brotteaux in Lyon continued to be praised by bourgeois newspapers like *Le journal du commerce* throughout the 1820s, and women appeared with regularity in theaters, dance halls, intellectual gatherings, and other venues.

Why would women's presence in all of these spaces have seemed so important? Why would it have been commented upon with such frequency in newspapers, by the police, and in countless other places? In the postrevolutionary period, women's behavior and "morality" seemed central to building a stable and healthy society. Several publications expressed with great clarity this obsession with women and their influence on society. In an essay published in 1819, *De la politesse, ouvrage critique, moral et philosophique,* Louis-Damien Eméric made an impressive generalization: "Social bonds, order, and general prosperity depend on the behavior of women."[2] Many members of the French intellectual community, and no doubt others who left fewer traces, agreed with Eméric. In 1825, Julien-Joseph Virey, a prolific author and doctor, published a "physiological, moral, and literary" study of women. The concluding paragraph of this lengthy work began by urging women to recognize their vital role in society: "Woman! inconsistent object of idolatry and of hatred, sensitive, enlightened companion to man; wife, tender [other] half, or rather the whole of a citizen and of his family, your praise or your blame will decide the destiny of the world."[3] As the centrality of "woman" to the future health of French society became a matter of acceptance, debates about women's nature and roles took on great intensity. Watching their behavior in public functioned as a way to gauge the extent to which France appeared to be moving in the right direction, regardless of the observers' views on which direction was the right course to follow.

Of course, turning women into symbols did not erase the realities of their lives. Women and men of all classes dealt with the joys and hardships of their lives in whatever ways they could. They celebrated their successes and profited from their moments of leisure as they saw fit, regardless of how their behavior may have contradicted the prescriptions or the symbolic readings of moralists. Men and women reacted to the changes brought by the Revolution and the ensuing regimes as seemed suitable to their particular situations. Their responses depended on their social positions, their locations, their employment, as well as their sense of whether they received fair or unfair treatment from local and national authorities.

That is why local conditions need to be considered when examining the significance of social interaction in urban spaces. Ambiguities in social structures and then their growing clarification help to explain the trajectory visible in the case of the Parisian Boulevard. A desire to observe different social groups so as to comprehend how one's position in society was defined explains elites' attraction to the Boulevard and melodrama during the genre's heyday. Fewer ambiguities about the class structure and how it was represented through dress and behavior existed in Lyon, except among those at the very top of the social scale. Class structures similar to those of the later nineteenth century were already in existence in Lyon by the mid-eighteenth century: a large, confident bourgeoisie secure in its social position and wealth, and a relatively weak, small aristocracy. Whereas Lyon's social structures could be described as ahead of their time, those in Nantes were, if anything, behind the times. The stagnant economy in Nantes helps to explain the relative lack of social change there. With "traditional" class structures intact, the distinctions between women's lives among the different social groups that seemed so significant in Lyon mattered less in Nantes. Wealthy men and women had plenty of leisure time, and they spent much of that time together. Poorer men and women had little time for amusement, but their lifestyles also brought both sexes and the different generations together for work and pleasure.

Despite numerous local variables, we can make some generalizations.

First, as an analytical tool, "separate spheres" helps little in understanding male and female roles and experiences. Men and women of all classes occupied both public and private spaces, and many spaces cannot be categorized as either purely public or private. However, denying the relevance of "separate spheres" ideology does not mean that the women and men participated in public activities on an equal footing. Though both sexes may have shared many spaces, those spaces were nonetheless shaped by, while simultaneously shaping, ideas about gender and sexuality. In particular, they reflected the profound belief in "natural" gender complementarity. Second, despite demonstrating the weaknesses of "separate spheres" as an analytical tool or a reflection of reality, we can see a change over time with regard to middle-class women's access and control over various kinds of venues. By the 1820s, bourgeois men had more places in which to amuse themselves, whereas women had fewer options available to them and less control over those spaces to which they did have access. Even theaters, which consistently welcomed and encouraged female spectators to serve as "ornaments," placed women under greater surveillance as prostitutes came under greater control. Middle-class women's lives thus began to reflect the "domestic ideology" prescribed by moralists and novelists since at least the time of Rousseau. The timing of the emergence of utopian socialism in the late 1820s reflects this trend. The Saint-Simonians' and Fourierists' rejection of "traditional" gender norms and sexual constraints implies a coherent set of "traditions" against which to rebel.[4] In other words, the first body of texts arguing for women's "domestic" existence needed to be created and internalized before subversive discourses could come into existence in opposition to it. Similarly, the absence of a true feminist movement until after 1830 reflects the ambiguity of gender norms during the postrevolutionary period. Clearer, more stable rules of behavior for men and women and for the various classes were a prerequisite for individual and group efforts to revolt against them. The construction and comprehension of these rules of behavior emerged in large part through the practices and in the spaces examined in this book. Ordinary men and women contributed in real and important ways to the emergence of an increasingly solid, visible, and contested postrevolutionary order.

Abbreviations

Notes

List of Primary Sources

Index

# Abbreviations

| | |
|---|---|
| AN | Archives Nationales, Paris |
| ADLA | Archives Départementales de la Loire-Atlantique, Nantes |
| ADR | Archives Départementales du Rhône, Lyon |
| ADSM | Archives Départementales de la Seine-Maritime, Rouen |
| AMB | Archives Municipales de Bordeaux |
| AML | Archives Municipales de Lyon |
| AMM | Archives Municipales de Montpellier |
| AMN | Archives Municipales de Nantes |
| AMT | Archives Municipales de Toulouse |
| BML | Bibliothèque Municipale de Lyon, département de fonds anciens |

# Notes

## Introduction

1. The essay was published as a pamphlet by the Academy: Jean-Baptiste-Louis Camel, *De l'influence des théâtres et particulièrement des théâtres secondaires sur les mœurs du peuple* ([Paris]: Nouzou, 1822), 1. Unless otherwise indicated, all translations are my own.

2. Ibid., 2–4.

3. Ibid., 13–14.

4. On Old Regime "habits of deference," see David Garrioch, *The Making of Revolutionary Paris* (Berkeley: University of California Press, 2002), 40. For an example of such forms of deference slipping, see Robert Darnton, "Workers Revolt: The Great Cat Massacre of the Rue Saint-Séverin," in *The Great Cat Massacre and Other Episodes in French Cultural History* (New York: Vintage, 1985).

5. A recent study of dress during the Revolution describes the "central feature of the politics of revolutionary appearances" as "an uncertain and frequently unresolved process of (mis)recognition whereby the heterogeneous spectacle of people visible in the street, club, and café had continually to be tested against expectations of how dress should signify new modes of identity." Richard Wrigley, *The Politics of Appearances: Representations of Dress in Revolutionary France* (Oxford: Berg, 2002), 250.

6. Ewa Lajer-Burcharth, *Necklines: The Art of Jacques-Louis David after the Terror* (New Haven: Yale University Press, 1999), 69, 244.

7. A discussion of early nineteenth-century views toward women, particularly their predilection for religious sentiment, appears in Darrin M. McMahon, *Enemies of the Enlightenment: The French Counter-Enlightenment and the Making of Modernity* (Oxford: Oxford University Press, 2001), 133–138. On the long-term significance of the association of women with the Church, see

Caroline Ford, *Divided Houses: Religion and Gender in Modern France* (Ithaca: Cornell University Press, 2005).

8. See Dena Goodman, "Enlightenment Salons: The Convergence of Female and Philosophic Ambitions," *Eighteenth-Century Studies* 22 (1989): 325–350; Goodman, *The Republic of Letters: A Cultural History of the French Enlightenment* (Ithaca: Cornell University Press, 1994); and Steven Kale, *French Salons: High Society and Political Sociability from the Old Regime to the Revolution of 1848* (Baltimore: Johns Hopkins University Press, 2004), ch. 1.

9. Daniel Roche, *The People of Paris: An Essay in Popular Culture in the Eighteenth Century,* trans. Marie Evans (Berkeley: University of California Press, 1987) and Robert M. Isherwood, *Farce and Fantasy: Popular Entertainment in Eighteenth-Century Paris* (Oxford: Oxford University Press, 1986).

10. I explore the theme of domesticity in prescriptive and popular literature in "*Bonnes Lectures:* Improving Women and Society Through Literature in Post-Revolutionary France," in *The French Experience from Republic to Monarchy, 1792–1824: New Dawns in Politics, Knowledge and Culture,* ed. Máire F. Cross and David Williams (Basingstoke: Palgrave, 2000), 155–171.

11. See Bonnie G. Smith, *Ladies of the Leisure Class: The Bourgeoises of Northern France in the Nineteenth Century* (Princeton: Princeton University Press, 1981) and Louise A. Tilly and Joan W. Scott, *Women, Work, and Family* (New York: Holt, Rinehart and Winston, 1978). For analysis of postrevolutionary French discourse and the exclusion of women from politics, see Geneviève Fraisse, *Reason's Muse: Sexual Difference and the Birth of Democracy,* trans. Jane Marie Todd (Chicago: University of Chicago Press, 1994).

12. See for example Joan Wallach Scott, " 'L'ouvrière! Mot impie, sordide . . .': Women Workers in the Discourse of French Political Economy, 1840–1860," in Scott, *Gender and the Politics of History* (New York: Columbia University Press, 1988); Laura L. Frader, "Engendering Work and Wages: The French Labor Movement and the Family Wage," in *Gender and Class in Modern Europe,* ed. Laura L. Frader and Sonya O. Rose (Ithaca: Cornell University Press, 1996); and Anna Clark, *The Struggle for the Breeches: Gender and the Making of the British Working Class* (Berkeley: University of California Press, 1995).

13. Elizabeth Colwill, "Epistolary Passions: Friendship and the Literary Public of Constance de Salm, 1767–1845," *Journal of Women's History* 12 (2000): 46; and Jann Matlock, "The Invisible Woman and Her Secrets Unveiled," *Yale Journal of Criticism* 9 (1996): 183. On problems inherent in the concept of separate spheres, see Linda Kerber, "Separate Spheres, Female Worlds, Woman's Place: The Rhetoric of Women's History," *Journal of American History* 75 (June 1988): 9–39. Two recent issues of the *Journal of Women's History* 15 (Spring and Summer 2003) are devoted to "Women's History in the New Millennium: Rethinking

Public and Private." See especially the articles by Leonore Davidoff, Mary Ryan, and Joan Landes.

14. Mona Ozouf, *Women's Words: Essay on French Singularity,* trans. Jane Marie Todd (Chicago: University of Chicago Press, 1997), 252–283.

15. On British domesticity, the classic work is Leonore Davidoff and Catherine Hall, *Family Fortunes: Men and Women of the English Middle Class, 1780–1850* (Chicago: University of Chicago Press, 1987). A more recent synthetic work is Robert B. Shoemaker, *Gender in English Society, 1650–1850: The Emergence of Separate Spheres?* (London: Longman, 1998). In the American context, Christine Stansell, *City of Women: Sex and Class in New York, 1789–1860* (Urbana: University of Illinois Press, 1987) and Lori D. Ginzberg, *Women and the Work of Benevolence: Morality, Politics, and Class in the Nineteenth-Century United States* (New Haven: Yale University Press, 1990) focus on women playing public roles despite domestic ideology. On French feminism, see Joan Wallach Scott, *Only Paradoxes to Offer: French Feminists and the Rights of Man* (Cambridge, Mass.: Harvard University Press, 1996) and Karen Offen's thoughtful comments in her review of Anne Verjus, *Le cens de la famille: Les femmes et le vote, 1789–1848* (Paris: Belin, 2002), *H-France Review* 3 (September 2003).

16. An insightful analysis of this and other Franco-American debates appears in Eric Fassin, "The Purloined Gender: American Feminism in a French Mirror," *French Historical Studies* 22 (1999): 113–138. The debate launched by Ozouf's study can be found in "Femmes: Une singularité française?" *Le débat* 87 (November–December 1995) with contributions by Bronislaw Baczko, Elisabeth Badinter, Lynn Hunt, Michelle Perrot, and Joan Wallach Scott, as well as a reaction by Ozouf. In a review essay discussing two other books, Geneviève Fraisse summed up the concerns regarding Ozouf's argument: "the choice of the historian [was] to speak of women's freedom without discussing sexual equality, thus sweeping under the rug (*escamotant*) recognition of the oppression of women." "Droit de cuissage et devoir de l'historien," *Clio* 3 (1996): 258. Although I emphasize women's freedom to access public spaces and the importance of mixed-sex sociability, I in no way mean to imply that women entered public life on equal terms with men or to deny the legal and political oppression of women.

17. Suzanne Desan, *The Family on Trial in Revolutionary France* (Berkeley: University of California Press, 2004), 11. A thoughtful discussion of the idea of gender complementarity as it functioned in France from about 1780 to 1830 appears in Susan K. Foley, *Women in France since 1789* (Basingstoke: Palgrave, 2004), 4–9.

18. The classic statement of this view is Joan Landes, *Women and the Public Sphere in the Age of the French Revolution* (Ithaca: Cornell University Press, 1988). For a thoughtful analysis of the arguments contrasting the eighteenth and nineteenth centuries, see Steven Kale, "Women, the Public Sphere, and the Persistence of Salons," *French Historical Studies* 25 (Winter 2002): 115–148.

Like Kale, I argue that both sides of this contrast have been exaggerated: women's political influence was not as great in the eighteenth century as some would have it; and women were never completely excluded from politics and the public in the nineteenth.

19. For example, Lynn Hunt argued that "between 1793 and 1804 . . . male hostility toward women's political participation began to crystallize into a fully elaborated domestic ideology in which women were scientifically 'proven' to be suitable only for domestic occupations." Hunt, *The Family Romance of the French Revolution* (Berkeley: University of California Press, 1992), 158. See Landes, *Women and the Public Sphere* and Fraisse, *Reason's Muse.* James F. McMillan, *France and Women, 1789–1914: Gender, Society, and Politics* (London: Routledge, 2000), ch. 3, goes over these arguments. For an approach more focused on practices than discourse, see Dominique Godineau, *The Women of Paris and Their French Revolution,* trans. Katherine Streip (Berkeley: University of California Press, 1998). Godineau examines women's political action during the Revolution, their first "encounter with citizenship" (xix).

20. McMillan, *France and Women,* 42.

21. Steven Kale, *French Salons* and "Women, Salons, and the State in the Aftermath of the French Revolution," *Journal of Women's History* 13 (2002): 54–80; Suzanne Desan, *The Family on Trial* and "Reconstituting the Social after the Terror: Family, Property, and the Law in Popular Politics," *Past and Present* 164 (1999): 81–121; Anne Verjus, *Le cens de la famille: Les femmes et le vote, 1789–1848* (Paris: Belin, 2002); Jennifer Ngaire Heuer, *The Family and the Nation: Gender and Citizenship in Revolutionary France, 1789–1830* (Ithaca: Cornell University Press, 2005); and Jennifer Heuer and Anne Verjus, "L'invention de la sphère domestique au sortir de la Révolution," *Annales historiques de la Révolution française* 327 (2002): 1–28. The importance of the family in Restoration politics and culture is a prominent theme in Elizabeth A. Fraser, *Delacroix, Art and Patriomony in Post-Revolutionary France* (Cambridge: Cambridge University Press, 2004).

22. Carla Hesse, *The Other Enlightenment: How French Women Became Modern* (Princeton: Princeton University Press, 2001) and Jo Burr Margadant, "Gender, Vice, and Political Imagery in Postrevolutionary France: Reinterpreting the Failure of the July Monarchy, 1830–1848," *American Historical Review* 104 (1999): 1460–1496. On the blurring of public and private, see Sharon Marcus, *Apartment Stories: City and Home in Nineteenth-Century Paris and London* (Berkeley: University of California Press, 1999) and Victoria E. Thompson, *The Virtuous Marketplace: Women and Men, Money and Politics in Paris, 1830–1870* (Baltimore: Johns Hopkins University Press, 2000).

23. Harold Mah, "Phantasies of the Public Sphere: Rethinking the Habermas of Historians," *Journal of Modern History* 72 (2000): 153–182. The quotation appears on page 166.

24. A recent article makes similar use of the concept of space, linking it to bourgeois identity in 1830s Paris. Victoria Thompson, "Telling 'Spatial Stories': Urban Space and Bourgeois Identity in Early Nineteenth-Century Paris," *Journal of Modern History* 75 (2003): 523–556. Although the majority of the French population lived outside of cities until well into the twentieth century, urban life made social interaction possible in ways rural life could not.

25. A valuable discussion of the terms "public" and "private" and the ways historians and social scientists have used them appears in Michael Warner, *Publics and Counterpublics* (New York: Zone, 2002), ch. 1. Warner's list of the attributes of the public and the private is particularly helpful (29).

26. Henri Lefebvre, *The Production of Space*, trans. Donald Nicholson-Smith (Oxford: Blackwell, 1991), 101. For a theoretical discussion of space "as a social product," see Edward W. Soja, *Postmodern Geographies: The Reassertion of Space in Critical Social Theory* (New York: Verso, 1989), especially ch. 3.

27. Quoted in Soja, *Postmodern Geographies*, 80. On the ways historians of women have made use of the concept of space, see Rebecca Rogers, "Le sexe de l'espace: Réflexions sur l'histoire des femmes aux XVIIIe et XIXe siècles dans quelques travaux américains, anglais et français," in *Les espaces de l'historien*, ed. Jean-Claude Waquet, Odile Goerg, and Rebecca Rogers (Strasbourg: Presses Universitaires de Strasbourg, 2000), 181–202. See also Richard Biernacki and Jennifer Jordan, "The Place of Space in the Study of the Social," in *The Social in Question: New Bearings in History and the Social Sciences*, ed. Patrick Joyce (London: Routledge, 2002).

28. Henri d'Alméras, "1801," in *La vie parisienne à travers le XIXe siècle: Paris de 1800 à 1900 d'après les estampes et les mémoires du temps*, vol. 1, *1800–1830, Le Consulat, le Premier Empire, la Restauration*, ed. Charles Simond [pseud.] (Paris: Plon, 1900), 20.

29. Many of these issues are addressed in Howard G. Brown and Judith A. Miller, eds., *Taking Liberties: Problems of a New Order from the French Revolution to Napoleon* (Manchester: Manchester University Press, 2002). The historiographical essay that opens the collection is relevant, as is Brown's essay, "The Search for Stability." Brown argues in part that with the Constitution of the Year X (1802), "the state's basis of legitimacy had shifted from providing the people with access to politics to providing personal security and stability" (30). Isser Woloch, *Napoleon and His Collaborators: The Making of a Dictatorship* (New York: W. W. Norton, 2001) explores how and why the political elite of France would have supported the regime. A new study by Pierre Serna places Napoleon's appeal into a broader context that he labels the "extreme center." See *La République des girouettes, (1789–1815 . . . et au-delà) une anomalie politique: La France de l'extrême centre* (Seyssel: Champ Vallon, 2005).

30. On the entire period, see Isser Woloch, *The New Regime: Transformations of the French Civic Order, 1789–1820s* (New York: W. W. Norton, 1994). On Napoleonic France, see Jean Tulard's numerous publications; Jean-Paul Bertaud, *Le Consulat et l'Empire, 1799–1815* (Paris: Armand Colin, 1989); and Louis Bergeron, *France under Napoleon*, trans. R. R. Palmer (Princeton: Princeton University Press, 1981). On the long-term effects of Napoleonic efforts to construct a new social order, see Natalie Petiteau, *Elites et mobilités: La noblesse d'Empire au XIXe siècle, 1808–1914* (Paris: Boutique de l'Histoire, 1997). The classic work on the Restoration is Guillaume de Bertier de Sauvigny, *The Bourbon Restoration*, trans. Lynn M. Case (Philadelphia: University of Pennsylvania Press, 1966).

31. Philip Dwyer makes this argument in a recent review essay, "New Avenues for Research in Napoleonic Europe," *European History Quarterly* 33 (2003): 101–124. According to Howard Brown and Judith Miller, "our knowledge of the activities and adherences of those living under the Napoleonic State . . . remains rather fragmentary." "New Paths from the Terror to the Empire," in *Taking Liberties*, 13.

32. One important exception is Sheryl Kroen, *Politics and Theater: The Crisis of Legitimacy in Restoration France, 1815–1830* (Berkeley: University of California Press, 2000), which treats the impossibility of the Restoration government's efforts to negate the effects of the Revolution; another, a detailed study of Restoration politics and the emergence of liberal opposition movements at the grassroots level, is Robert Alexander, *Re-Writing the French Revolutionary Tradition* (Cambridge: Cambridge University Press, 2003). The older and idiosyncratic work of Richard Cobb also treats the history of this period from the bottom up: *Reactions to the French Revolution* (Oxford: Oxford University Press, 1972) and *The Police and the People: French Popular Protest, 1789–1820* (Oxford: Clarendon Press, 1970). The Restoration is often treated along with the July Monarchy, as in André Jardin and André-Jean Tudesq, *Restoration and Reaction, 1815–1848*, trans. Elborg Forster (Cambridge: Cambridge University Press, 1983) and Jean-Claude Caron, *La France de 1815 à 1848* (Paris: Armand Colin, 1993). A valuable discussion of Restoration political culture with an emphasis on its long-term political ramifications appears in Raymond Jonas, *France and the Cult of the Sacred Heart: An Epic Tale for Modern Times* (Berkeley: University of California Press, 2000), 118–146.

33. William H. Sewell, Jr., *Work and Revolution in France: The Language of Labor from the Old Regime to 1848* (Cambridge: Cambridge University Press, 1980); Jacques Rancière, The *Nights of Labor: The Workers' Dream in Nineteenth-Century France*, trans. John Drury (Philadelphia: Temple University Press, 1989); and Cynthia Maria Truant, *The Rites of Labor: Brotherhoods of Compagnonnage in Old and New Regime France* (Ithaca: Cornell University Press, 1994).

34. Sarah Maza, *The Myth of the French Bourgeoisie: An Essay on the Social Imagi-nary, 1750–1850* (Cambridge, Mass.: Harvard University Press, 2003); Carol E. Harrison, *The Bourgeois Citizen in Nineteenth-Century France: Gender, So-ciability, and the Uses of Emulation* (Oxford: Oxford University Press, 1999); and Adeline Daumard, *Les bourgeois de Paris au XIXe siècle* (Paris: Flammar-ion, 1970).

35. Robert A. Nye, *Masculinity and Male Codes of Honor in Modern France* (Berkeley: University of California Press, 1997) and William M. Reddy, *The Invisible Code: Honor and Sentiment in Postrevolutionary France, 1814–1848* (Berkeley: University of California Press, 1997).

36. In the introduction to a recent collection of essays treating "practice theory," a postlinguistic-turn trend in historiography, Gabrielle Spiegel describes the approach taken by the various authors whose work appears in the collection: "These scholars begin from a belief in individual perception as the agent's own source of knowledge about, and action in, the world, a perception medi-ated and perhaps constrained, but *not* wholly controlled, by the cultural scaf-folding or conceptual schemes within which it takes place." Spiegel then in-cludes a quotation from sociologist Andreas Rechwitz, one of her contributors: "The social then . . . is the subjective *idea* of a common world of meanings" (ellipses and emphasis in original). *Practicing History: New Directions in His-torical Writing after the Linguistic Turn,* ed. Gabrielle M. Spiegel (New York: Routledge, 2005), 13. Another good overview of this new approach is Richard Biernacki, "Language and the Shift from Signs to Practices in Cultural In-quiry," *History and Theory* 39 (2000): 289–310.

37. On Parisian uniqueness during the revolutionary period, see Garrioch, *The Making of Revolutionary Paris,* 9–10.

38. Gavin Daly, *Inside Napoleonic France: State and Society in Rouen, 1800–1815* (Aldershot: Ashgate, 2001), 1. Another local study is Jeff Horn, "Building the New Regime: Founding the Bonapartist State in the Department of the Aube," *French Historical Studies* 25 (2002): 225–263. Robert Alexander reflects on the relative neglect of the Restoration period, particularly with regard to local studies, in *Re-Writing the French Revolutionary Tradition.*

39. The best source for urban population statistics is Bernard Lepetit, *The Prein-dustrial Urban System: France, 1740–1840,* trans. Godfrey Rogers (Cam-bridge: Cambridge University Press, 1994). The numbers cited here appear in Appendix B, p. 449.

40. On Nantes' role in the slave trade during the Restoration, see William B. Co-hen, *The French Encounter with Africans: White Response to Blacks, 1530–1880* (Bloomington: University of Indiana Press, 1980), 187.

41. General works on the history of these cities include Jean-Pierre Gutton, ed., *Histoire de Lyon et du Lyonnais,* 2nd ed. (Paris: Presses Universitaires de

France, 2000); Françoise Bayard and Pierre Cayez, eds., *Histoire de Lyon des origines à nos jours,* 2 vols. (Le Coteau: Horvath, 1990); Paul Bois, ed., *Histoire de Nantes* (Toulouse: Privat, 1977); Emilienne Leroux, *Histoire d'une ville et de ses habitants: Nantes,* 2 vols. (Nantes: Editions ACL, 1984); and Armel de Wismes, *Nantes et le pays nantais* (Paris: Editions France-Empire, 1995).

42. Maza, *The Myth of the French Bourgeoisie.* The phrase "social imaginary" is more common among French scholars than in the Anglophone world. Maza defines it as "the cultural elements from which we construct our under-standing of the social world" (10). Historians have increasingly drawn at-tention to ways people construct their identities through performance. See for example, Jo Burr Margadant, ed., *The New Biography: Performing Femi-ninity in Nineteenth-Century France* (Berkeley: University of California Press, 2000) and Mary Louise Roberts, *Disruptive Acts: The New Woman in Fin-de-Siècle France* (Chicago: University of Chicago Press, 2002). Judith Butler's work on gender and performance has inspired much of this scholar-ship. See especially *Gender Trouble: Feminism and the Subversion of Identity* (New York: Routledge, 1990).

43. Michel de Certeau, *The Practice of Everyday Life* (Berkeley: University of Cali-fornia Press, 1984), xi. For a discussion of practice theory and feminism, see Sherry B. Ortner, "Making Gender: Toward a Feminist, Minority, Postcolonial, Subaltern, Etc., Theory of Practice," in Ortner, *Making Gender: The Politics and Erotics of Culture* (Boston: Beacon Press, 1996).

44. The most relevant work by Pierre Bourdieu on cultural consumption and so-cial structures is *Distinction: A Social Critique of the Judgment of Taste* (Cam-bridge, Mass.: Harvard University Press, 1984).

45. James C. Scott, *Domination and the Arts of Resistance: Hidden Transcripts* (New Haven: Yale University Press, 1990), 4–5.

46. Ibid., 120–124.

47. In *Only Paradoxes to Offer,* Joan Scott's study of French feminism from 1798 to 1944, each chapter treats an individual feminist. Scott goes directly from Olympe de Gouges, who was executed in 1793, to Jeanne Deroin and the Revolution of 1848, implying that little feminist activity took place between the two. In fact, a vocal feminist movement evolved out of and along with utopian socialism by about 1830. See Susan K. Grogan, *French Socialism and Sexual Difference: Women and the New Society, 1803–44* (Basingstoke: Macmillian, 1992). Claire Goldberg Moses discusses the silencing of femi-nism during the thirty-five years before 1830 in *French Feminism in the Nineteenth Century* (Albany: State University of New York Press, 1984), 41. Jeremy Popkin analyzes Lyon's feminist press after the 1830 revolution in *Press, Revolution, and Social Identities in France, 1830–1835* (University Park: Pennsylvania State University Press, 2002), ch. 3.

48. The connections Foucault draws between power, knowledge, and the expert's gaze run though much of his work, expressed most clearly perhaps in *Discipline and Punish: The Birth of the Prison,* trans. Alan Sheridan (New York: Vintage, 1977), 184–194. Jann Matlock discusses some of the strengths and weakness of Foucault's theories in *Scenes of Seduction: Prostitution, Hysteria, and Reading Difference in Nineteenth-Century France* (New York: Columbia University Press, 1994), 10–13, 39–40. See also her analysis of the "specularization of women's processes of looking" and the issue of the female gaze more generally in "The Invisible Woman and Her Secrets Unveiled," 203–209. Discussions of the *flâneur* and the impossible *flâneuse* can be found in Priscilla Parkhurst Ferguson, *Paris as Revolution: Writing the Nineteenth-Century City* (Berkeley: University of California Press, 1994), ch. 3; and Janet Wolff, "The Invisible *Flâneuse:* Women and the Literature of Modernity," in Wolff, *Feminine Sentences: Essays on Women and Culture* (Berkeley: University of California Press, 1990), 34–50. In contrast, Erika Diane Rappaport argues for the possibility of the *flâneuse* in *Shopping for Pleasure: Women in the Making of London's West End* (Princeton: Princeton University Press, 2000), 116–122. Work on the *flâneur* builds on Walter Benjamin's analysis of Baudelaire, some of which appears in his *Paris, Capitale du XIXe siècle: Le livre des passages,* trans. Jean Lacoste (Paris: Editions du Cerf, 1993), 434–472. Joan Landes works through these debates in *Visualizing the Nation: Gender, Representation, and Revolution in Eighteenth-Century France* (Ithaca: Cornell University Press, 2001), 15–17.

49. Vanessa R. Schwartz emphasizes the active role of spectators in creating the "spectacle of the city," in *Spectacular Realities: Early Mass Culture in Fin-de-Siècle Paris* (Berkeley: University of California Press, 1998). In *City of Dreadful Delight: Narratives of Sexual Danger in Late-Victorian London* (Chicago: University of Chicago Press, 1992), Judith R. Walkowitz analyzes the significance of women in public as spectators and spectacle. Richard Sennett's work on urban observation and interaction inspired my own. See for example, *The Fall of Public Man* (New York: Norton, 1974). I discuss these issues at greater length in "Making Society 'Legible': People-Watching in Paris after the French Revolution," *French Historical Studies* 28 (2005): 265–296.

50. I do not mean to suggest that classes exist as concrete entities. As Joan Scott explained, "Class and class consciousness are the same thing—they are political articulations that provide an analysis of, a coherent pattern to impose upon, the events and activities of daily life" (*Gender and the Politics of History,* 56). Here, I am interested in exploring how "the events and activities of daily life" in turn made these "political articulations" have meaning for the people using and applying these labels.

51. In *The Myth of the French Bourgeoisie,* Sarah Maza questions the very existence of a self-identified bourgeoisie. The classic, and still unequaled, study of

the nineteenth-century Parisian bourgeoisie is Daumard, *Les bourgeois de Paris*. Also useful is David Garrioch, *The Formation of the Parisian Bourgeoisie, 1690–1830* (Cambridge, Mass.: Harvard University Press, 1996). A significant provincial study is Jean-Pierre Chaline, *Les bourgeois de Rouen: Une élite urbaine au XIXe siècle* (Paris: Presses de la Fondation Nationale des Sciences Politiques, 1982).

52. A. Guépin and E. Bonamy, *Nantes aux XIXe siècle: Statistique topographique, industrielle et morale* ([1835] Nantes: Université de Nantes, 1981), 277 (orig. pagination, 455).

53. See Louis Chevalier's classic, though criticized, *Laboring Classes and Dangerous Classes in Paris during the First Half of the Nineteenth Century*, trans. Frank Jellinek (New York: H. Fertig, 1973) and Barrie M. Ratcliffe, "Classes laborieuses et classes dangereuses pendant la première moitié du XIXe siècle? The Chevalier Thesis Reexamined," *French Historical Studies* (Fall 1991): 542–574.

54. Maurice Agulhon, "The Center and the Periphery," in *Rethinking France: Les Lieux de Mémoire*, vol. 1, *The State*, ed. Pierre Nora, trans. Mary Trouille (Chicago: University of Chicago Press, 2001), 61–64. John Merriman makes a similar argument in *The Margins of City Life: Exploration on the French Urban Frontier, 1815–1851* (Oxford: Oxford University Press, 1991).

55. Maza, *Myth of the French Bourgeoisie*, ch. 5. Citing Maza, Lenard Berlanstein has argued, "The bourgeoisie was born after the Bourbon Restoration, as a result of political and ideological conflict over how to rule postrevolutionary France." *Daughters of Eve: A Cultural History of French Theater Women from the Old Regime to the Fin de Siècle* (Cambridge, Mass.: Harvard University Press, 2001), 87.

56. On "bourgeois ideals" and domesticity, see McMillan, *France and Women*, 47–52; and Foley, *Women in France*, ch. 1.

## 1. Staging the Napoleonic State

1. AN F$^7$ 3681 (7), commissaire central to minister of the interior, 21 Ventôse Year VII (12 March 1799). On resistance to the *décadis*, see Mona Ozouf, *Festivals and the French Revolution*, trans. Alan Sheridan (Cambridge, Mass.: Harvard University Press, 1988), 228–229; and Howard G. Brown, "The Search for Stability," in *Taking Liberties: Problems of a New Order from the French Revolution to Napoleon*, ed. Howard G. Brown and Judith A. Miller (Manchester: Manchester University Press, 2002), 46.

2. AN F$^7$ 3681 (7), Minutes of 2nd Division Meeting, Situation Politique du Dép. de la Loire-Inférieure, 6 Germinal Year VII (27 March 1799).

3. See Suzanne Desan, *Reclaiming the Sacred: Lay Religion and Popular Politics in Revolutionary France* (Ithaca: Cornell University Press, 1990), 13.

4. S. de Naurois, "Les fêtes de pouvoir avant 1789," in B. de Andia et al., *Fêtes et Révolution* (Paris: Délégation à l'Action Artistique de la Ville de Paris, 1989), 43.

5. Little work has been done on Napoleonic festivals, but revolutionary festivals attracted a spate of attention in the 1970s. See Ozouf, *Festivals;* de Andia et al., *Fêtes et Révolution;* Jean Ehrard et al., *Les fêtes de la Révolution: Colloque de Clermont Ferrand (Juin 1974)* (Paris: Société des Etudes Robespierristes, 1977); and *Annales historiques de la Révolution française* 47, no. 221 (1975), which published papers given at the Clermont-Ferrand conference on revolutionary festivals. Despite its title, Michel Vovelle, *Les métamorphoses de la fête en Provence de 1750 à 1820* (Paris: Aubier/Flammarion, 1976) devotes scant attention to the evolution of festivals after 1799.

6. Lynn Hunt, *Politics, Culture, and Class in the French Revolution* (Berkeley: University of California Press, 1984), 229. Valuable analyses of the methods used by Napoleon and his supporters to build his image appear in Jean Tulard, *Napoleon: The Myth of the Savior,* trans. Teresa Waugh (London: Weidenfeld and Nicolson, 1984) and, more recently, Annie Jourdan, *Mythes et légendes de Napoléon: Un destin d'exception entre rêve et réalité* (Toulouse: Privat, 2004), ch. 1.

7. On Rouennais "moderation" during the Revolution, see Gavin Daly, *Inside Napoleonic France: State and Society in Rouen, 1800–1815* (Aldershot: Ashgate, 2001), 27–32.

8. On the effects of the Revolution on Rouen, see Claude Mazauric, "Une histoire urbaine dans la Révolution française: A Rouen rien ne change mais tout a changé," in *Pouvoir local et Révolution, 1780–1850: La frontière intérieure,* ed. Roger Dupuy (Rennes: Presses Universitaires de Rennes, 1995), 356. On Rouennais traits, particularly bourgeois perspectives on politics, see Jean-Pierre Chaline, *Les bourgeois de Rouen: Une élite urbaine au XIXe siècle* (Paris: Presses de la Fondation Nationale des Sciences Politiques, 1981), 97–100, 251–259.

9. On regional as opposed to national identities see Pierre-Yves Saunier, *L'esprit lyonnais XIXe–XXe siècles* (Paris: CNRS, 1995) and "La ville comme antidote? ou à la rencontre du troisième type (d'identité régionale)," in *Regional and National Identities in Europe in the XIXth and XXth Centuries,* ed. Heinz-Gerhard Haupt, Michael G. Müller, and Stuart Woolf (The Hague: Kluwer Law International, 1998).

10. Maurice Garden, "Effacement politique, contradictions culturelles et tensions sociales," in *Histoire de Lyon et du Lyonnais,* ed. André Latreille (Toulouse: Privat, 1975), 279.

11. Anne-Claire Déré, *Fêtes révolutionnaires à Nantes* (Nantes: Ouest Editions, 1989).

12. ADSM 1M 364, Rapport présenté à sa majesté impériale et royale par le ministre des cultes, le 19 février 1806, printed in circular to prefects from minister of the interior, 26 July 1806. The circular gave instructions for how to celebrate August 15th, the Fête de Saint-Napoléon.

13. Quoted in John Merriman, *A History of Modern Europe* (New York: Norton, 1996), 567. On the Civil Code and women's status see Xavier Martin, "Fonction paternelle et code Napoléon," *Annales historiques de la Révolution française*, no. 305 (1996): 471–475; and Jennifer Heuer and Anne Verjus, "L'invention de la sphère domestique au sortir de la Révolution," *Annales historiques de la Révolution française* 327 (2002): 25–27. In his examination of the biological arguments used to bolster "separate spheres" in postrevolutionary France, Robert Nye describes the Civil Code as "the legal apotheosis of . . . sexual separation and inequality," in *Masculinity and Male Codes of Honor in Modern France* (Berkeley: University of California Press, 1998), 55. A regional examination of the Napoleonic regime's treatment of women appears in Nicole Vray, *Les femmes dans l'Ouest au XIXe siècle, 1800–1870* ([Rennes]: Editions Ouest-France, 1990), 37–43.

14. According to Steven Kale, Napoleon viewed de Staël as a perpetual troublemaker. When her son tried to convince the emperor to allow her to return, he responded that "to talk of literature, morals, the fine arts, and everything under the sun is to indulge in politics. . . . Women should knit." Quoted in Kale, *French Salons: High Society and Political Sociability from the Old Regime to the Revolution of 1848* (Baltimore: Johns Hopkins University Press, 2004), 89.

15. Suzanne Desan makes a similar argument for the Directory period in *The Family on Trial in Revolutionary France* (Berkeley: University of California Press, 2004).

16. In an essay challenging standard views about the meaninglessness of Napoleonic elections, Malcolm Crook argues that "the preservation of the electoral system played a vital role in the process of political acculturation" but acknowledges that these were "elections without choice." "The Uses of Democracy: Elections and Plebiscites in Napoleonic France," in *The French Experience from Republic to Monarchy, 1792–1824: New Dawns in Politics, Knowledge, and Culture*, ed. Máire Cross and David Williams (Basingstoke: Palgrave, 2000), 58–71, quotation p. 68.

17. Ozouf, *Festivals*, 19. Ozouf's comments are based on her reading of Jules Michelet's *Le banquet* (Paris: Calmann-Lévy, 1879) and *Nos fils* (Paris: A. Lacroix, Verboekhoven, 1870). On more immediate reactions to women's presence in revolutionary festivals, see Ozouf, *Festivals*, 101. Ozouf's reading of Michelet foreshadows her argument in *Women's Words: Essay on French Singularity*, trans. Janet Marie Todd (Chicago: University of Chicago Press, 1997).

18. AMN I[1] 11, prefect to mayor, 4 Aug. 1807.

19. Malcolm Crook, *Napoleon Comes to Power: Democracy and Dictatorship in Revolutionary France, 1795–1804* (Cardiff: University of Wales Press, 1998), 72–73. In 1799, an official in Nantes complained: "The festival of the sovereignty of the people took place yesterday in a shabby manner considering the

wealth and size of this town." Two days later, the same official reported that "the indifference of the Nantais is inconceivable"; even the army's victories against England "create little sensation." AN F⁷ 3681 (7), commissaire central to minister of the Interior, 1 Germinal Year VII (22 March 1799) and 3 Germinal Year VI (24 March 1799). On the coup and the consolidation of the Napoleonic regime, see Isser Woloch, *Napoleon and His Collaborators: The Making of a Dictatorship* (New York: W. W. Norton, 2001).

20. AN F⁷ 3681 (7), miscellaneous correspondence, Years VII–IX (1799–1801).

21. A. Lloyd Moote, *Louis XIII, the Just* (Berkeley: University of California Press, 1989), 260. Solange Bidou refers to 15 August and the *vœu de Louis XIII* as the "'fête nationale' de l'Ancien Régime." "Les fêtes officielles à Charleville sous le Premier Empire," in *Fêtes et politiques en Champagne à travers les siècles,* ed. S. Guibert (Nancy: Presses Universitaires de Nancy, 1992), 112. Annie Jourdan argues that the mixture of the sacred and the profane exemplified by the festival of 15 August helped to produce an image of Napoleon as a demigod. See *Mythes et légendes de Napoléon,* 30–33. On Saint-Napoleon and religious propaganda during the Empire, see Barbara Ann Day-Hickman, *Napoleonic Art: Nationalism and the Spirit of Rebellion in France (1815–1848)* (Newark: University of Delaware Press, 1999), 93. Sudhir Hazareesingh's *The Saint-Napoleon: Celebrations of Sovereignty in Nineteenth-Century France* (Cambridge, Mass.: Harvard University Press, 2004) deals mostly with the Second Empire, but treats the earlier Saint-Napoleon festivities as background and as a memory invoked by Napoleon III's regime.

22. For a complete list of festivals, see the entry "Fêtes" in Alfred Fierro, André Palluel-Guillard, and Jean Tulard, *Histoire et dictionnaire du Consulat et de l'Empire* (Paris: Robert Laffont, 1995), 772; and Bidou, "Les fêtes officielles à Charleville," 111–118.

23. Jean-Paul Bois, *Histoire des 14 juillet 1789–1914* (Rennes: Editions Ouest-France, 1991), 100.

24. See Louis Bergeron, "Evolution de la fête révolutionnaire: Chronologie et typologie," *Annales historiques de la Révolution française* 47 (1975): 377–378 on the give-and-take between *fêtes populaires* and *fêtes officielles.* These trends have roots in the Old Regime. See Antoine de Baecque, "'Les ris et les pleurs.' Spectacles des affections 1790–1791," in *Fêtes et Révolution,* 149. According to the authors of the *Histoire et dictionnaire du Consulat et de l'Empire,* traditional local festivals brought greater pleasure than official ones: "To entertain citizens, there were also the official festivals where, under the direction of mayors and other authorities, balls, fireworks, parades, and releasing of balloons were organized: but their governmental and at times obligatory character removed much of their spontaneity and thus much of their pleasure. People amused themselves much more at familial, village, or local celebrations *(fêtes),*

[which were] more or less traditional [and] where they felt more at home *(entre soi)* to laugh, sing, drink and eat to excess *(s'empiffrer)*, and dance" (243).

25. Alan Forrest, "The Military Culture of Napoleonic France," in *Napoleon and Europe,* ed. Philip G. Dwyer (Harrow: Longman, 2001), 55.

26. ADLA 161 T 1, circular from the Baron de Pommereul, directeur général de l'Imprimerie et de la Librarie à MM les Imprimeurs, 30 June 1811.

27. *Feuille nantaise,* no. 108, 8 Jan. 1805.

28. Dances constituted part of Old Regime festivities, too. According to Abel Poitrineau, the eighteenth century brought "a great passion for dancing *(un véritable engouement pour la danse)."* "La Fête traditionnelle," in *Fêtes de la Révolution,* 16.

29. Père Letuaire, quoted in Malcolm Crook, *Toulon in War and Revolution* (Manchester: Manchester University Press, 1991), 207.

30. ADLA 1M 669, draft copy of letter from prefect to ministers of police and of the interior, 10 June 1811. Ozouf comments on the formulaic nature of such comments. Local officials would copy verbatim the language used in their orders, particularly phrases like "ordre et décence," which was used in the passage quoted here. *Festivals,* 305–306n46.

31. ADSM 1M 365, mayor to prefect, 22 March 1811.

32. AMN, I¹ 29, poster announcing locations of food distribution, 14 Nivôse Year XIII (4 Jan. 1805). Thirteen public squares were listed, as well as the hospital and prison.

33. AMN, I¹ 29, form letter from mayor to "Dame de Charité," 3 Dec. 1813. Women's charitable groups are discussed at greater length in Chapter 5.

34. AMN P¹ 8, poster announcing rules for Fête du 15 août 1806. The poster published for the Fête de la Naissance du Roi de Rome made similar specifications. AMN I¹ 30, 9 June 1811.

35. *Feuille nantaise,* no. 108, 8 Jan. 1805.

36. AMN I¹ 29, prefect to mayor, 24 Nov. 1813. This document dates from after Napoleon's defeat in the Russian campaign and the ensuing declaration of war by most of the European powers. Napoleon's defeat at Leipzig in October 1813 spelled the beginning of the end of Napoleon's reign. At this point it was clear that the regime was on its last legs; coffers were empty and public discontent was rising. See Jean-Paul Bertaud, *Le Consulat et l'Empire, 1799–1815* (Paris: Armand Colin, 1989), 119–122. On economic fluctuations during the period, see A. Chabert, *Essai sur les mouvements des revenus et de l'activité économique en France de 1798 à 1820* (Paris: Librairie de Médicis, 1949), 369–397.

37. Rouen was emerging as a center of cotton textile production during this period, and most of the *manufactures* were in such suburbs. See Chaline, *Les bourgeois de Rouen,* 102–112.

38. *Journal de Rouen et du département de la Seine-Inférieure,* no. 152, 1 June 1810.

39. *Journal de Rouen*, no. 154, 3 June 1810. My rendering of the event is also based on an account by the older sister of one of the girls who presented the basket. AML Fonds Vitet 84 II 11, letter from Amélie Vitet née Arnaud-Tizon to her husband, Pierre Vitet, 3 June 1810. On Napoleon's visit to the city, see Jean-Pierre Chaline, "Napoléon et Rouen," *Connaître Rouen* 5 (Boisguillaume, 1984): 8; and M. H. Geispitz, "Voyage de Napoléon Ier à Rouen en 1810," in *Bulletin de la Société Libre d'Emulation du Commerce et de l'Industrie de la Seine-Inférieure*, Exercises 1926, 1927 (Rouen, 1928).

40. Serge Charléty, "La vie politique à Lyon sous Napoléon Ier," *Revue d'histoire de Lyon* 4 (1905): 379.

41. Joseph Camelin, *Napoléon à Lyon* (Lyon: Anciens Etablissements Legendre, 1921), 33.

42. On the imperial court in Paris and elsewhere, see Claire de Rémusat, *Mémoires de Madame de Rémusat* (Paris: Les Amis de l'Histoire, 1968).

43. AML I$^1$ 155, handwritten account of the couple's stay in Lyon, 23 Germinal Year XIII (13 April 1805). A discussion of this visit can be found in Arthur Kleinclausz, *Histoire de Lyon*, Tome II de 1595 à 1814 (Lyon: Pierre Masson, 1948), 405.

44. Marie-Jeanne-Pierette Avrillon, *Mémoires de Mademoiselle Avrillon première femme de chambre de l'impératrice sur la vie privée de Joséphine, sa famille et sa cour* ([1833] Paris: Mercure, 1986), 90.

45. Much work has been done on Napoleon's efforts to build a group of "notables" who would be loyal to him, but none draws attention to the role of women in such projects. See Natalie Petiteau, *Elites et mobilités: La noblesse d'Empire au XIXe siècle (1808–1914)* (Paris: Boutique de l'Histoire, 1997); Jean Tulard, *Napoléon et la noblesse d'Empire* (Paris: Tallandier, 1986); Jean-Paul Bertaud, "Napoleon's Officers," *Past and Present* 112 (1986): 91–111; and Rafe Blaufarb, "The Social Contours of Meritocracy in the Napoleonic Officer Corps," in *Taking Liberties*, ed. Brown and Miller, 126–146. One study that does draw attention to women's roles in building this elite, though it extends its analysis well beyond the First Empire, is Rebecca Rogers, *Les demoiselles de la Légion d'honneur: Les maisons d'éducation de la Légion d'honneur au XIXe siècle* (Paris: Plon, 1992).

46. According to Madame de Rémusat, Napoleon was bored even when surrounded by a hand-picked group of courtiers at Fontainebleau. He always seemed to want to say, "Let's go, ladies and gentlemen, forward, march!" Talleyrand described him as "the 'unamusable' one" *(l'inamusable)*. *Mémoires de Madame de Rémusat*, 363.

47. *Journal de Rouen*, no. 151, 31 May 1810.

48. AML Fonds Vitet 84 II 11, letter from Amélie Vitet to Pierre Vitet, Rouen, 31 May [1810]. This collection includes a large number of this family's letters. Although they were far from happy about the frequent wars during the Empire and the resulting disruption of commerce, the family generally supported

the Napoleonic government. For more on the family, see my "Pleasure and Politics in Rouen: Bourgeois Provincial Sociability, 1805–1816," *Proceedings of the Western Society for French History* 28 (2002): 364–371.

49. AML Fonds Vitet 84 II 11, letter from Amélie Vitet to Pierre Vitet, Rouen, 31 May [1810].

50. See Frédéric Masson, *L'Impératrice Marie-Louise* (Paris: Goupil et Cie, 1902), 83–84; and Henri d'Alméras, *La vie parisienne sous le Consulat et l'Empire* (Paris: Albin Michel, [1909]), 273. According to one biographer, Marie-Louise's "lack of manners" was "due almost entirely to intense shyness." Patrick Turnbull, *Napoleon's Second Empress* (New York: Walker and Co., 1971), 74. When she returned to Rouen in 1813, Marie-Louise was snubbed by the elite and ignored by the popular classes, indicating the people's dissatisfaction with both the empress and the regime. Daly, *Inside Napoleonic France*, 253–254.

51. Bauche lived from 1797 to 1867. For biographical information, see André Dubuc, "Une Rouennaise de 1837 face à son passé," in *La femme en Normandie: Actes du XIXe congrès des sociétés historiques et archéologiques de Normandie* (Caen: Archives Départementales du Calvados, 1986), 350–353.

52. ADSM 1 Mi 1137, Souvenirs d'Adélaïde Bauche, 158. Cited (with some changes in language) in Dubuc, "Une Rouennaise de 1837," 356–357.

53. Dubuc, "Une Rouennaise de 1837," 356.

54. Julie Pellizzone, *Souvenirs,* vol. 1 *(1781–1815),* ed. Pierre Echinard, Hélène Echinard, and Georges Reynaud (Paris: Indigo et Côté-femmes, 1995), 394.

55. Isser Woloch refers to Napoleon as a "masterly manipulator of public opinion." *Napoleon and His Collaborators,* 135.

56. On 25 Messidor Year VIII (14 July 1800), the mothers, sisters, widows, and daughters of men killed in battle paraded through Lyon. AML I¹ 155, prefect to deputy mayor of northern division of Lyon, 22 Messidor Year VIII (11 July 1800).

57. ADSM 1M 364, speech dated 4 Dec. 1808.

58. Ibid.

59. See Maurice Agulhon, *Marianne into Battle: Republican Imagery and Symbolism in France, 1789–1880,* trans. Janet Lloyd (Cambridge: Cambridge University Press, 1981). Hunt discusses the use of female allegorical figures during the Revolution in *Politics, Culture, and Class,* 60–65, 118–119.

60. ADSM 1M 364, speech dated 4 Dec. 1808.

61. Sarah Maza, *Private Lives and Public Affairs: The Causes Célèbres of Prerevolutionary France* (Berkeley: University of California Press, 1993), 69.

62. Ozouf, *Festivals,* 51.

63. Lynn Hunt, *The Family Romance of the French Revolution* (Berkeley: University of California Press, 1992), 154. On images of the family in revolutionary festivals, see Desan, *The Family on Trial,* 75–80.

64. Reprinted in Edmond-Jacques Chardon, *Dix ans de fêtes nationales et de cérémonies publiques à Rouen 1790–1799* (Rouen: Léon Gy, 1911), 268.

65. One occurrence of the term "rosière" appears in "Fête du Couronnement à Nantes," *Feuille nantaise,* no. 108, 8 Jan. 1805.

66. On hostility toward the draft, see Isser Woloch, *The New Regime: Transformations of the French Civic Order, 1789–1820s* (New York: W. W. Norton, 1994), 418–426. Woloch expresses surprise at the state's ability to finally prevail over resistance to conscription (424). Perhaps these festivals contributed to that endeavor.

67. Here, too, we can see continuities with revolutionary festivals. Anne-Claire Déré found that at the first anniversary of the fall of the Bastille, "the roles for the festival were already irrevocably distributed; for women tenderness, sweetness, and purity." *Fêtes révolutionnaires à Nantes,* 11.

68. AML I¹ 155, vice president of benevolent committee to deputy-mayor of southern section, 23 Brumaire Year XIII (14 Nov. 1804). On problems finding suitable couples in Champagne, see Bidou, "Les fêtes officielles à Charleville," 115–116.

69. ADLA 1M 669, mayor to prefect, 28 Nov. 1807.

70. "*Filles pauvres mais 'vertueuses'* " were selected to receive more than 6000 dowries of 600 francs which were distributed in honor of the emperor's marriage. Olivier Ihl, *La fête républicaine* (Paris: Gallimard, 1996), 80. For Lyon, the sources disagree with Ihl on the amount of the dowry, but not on the criteria for choosing brides. Ihl also discusses the "*universalisation* of civic participation. . . . Everyone, without exception, was convoked for these civic raptures *(transports civiques)*" (80).

71. AML I¹ 156, minutes of Conseil Municipal, meeting of 24 March 1810.

72. ADSM 1M 364, copy of mayor's speech, 2 Dec. 1810.

73. AML I¹ 156, report on the celebration, 8 April 1810.

74. AML I¹ 156, poster listing police ordinances for festival of 29 April 1810. See also Kleinclausz, *Histoire de Lyon,* 415–417. For details on such games and other activities, see Claude Ruggieri, *Précis historique sur les fêtes, les spectacles et les réjouissances publiques* (Paris: L'Auteur, 1830), 181–205.

75. In his study of Italian Communism, David Kertzer emphasizes a similar point about the ability of ritual to create and renew bonds of solidarity, regardless of whether the desired message was thoroughly absorbed. "Less well appreciated is the fact that ritual produces such solidarity without presupposing that the people involved actually interpret the rite in the same way. . . . While some [participants at a Communist gathering] see the rally as a step toward bringing about the end of capitalism, others view it simply as a pleasant way to spend an evening." *Politics and Symbols: The Italian Communist Party and the Fall of Communism* (New Haven: Yale University Press, 1996), 129.

76. ADLA 1M 669, prefect to the ministers of police and of the interior, 10 June 1811.

77. Charléty, "La vie politique à Lyon," 383–384. This "dialogue" appears as an attachment to the mayor's prepared speech, a document dated 9 June 1811 and held in AML I¹ 156.

78. ADLA 161 T 1, circular from the Baron de Pommereul, directeur général de l'Imprimerie et de la Librairie à MM les Imprimeurs, 30 June 1811.

79. AML I¹ 156, copy of mayor's speech, 25 Aug. 1813.

80. Robert Alexander, *Re-Writing the French Revolutionary Tradition* (Cambridge: Cambridge University Press, 2003), 8.

81. *Journal de Nantes et du département de la Loire-Inférieure,* no. 667, 1 Aug. 1815.


## 2. Renewing Ties with the Bourbon Monarchy

1. AMN, I¹ 11, mayor's proclamation, Nantes, 11 March 1815. A copy of the proclamation is also held at the Médiathèque de Nantes, bound with the *Journal de Nantes et du département de la Loire-Inférieure* of 1815.

2. M. de Maisonfort, quoted in Ernest Sevrin, *Les missions religieuses en France sous la Restauration,* vol. 2, *Les Missions (1815–1820)* (Paris: Vrin, 1959), 40.

3. See Sheryl Kroen, *Politics and Theater: The Crisis of Legitimacy in Restoration France, 1815–1830* (Berkeley: University of California Press, 2000) and Françoise Waquet, *Les fêtes royales sous la Restauration, ou l'Ancien Régime retrouvé* (Geneva: Droz, 1981). Both provide extensive information on festival activities, goals, successes, and failures. Waquet focuses solely on Paris, whereas Kroen's work deals mostly with the provinces. Kroen refers to the largely unsuccessful Restoration efforts to erase the memory of the Revolution, as a "politics of *oubli.*" See her *Politics and Theater,* ch. 1 and "Revolutionizing Religious Politics during the Restoration," *French Historical Studies* 21 (1998): 27–53. Often, the regime's vehement supporters frustrated this policy of "forgetting." See Raymond Jonas, *France and the Cult of the Sacred Heart: An Epic Tale for Modern Times* (Berkeley: University of California Press, 2000), 119.

4. ADLA 1M 670, poster dated 22 Aug. 1818. Under Napoleon, authorities made as many as thirteen locations for distributions of free food and wine available. The Bourbons were less willing to spend the money needed to pay for the food; they also feared having too many locations at which potentially unruly crowds gathered.

5. Waquet, *Fêtes royales,* 155.

6. AML 2 Mi 52, 6 Fi 05934 (microfilm), poster announcing the return of the king's brother, 23 Sept. 1814.

7. Sharif Gemie, *Women and Schooling in France, 1815–1914: Gender, Authority, and Identity in the Female Schooling Sector* (Keele: Keele University Press, 1995), 60–61.

8. *L'ami de la Charte: Journal politique, littéraire et d'avis de Nantes* 98, 14 Feb. 1820. The year 1815 brought the "Second" Restoration, when the Bourbons returned following Napoleon's failed attempt to come back to power after being sent into exile. Marked by reprisals against Jacobins and Bonapartists, known as the "White Terror," the atmosphere of the early Second Restoration made it possible for "ultra" monarchists to undermine the more moderate constitutional monarchy established by the Charter of 1814.

9. *Journal de Nantes*, no. 235, 24 May 1814.

10. *Journal de Nantes*, no. 191, 10 April 1814, and no. 192, 11 April 1814.

11. *Journal de Nantes*, no. 247, 5 June 1814, and no. 248, 6 June 1814.

12. *Journal de Nantes*, no. 331, 26 Aug. 1814.

13. Julie Pellizzone, *Souvenirs*, vol. 1 *(1781–1815)*, transcribed and annotated by Hélène Echinard and Georges Reynaud (Paris: Indigo and Côté-femmes, 1995), 364.

14. P. Tezenas de Montcel, "Journal de Mlle Audouard de Monviol," *Revue d'histoire de Lyon* (1911): 100.

15. Olwen H. Hufton, "In Search of Counter-Revolutionary Women," in *Women and the Limits of Citizenship in the French Revolution* (Toronto: University of Toronto Press, 1992) provides many rich examples that help to illuminate how and why so many women resisted the Revolution.

16. Pellizzone, *Souvenirs*, 1: 366–367.

17. Ibid., 370.

18. Pellizzone, *Souvenirs: Journal d'une Marseillaise*, vol. 2 *(1815–1824)*, transcribed by Hélène Echinard, introduced and annotated by Pierre Echinard, Hélène Echinard, and Georges Reynaud (Paris: Indigo and Côté-femmes, 2001), 87.

19. Carla Hesse, *The Other Enlightenment: How French Women Became Modern* (Princeton: Princeton University Press, 2001), ch. 1.

20. Waquet, *Fêtes royales*, 34, 92–95.

21. ADLA 1M 670, *Procès-verbal du passage du duc d'Angoulême* (Nantes, 1814), 7, 12–13. Julie Pellizzone recounts a similar visit by the duke and duchess de Berry in Marseille in July 1814. *Souvenirs*, 1: 409–421. For a description of the royal family in 1814, see Guillaume Bertier de Sauvigny, *The Bourbon Restoration*, trans. Lynn M. Case (Philadelphia: University of Pennsylvania Press, 1966), 57–60.

22. ADLA 1M 670, *Procès-verbal du passage du duc d'Angoulême*, 11.

23. AML I¹ 157A, poem read to the duchesse d'Angoulême while she was visiting Lyon's library.

24. *Procès-verbal de l'arrivée et du séjour à Lyon de SAR le comte d'Artois frère du roi* (Lyon, 1814), 7. Both the comte d'Artois and the duchesse d'Angoulême were ultras, members of the Restoration's extreme right, and hated all the Revolution stood for. See Georges Ribe, *L'opinion publique et la vie politique à Lyon lors des premières années de la seconde Restauration* (Paris: Librairie du Recueil Sirey, 1957), 7–8.

25. *Procès-verbal de l'arrivée et du séjour à Lyon de SAR le comte d'Artois,* 10, 22.

26. Ibid., 60. Pellizzone recounts similar scenes from the comte d'Artois' visit to Marseille a month later. "During the evening he attended the theater, the seats were filled by 3 P.M. He only arrived at 8:00 . . . [but] the prince stayed until the end." The next day he visited the city's *manufactures. Souvenirs,* 1: 449–450.

27. Gérard Chauvy and Serge Blanchon, *Histoire des Lyonnais: Forez, Bugey, Dombes, Gex* (Paris: Fernand Nathan, 1981), 205.

28. "Le vœu accompli: Vers adressés aux dames de Lyon, qui ont fait un vœu pour le retour du Roi, et récités au Grand-Théâtre de Lyon, le 25 Août 1815." (Pamphlet held in AML, code 656.)

29. *Journal de Nantes,* no. 667, 1 Aug. 1815.

30. Steven D. Kale, "Women, Salons, and the State in the Aftermath of the French Revolution," *Journal of Women's History* 13 (2002): 71–72.

31. Letter from mayor to minister of the interior dated 10 Jan. 1816, *Journal de Nantes,* no. 842, 30 Jan. 1816.

32. *Madame la duchesse d'Angoulême à Nantes les 19, 20, 21, 22 septembre 1823* (Nantes: Mellinet-Melassis, 1823), 7. (Held in ADLA 1M 671.)

33. ADLA 1M 671, "Extrait d'une lettre sur le passage et le séjour de madame, duchesse d'Angoulême, dans le département de la Loire-Inférieure," Nantes, 24 Sept. 1823, 10–11.

34. Ibid., 11.

35. Due to a series of unexpected circumstances, Louis XVIII never managed to stage a coronation for himself, but Charles X made every effort to ensure that his coronation, which took place in Reims Catheral on 29 May 1825, would invoke every possible Bourbon tradition. See Kroen, *Politics and Theater,* 116–120.

36. *Journal du commerce,* no. 230, 10 June 1825.

37. ADLA 1M 671, mayor to prefect, 1 June 1825.

38. Ibid.

39. ADLA 1M 671, president of Société Académique to prefect, 22 Jan. 1825.

40. Waquet, *Fêtes royales,* 149.

41. AMN I¹ 30, booklet describing the Fête du Baptême du duc de Bordeaux, 1 May 1821, and poster announcing it, 25 April 1821.

42. AMN I¹ 11, poster announcing events for 25 Aug. 1814 and AML 2 Mi 52, 6 Fi 05923 (microfilm), poster announcing events for 25 Aug. 1814.

43. AML 2 Mi 52, 6 Fi 05942 (microfilm), poster announcing events for 20 Aug. 1819. "Nightfall" in August would have meant nearly 10 P.M., too.

44. AML I¹ 157A, "Dispositions relatives à la réception de S.A.R. Madame la duchesse d'Angoulême, . . ." and AML 2 Mi 52, 6 Fi 05915 (microfilm), poster announcing events to be held during the duchesse d'Angoulême's visit, 3 Aug. 1814.

45. *Journal de Nantes*, no. 285, 20 Oct. 1823. For details on what took place at Parisian balls organized by the Bourbons, see Waquet, *Fêtes royales*, 64–65, 152–153.

46. On Boilly's art as social commentary and his capacity to reveal a bourgeois "disdain for *le peuple*," see Susan L. Siegfried, *The Art of Louis-Léopold Boilly: Modern Life in Napoleonic France* (New Haven: Yale University Press, 1995), 54.

47. AN F⁷ 9898, "Fête aux Champs-Elysées, rapport," 3 Nov. 1825, cited in Waquet, *Fêtes royales*, 148.

48. On depictions of heterogeneous crowds, see my "Making Society 'Legible': People-Watching in Paris after the Revolution," *French Historical Studies* 28 (2005): 265–296. On the growing desire for separate spaces for distinct social groups, see Victoria E. Thompson, "Telling 'Spatial Stories': Urban Space and Bourgeois Identity in Early Nineteenth-Century Paris," *Journal of Modern History* 75 (2003): 523–566.

49. Much work has been done on women's roles in food riots. One example is Cynthia A. Bouton, *The Flour War: Gender, Class, and Community in Late Ancien Régime French Society* (University Park: Pennsylvania State University Press, 1993). During the Enlightenment, "women came to be seen as a civilizing force that tempered the violent and destructive behavior of men." James Van Horn Melton, *The Rise of the Public in Enlightenment Europe* (Cambridge: Cambridge University Press, 2001), 203.

50. Philippe Le Bas, *Dictionnaire encyclopédique de l'histoire de France* (Paris: F. Didot Frères, 1840–1845), quoted in Emmanuel Lemaire, *Les fêtes publiques à Saint-Quentin pendant la Révolution et sous le Premier Empire* (Saint-Quentin: Jules Moreau et fils, 1884), 215–216.

51. Lemaire, *Les fêtes publiques,* 217. Both Lemaire's and Le Bas' commentaries in many ways shed more light on Third Republic sensibilities about the "crowd" than about what actually took place during the Empire and the Restoration. See Suzanna Barrows, *Distorting Mirrors: Visions of the Crowd in Late Nineteenth-Century France* (New Haven: Yale University Press, 1981).

52. AMN I¹ 11, letter prefect to mayor, 9 Oct. 1815.

53. *Journal de Nantes*, no. 331, 26 Aug. 1814.

54. According to F. W. J. Hemmings, "Probably because of the deep-seated unease felt by the governing classes in France at this period, confronting a discontented

proletariat suffering wage-cuts and layoffs as the industrial revolution gathered pace, free performances for the working class seem to have been discontinued later in the Restoration and were not resumed under Louis-Philippe." *The Theatre Industry in Nineteenth-Century France* (Cambridge: Cambridge University Press, 1993), 120.

55. AML 2 Mi 52, 6 Fi 05944 (microfilm), poster announcing program of events, 11 April 1821.

56. AML 2 Mi 52, 6 Fi 05946 (microfilm), poster announcing Fête de Saint-Charles, 23 Oct. 1826. Catherine Duprat discusses depictions of the Bourbons performing charitable deeds in *Usage et pratiques de la philanthropie: Pauvreté, action sociale et lien social, à Paris, au cours du premier XIXe siècle,* vol. 2 (Paris: Association pour l'Etude de l'Histoire de la Sécurité Sociale, 1997), 982–987.

57. AMN I$^1$ 30, poster announcing fête du mariage du duc de Berry, 17 June 1816. In a contradictory example, sixteen young women received dowries from the city of Paris in 1821 at the celebration for the duc de Bordeaux's baptism on 30 April. *Relation des fêtes données par la ville de Paris et de toutes les cérémonies qui ont eu lieu dans la capitale à l'occasion de la naissance et du baptême de son altesse royale Monseigneur le duc de Bordeaux* (Paris: Petit, 1822). (Held in AMN I$^1$ 30.) This appears to have been the one Restoration festival for which wedding ceremonies were deemed suitable.

58. *Relation des fêtes données par la ville de Paris,* 46. AML 2 Mi 52, 6 Fi 05944 (microfilm), poster announcing the program for the celebrations of the baptism, 11 April 1821.

59. AMN I$^1$ 30, copy of papers given to parents of these children dated 1 May 1821.

60. L'abbé Ernest Sevrin, *Les missions religieuses en France sous la Restauration (1815–1830),* vol. 1, *Le missionnaire et la mission* (Saint-Mandé: Procure des Prêtres de la Miséricorde, 1948), 254. Jonas analyzes these missions as spectacular events meant to emphasize "a dramatic break with the past" in *France and the Cult of the Sacred Heart,* 124–129.

61. *Discours sur le prix de vertu, prononcé dans la séance publique du 25 août 1824 par le comte de Sèze, directeur* (Paris: Firmin Didot, 1824). (Held in ADLA 1M 468.)

62. ADLA 1M 468, prefect to sous-préfets et maires du département, 23 Dec. 1824.

63. Adélaide-Gilette Billet Dufrénoy, *Biographie des jeunes demoiselles, ou vies des femmes célèbres depuis les Hébreux,* vol. 1 (Paris: Eymery, 1816), iv. Mid-eighteenth-century authors expressed similar views toward male and female virtues; many believed women had a special affinity for benevolence. See Marisa Linton, "Virtue Rewarded? Women and the Politics of Virtue in Eighteenth-Century France, Part II," *History of European Ideas* 26 (2000): 51–65. On connections between evolving gender norms and the issue of

sentiment, see William M. Reddy, *The Invisible Code: Honor and Sentiment in Postrevolutionary France, 1814–1848* (Berkeley: University of California Press, 1997).

64. On Montyon, see Duprat, *Usage et pratiques de la philanthropie,* 2: 975.

65. The December 2002 speech by Marc Fumaroli, which includes a history of the prize, is available at the website of the Académie française, http://www .academie-francaise.fr/ (accessed 20 February 2006).

66. Quoted in Duprat, *Usage et pratiques de la philanthropie,* 2: 675.

67. Ibid., 982.

68. [Elizabeth-Félicie Bayle-Mouillard], *La bonne cousine, ou conseils de l'amitié par Mme Elisabeth Celnart* (Paris: Villet, 1822), ii–iv. "Virtue" was a frequent trope in early American literature as well. See Carroll Smith-Rosenberg, "Domesticating 'Virtue': Coquettes and Revolutionaries in Young America," in *Literature and the Body: Essays on Populations and Persons,* ed. Elaine Scarry (Baltimore: Johns Hopkins University Press, 1988).

69. Olivier Ihl, *La fête républicaine* (Paris: Gallimard, 1996), 58. Other works on the long-term evolution of political festivals in France include Jean-Pierre Bois, *Histoire des 14 juillet 1789–1914* (Rennes: Editions Ouest-France, 1991); Alain Corbin, Noëlle Gérome, and Danelle Tartakowsky, eds., *Les usages politiques des fêtes aux XIXe–XXe siècles: Actes du colloque organisé les 22 et 23 novembre 1990 à Paris* (Paris: Publications de la Sorbonne, [1994]); and Matthew Truesdell, *Spectacular Politics: Louis-Napoleon Bonaparte and the Fête Impériale, 1849–1870* (Oxford: Oxford University Press, 1997).

70. These events continued revolutionary precedents. According to Anne-Claire Déré, the "grands spectacles" staged in Nantes during the Year 2 incorporated parades of ordinary people early in the day and then "*illuminations, danses et spectacles*" in the evening. *Fêtes révolutionnaires à Nantes* (Nantes: Ouest Editions, 1989), 21–25.

71. For an examination of prerevolutionary attitudes toward festivals, see Jean Ehrard, "Le peuple en fête avant la Révolution," in B. de Andia et al., *Fêtes et Révolution* (Paris: Délégation à l'Action Artistique de la Ville de Paris, 1989), 24–35.

72. Mona Ozouf, *Festivals and the French Revolution,* trans. Alan Sheridan (Cambridge, Mass.: Harvard University Press, 1988), 25.

73. On the importance of the Restoration period in cementing a broad, popular movement—devotion to the sacred heart—defined by its animosity to the revolutionary/republican tradition and that involved many women at the grassroots level, see Jonas, *France and the Cult of the Sacred Heart,* 118–146. On the problematic relationship between women and republicanism because of their supposed propensity toward religiosity, see Joan Wallach Scott, *Only Paradoxes to Offer: French Feminists and the Rights of Man* (Cambridge, Mass.: Harvard University Press, 1996), 102–103.

## 3. Melodramatic Spectatorship on the Parisian Boulevard

1. Peter Hervé, *How to Enjoy Paris: Being a Guide to the Visitor of the French Metropolis*, vol. 1 (London, 1816), 51–54. This atmosphere is echoed in Jules Bertaut, *La vie à Paris sous le Premier Empire* (Paris: Editions Balzac, 1943), 14. For analysis of "exotic" themes in Boulevard plays, with parallels to the reference to "Arabian tales," see Angela C. Pao, *The Orient of the Boulevards: Exoticism, Empire, and Nineteenth-Century French Theater* (Philadelphia: University of Pennsylvania Press, 1998).

2. Hyppolyte Auger, *Physiologie du théâtre*, vol. 2 (Paris: Didot Frères, 1839), 51.

3. On eighteenth-century Boulevard theater, see Robert M. Isherwood, *Farce and Fantasy: Popular Entertainment in Eighteenth-Century Paris* (New York: Oxford University Press, 1986), ch. 7; and Michèle Root-Bernstein, *Boulevard Theater and Revolution in Eighteenth-Century Paris* (Ann Arbor: UMI Research Press, 1984). On the evolution of "bourgeois drama" into melodrama, see Sarah Maza, *Private Lives and Public Affairs: The Causes Célèbres of Prerevolutionary France* (Berkeley: University of California Press, 1993), 61–67. Vanessa Schwartz traces the evolution of Boulevard culture into the late nineteenth century in *Spectacular Realities: Early Mass Culture in Fin-de-Siècle Paris* (Berkeley: University of California Press, 1998), 16–26.

4. The author of an 1809 discussion of the genre insisted that M. Cuvelier was the first playwright to bring what would be termed melodrama to the Boulevard, though he admits that Pixérécourt was "the most profilic and indefatigable of all the authors who devoted their talents to the boulevards." Armand Charlemagne, *Le mélodrame aux boulevards: Facétie littéraire, historique et dramatique* (Paris: l'Imprimerie de la rue Beaurepaire, 1809), 21. Edmond Estève agrees with the playwright's appellation as "the father of melodrama," and "the Corneille of the Boulevard" in his *Etudes de littérature préromantique* (Paris: Librairie Ancienne Honoré Champion, 1923), 152. Estève also provides a brief biographical discussion of the playwright and an examination of his influence and his milieu (139–168).

5. Frederick Brown, *Theater and Revolution: The Culture of the French Stage* (New York: Viking, 1980), 89–90.

6. Sharon Marcus, *Apartment Stories: City and Home in Nineteenth-Century Paris and London* (Berkeley: University of California Press, 1999), 17–18. For Marcus, even domestic space was open to urban observers.

7. "Cadet Buteux au boulevard du Temple," reprinted in Henri d'Alméras, *La vie parisienne sous le Consulat et l'Empire* (Paris: Albin Michel, [1909]), 47–50.

8. *Journal des dames et des modes*, 25 Thermidor Year XII (13 Aug. 1805), quoted in Alphonse Aulard, *Paris sous le Premier Empire: Recueil de documents pour l'histoire de l'esprit public à Paris*, vol. 2 (Paris: Cerf, 1914), 115–116. A long-needed

complete history of this publication has appeared: Annemarie Kleinert, Le "Journal des dames et des modes," ou la conquête de l'Europe féminine (1797–1839) (Stuttgart: Verlag, 2001).

9. According to a history of Restoration Paris, there were few convenient places to go for a stroll, which explains the "importance in the social life of the period of two privileged spaces: The Boulevard and the Palais Royal." Guillaume Bertier de Sauvigny, Nouvelle histoire de Paris: La Restauration, 1815–1830 (Paris: Hachette, 1977), 379.

10. ADLA 133 J 43 Fonds Louis Bouchaud letter dated 21 Sept. 1821. "Grandes poupées" was underlined in the original. I am grateful to Monsieur Gabriel Perchet for his permission to read and cite these letters.

11. On this notion of the city as a site of consumption, see Rebecca L. Spang, The Invention of the Restaurant: Paris and Modern Gastronomic Culture (Cambridge, Mass.: Harvard University Press, 2000), ch. 6. Spang also discusses women's presence in Parisian restaurants and foreigners' surprised reaction to this fact (199–202).

12. Guide de l'étranger dans Paris (Paris: Barba, 1805), 124. Some of the petits spectacles listed here were "les grands phantocchini, les ombres chinoises, le cabinet de Curtius, les chanteurs, les baladins, les paillasses, les danseurs de corde, les escamoteurs, etc." Not insignificantly, the publisher of this guide, Barba, also published most of the plays performed at Boulevard theaters. On guidebooks as historical sources and a literary genre, see Priscilla Parkhurst Ferguson, Paris as Revolution: Writing the Nineteenth-Century City (Berkeley: University of California Press, 1994).

13. Victor Fournel, Le vieux Paris: Fêtes, jeux, spectacles (Tours, 1887) quoted in Bertier de Sauvigny, Nouvelle histoire de Paris, 374.

14. Schwartz, Spectacular Realities.

15. It has been estimated that Parisian drinking establishments numbered between three thousand and four thousand in 1800. See Henry-Melchior de Langle, Le petit monde des cafés et débits parisiens au XIXe siècle: Evolution de la sociabilité citadine (Paris: Presses Universitaires de France, 1990), 14; and Scott Haine, The World of the Paris Café: Sociability among the French Working Class, 1789–1914 (Baltimore: Johns Hopkins University Press, 1996), 3. Contemporary estimates of their numbers include: "more than 3,000" (P. Villiers, Manuel du voyageur à Paris ou Paris ancien et moderne [Paris: Delaunay, 1811], 239); "more than 2,500" (Voyage descriptif et historique de Paris, vol. 1 [Paris: l'Auteur, 1814], 12); and "more than 1,000 cafés" (Le guide du voyageur à Paris [Paris: Dabo, 1814], 377).

16. Décade philosophique 10 Fructidor Year VIII (28 Aug. 1800), quoted in Charles Simond [pseud.], La vie parisienne à travers le XIXe siècle: Paris de 1800 à 1900 d'après les estampes et les mémoires du temps, vol. 1, 1800–1830, Le Consulat,

*le Premier Empire, la Restauration* (Paris: Plon, 1900), 7–8. An engraving entitled "Departure for Frascati," which depicts a self-possessed woman wearing a transparent, breast-exposing dress with a long train and examining herself in a mirror while a man looks on "in awe or stupefaction," is reproduced and analyzed in Ewa Lajer-Burcharth, *Necklines: The Art of Jacques-Louis David after the Terror* (New Haven: Yale University Press, 1999), 261.

17. *Le cicérone ou l'indicateur de Paris* (Paris: Debray, 1811), 382.

18. Louis Gabriel Montigny, *Le provincial à Paris: Esquisses des mœurs parisiennes,* vol. 1 (Paris: Ladvocat, 1825), 213.

19. Louis-Sébastien Mercier, *Tableau de Paris,* quoted in David Garrioch, *Neighborhood and Community in Paris, 1740–1790* (Cambridge: Cambridge University Press, 1986), 192–193.

20. *Journal des dames et des modes,* vol. 20, no. 54, 30 Sept. 1816, 426.

21. Peter Brooks, *The Melodramatic Imagination: Balzac, Henry James, Melodrama, and the Mode of Excess* ([1976] New Haven: Yale University Press, 1995), 11–16.

22. Julia Przybos, *L'entreprise mélodramatique* (Paris: José Corti, 1987), 173. Przybos argues that melodrama represented the first modern, "industrial" form of mass culture. See also Jean-Marie Thomasseau, *Le mélodrame* (Paris: Presses Universitaires de France, 1984). Thomasseau coined the term "classical melodrama" for plays written between 1800 and 1823, but Przybos argues it may be applied to those created until about 1830.

23. According to Przybos, "melodramas always portray a harmoniously hierarchical social order. In this stratified universe, everyone is quick to fulfill the role to which they were assigned at birth." *L'entreprise mélodramatique,* 63.

24. Brooks, *Melodramatic Imagination,* 11–13.

25. Ibid., 20.

26. See the AHR Forum built around Lawrence W. Levine, "The Folklore of Industrial Society: Popular Culture and Its Audiences," *American Historical Review* 97 (1992): 1369–1399, with essays by Robin Kelly, Natalie Davis, and Jackson Lears. Focusing on 1930s radio, Levine argues that though consumers did not create mass-produced culture, they chose which to support and which to ignore. The impact of consumers in melodramatic theater was even more direct than for later forms of popular culture.

27. A discussion of these issues appears in Pao, *The Orient of the Boulevards,* 6–14.

28. Przybos, *L'entreprise mélodramatique,* 29. On the power and influence of journalists in shaping these plays, see ibid., 24–25.

29. Marie-Antoinette Allévy discusses the great effort and expense involved in creating these backdrops in *La mise en scène en France dans la première moitié du dix-neuvième siècle* ([1938] Geneva: Slatkine Reprints, 1976), 23–29. One of the important theatrical artists was Louis Jacques Mande Daguerre. After

working at the Ambigu-Comique, he would go on to invent an early form of photography, the daguerreotype. Ibid., 41–50.

30. *Le miroir des spectacles, des lettres, des mœurs et des arts,* no. 228, 29 Sept. 1821.

31. *Le miroir des spectacles,* no. 150, 13 July 1821.

32. *Traité du mélodrame, par MM. A! A! A!* [Abel Hugo, Armand Malitourne, J. Adler] (Paris: Delaunay, 1817), 35–37. "MM." is the abbreviation for "*messieurs*" or "misters" and "A! A! A!" is pronounced in French as "Ah! Ah! Ah!" A discussion of this pamphlet appears in John McCormick, *Popular Theatres of Nineteenth-Century France* (London: Routledge, 1993), 166.

33. Paul Ginisty, *Le mélodrame* (Paris: Louis-Michaud, [1910]), 14.

34. René-Charles Guilbert de Pixérécourt, *Cœlina ou l'enfant de mystère* (Paris, 1801), 37.

35. *Gazette de France,* no. 2814, 12 Vendémiaire Year XIV (4 Oct. 1805).

36. *Courrier des spectacles,* no. 2253, 17 Floréal Year XI (8 May 1803). On the eighteenth-century forerunners of such techniques, see Isabelle Martin, *Le théâtre de la foire: Des tréteaux aux boulevards* (SVEC 2002:10) (Oxford: Voltaire Foundation, 2002), ch. 5.

37. *Courrier des spectacles,* no. 2982, 25 Germinal Year XIII (15 April 1805).

38. According to Brooks, melodramatic rhetoric functioned similarly: "Such bombastic sublimity forcibly removes us—and no doubt is intended to remove us—from the plane of actuality, to place us in a more rarefied atmosphere where each statement is a total and coherent gesture toward the representation of the cosmic moral drama." *Melodramatic Imagination,* 40–41. The emphasis on the technical side of performances, which was often truly innovative for the period despite seeming simplistic today, brings to mind the fascination with technical effects in 1980s and 1990s science-fiction and adventure films like *The Terminator,* and more recently, films like *The Matrix.*

39. Brooks, *Melodramatic Imagination,* 32–33. Brooks makes no attempt to explain this preference for female characters. See also James L. Smith, *Melodrama* (London: Methuen, 1973), 1–3. The association of virtue with women can be found in the Prix de Vertu discussed in Chapter 2.

40. Doris Kadish, *Politicizing Gender: Narrative Strategies in the Aftermath of the French Revolution* (New Brunswick, N.J.: Rutgers University Press, 1991), 9.

41. I analyze such prescriptive literature in "*Bonnes Lectures:* Improving Women and Society through Literature in Post-Revolutionary France," in *The French Experience from Republic to Monarchy, 1792–1824: New Dawns in Politics, Knowledge and Culture,* ed. Máire F. Cross and David Williams (Basingstoke: Palgrave, 2000), 155–171 and "Constructing Order in Post-Revolutionary France: Women's Identities and Cultural Practices, 1800–1830" (Ph.D. diss., University of Pennsylvania, 1997), ch. 1.

42. On the dramatic structures of these plays, see Przybos, *L'entreprise mélodra-matique*, 123–150.

43. René-Charles Guilbert de Pixérécourt, *Tékéli, ou le siège de Montgatz* (Paris: Barba, 1804), 14.

44. A classic analysis of the gender dimensions of cinematic spectatorship is Laura Mulvey, "Visual Pleasure and Narrative Cinema," *Screen* 16 (1975): 6–18. A thoughtful discussion of Mulvey's argument and debates about the male and female "gaze" appears in Joan B. Landes, *Visualizing the Nation: Gender, Representation, and Revolution in Eighteenth-Century France* (Ithaca: Cornell University Press, 2001), 16–17.

45. In an essay on Chateaubriand's novels, *Atala* and *René*, Margaret Waller argues that the female title character of *Atala* resonated in the early 1800s because she represented the dual nature of female piety and sexual desires. *René*, in contrast, with its male central character, only became popular as Romanticism took hold. He served as a model for Romantic authors in the 1820s. See her "Being René, Buying Atala: Alienated Subjects and Decorative Objects in Postrevolutionary France," in *Rebel Daughters: Women and the French Revolution*, ed. Sara E. Melzer and Leslie W. Rabine (Oxford: Oxford University Press, 1992). Waller came to similar conclusions with regard to Romantic novels whose male characters, she argues, valorized the feminine in the male. See *The Male Malady: Fictions of Impotence in the French Romantic Novel* (New Brunswick, N.J.: Rutgers University Press, 1993), 13–17.

46. See Ruth Harris, "Melodrama, Hysteria and Feminine Crimes of Passion in the Fin-de-Siècle," *History Workshop Journal* 25 (1988): 31–63.

47. Marie-Pierre Le Hir, "La représentation de la famille dans le mélodrame du début du dix-neuvième siècle: De Pixérécourt à Ducange," *Nineteenth-Century French Studies* 18 (1989): 15–24.

48. Jean-Marie Thomasseau, "Le mélodrame et la censure sous le Premier Empire et la Restauration," *Revue des sciences humaines: Le mélodrame* 162 (1976): 171–182. Thomasseau also sees a transition in the form of melodramatic plays, with "classical melodrama" dominating before 1823 and "romantic melodrama" emerging after that date. On late 1820s efforts to "refresh a genre exhausted by thirty years of triumphs," see Maurice Albert, *Les théâtres des Boulevards (1789–1848)* ([1902] Geneva: Slatkine Reprints, 1969), 300–301.

49. *Le miroir des spectacles*, no. 181, 13 Aug. 1821, emphasis in original.

50. Ibid., no. 751, 15 Feb. 1823, emphasis added; note parallel language.

51. Waller, "Being René, Buying Atala."

52. The spectators who filled this *parterre* differed greatly from those in the *parterre* of elite theaters. In the latter, which were for men only and until the mid-eighteenth century had no benches, spectators stood up during the performances. In his study of these spaces, Jeffrey Ravel includes Jean-François

Marmontel's commentary about the significance of putting benches in the *parterre* that appeared as an entry in Diderot's *Encyclopédie*. Summarizing that entry, Ravel explains that "the seated spectator . . . is more at ease but colder, more reflective, less susceptible to illusion. . . . Furthermore, . . . the press of people multiplies the individual's emotional output." *The Contested Parterre: Public Theater and French Political Culture 1680–1791* (Ithaca: Cornell University Press, 1999), 215. Perhaps the fact that audiences were seated helps to explain the need for melodrama's over-the-top techniques in order to move its spectators.

53. See Richard Sieburth, "Une Idéologie du lisible: Le phénomène des "Physiologies," *Romantisme* 15 (1985): 39–60. Other discussions of the "phenomenon" of "physiologies" include Marcus, *Apartment Stories,* ch. 1; and Richard Terdiman, *Discourse/Counter-Discourse: The Theory and Practice of Symbolic Resistance in Nineteenth-Century France* (Ithaca: Cornell University Press, 1985), ch. 3.

54. Pierre Bourdieu, *Distinction: A Social Critique of the Judgement of Taste* (Cambridge, Mass.: Harvard University Press, 1984), especially chs. 2 and 3 on social space and the habitus. On cultural capital more generally, see Bourdieu, *The Logic of Practice* (Stanford: Stanford University Press, 1980), 124–125 and *Outline of a Theory of Practice* (Cambridge: Cambridge University Press, 1977), especially 187–188.

55. See Christine Stansell, *City of Women: Sex and Class in New York, 1789–1860* (Urbana: University of Illinois Press, 1987), 92–95 on popular entertainment giving the working classes a chance to dress up and temporarily forget their difficulties.

56. *Journal d'indications,* Fructidor Year X (1802), quoted in René-Charles Guilbert de Pixérécourt, *Théâtre choisi,* vol. 1 (Paris: Tresse, 1841), 251–252.

57. Lady Morgan, *France* (Philadelphia: M. Thomas, 1817), 90. For background on Lady Morgan, see Sydney Owenson (Lady Morgan), *The Missionary: An Indian Tale,* ed. Julia M. Wright (Peterboro, Ontario: Broadview Press, 2002), introduction.

58. Prices were low enough on the Boulevard to allow even the most humble of Parisians to attend the theater occasionally. In 1810, for example, seats at the Ambigu-Comique cost as little as sixty centimes. *Le nouveau Pariseum, ou curiosités de Paris* (Paris: Marchand, 1810), 192.

59. Odile Krakovitch, *Les pièces de théâtre soumises à la censure, 1800–1830* (Paris: Archives Nationales, 1982), 18.

60. Charlemagne, *Le mélodrame aux boulevards,* 6–7.

61. *Essai sur l'état actuel des théâtres de Paris et des principales villes de L'Empire, leurs administrations, leurs acteurs, leur répertoire, les journalistes, le conservatoire, etc. etc.* (Paris: L'Huillier, 1813), 86.

62. On upper-class attendance at Boulevard theaters, see Maurice Descotes, *Le public de théâtre et son histoire* (Paris: Presses Universitaires de France, 1964), 220–222.

63. *Gazette de France*, 5 Sept. 1806. Reprinted in Aulard, *Paris sous le Premier Empire*, 2: 676, emphasis added. Though ambiguous, the language of changing "état" would no doubt have brought recent political developments to mind.

64. Writing in 1839, Auger explained that "the peuple, that is to say the laboring classes *(gens laborieux)* only go to the theater on Sundays and Mondays: the other five days attract audiences from higher up the social hierarchy." *Physiologie du théâtre*, 3: 112.

65. Jean Baptiste Augustin Hapdé, *De l'anarchie théâtrale, ou de la nécessité de remettre en vigueur les lois et règlemens relatifs aux différens genres de spectacles de Paris* (Paris: J. G. Dentu, 1814), 44–45.

66. *Le miroir des spectacles*, no. 111, 4 June 1821.

67. Hapdé complained that "beginning at 4:00, the doors of the theater are obstructed by several hundred people." Hapdé, *De l'anarchie théâtrale*, 7–8. Upper-class spectators, however, did not appear in these crowds as they rented their loges in advance.

68. Hyppolite Auger argued that "during the performance, spectators at melodramatic theaters forget their own situations; . . . they become someone else. Upon leaving the theater, the fever of emotion still holds on to them." *Physiologie du théâtre*, 3: 280. Many nineteenth-century theorists derided melodrama as simply a form of escapism. See Lynn Hunt, *The Family Romance of the French Revolution* (Berkeley: University of California Press, 1992), 183–184.

69. Auger, *Physiologie du théâtre*, 3: 113.

70. Men in the parterre of eighteenth-century theaters certainly found it easy to observe the ladies in the balconies above. See Ravel, *Contested Parterre*, 50.

71. Margaret Cohen, *The Sentimental Education of the Novel* (Princeton: Princeton University Press, 1999), 14.

72. Born Constance de Théis in Nantes in 1767, she received a thorough education from her father, a naturalist. With her first marriage, she became Constance Pipelet; after a divorce, she married the prince de Salm. She held a salon in Paris and published widely throughout the early nineteenth century. See Elizabeth Colwill, "Epistolary Passions: Friendship and the Literary Public of Constance de Salm, 1767–1845," *Journal of Women's History* 12 (2000): 39–68 and "Laws of Nature/Rights of Genius: The Drame of Constance de Salm," in *Going Public: Women and Publishing in Early Modern France*, ed. Elizabeth Goldsmith and Dena Goodman (Ithaca: Cornell University Press, 1995), 224–242. See also Geneviève Fraisse, *Reason's Muse: Sexual Difference and the Birth of Democracy*, trans. Jane Marie Todd (Chicago: University of Chicago Press, 1994), 131–137.

73. Constance de Salm, *Vingt-quatre heures d'une femme sensible*, in her *Œuvres complètes*, vol. 3 (Paris: Firmin Didot, 1842), 13.

74. See J. C. Flügel, *The Psychology of Clothes* ([1930] New York: International Universities Press, 1966). Lynn Hunt discusses Flügel's concept of "The Great Masculine Renunciation," when "men began to dress alike, whereas women's dress took on more of the burdens of class signification," in her "Freedom of Dress in Revolutionary France," in *From the Royal to the Republican Body: Incorporating the Political in Seventeenth and Eighteenth-Century France*, ed. Sarah E. Melzer and Kathryn Norberg (Berkeley: University of California Press, 1998), 231. On masculinity, see Robert A. Nye, *Masculinity and Male Codes of Honor in Modern France* ([1993] Berkeley: University of California Press, 1998) and William M. Reddy, *The Invisible Code: Honor and Sentiment in Postrevolutionary France, 1814–1848* (Berkeley: University of California Press, 1997).

75. These trends parallel those explained by Anne Vincent-Buffault in *A History of Tears: Sensibility and Sentimentality in France* (Basingstoke: Macmillan, 1991). Many behavioral changes were taking place during this period, and Buffault traces transformations in the rules guiding emotional expression as men lost the ability to cry in public while women's tears became increasingly prevalent. William Reddy, in contrast, argues that men did indeed remain emotional, though they couched their sentiment in terms like "honor" precisely because of the gender connotations of emotions. *Invisible Code*, 228–238.

76. On evolving attitudes toward actresses as "public women," see Lenard R. Berlanstein, *Daughters of Eve: A Cultural History of French Theater Women from the Old Regime to the Fin-de-Siècle* (Cambridge, Mass.: Harvard University Press, 2001) and Anne Martin-Fugier, *Comédienne: De Mlle Mars à Sarah Bernhardt* (Paris: Seuil, 2001).

77. Pixérécourt, *Théâtre choisi*, 4:497–498. This quotation raises questions about which variable had changed, the plays or the attitudes of "good society" toward them.

78. Descotes, *Le public de théâtre*, 243.

79. In her analysis of Parisian attitudes in the years preceding the 1832 cholera epidemic, Catherine Kudlick describes a "fundamental restructuring of how Parisians perceived the nature of their city in the 1820s." *Cholera in Post-Revolutionary Paris: A Cultural History* (Berkeley: University of California Press, 1996), 39.

80. Juste Olivier, *Paris en 1830*, quoted in Descotes, *Le public de théâtre*, 243.

81. Berlanstein, *Daughters of Eve*, 13–14.

82. On post-1830 trends in popular theater, see McCormick, *Popular Theatres*, ch. 12. F. W. J. Hemmings argues that some Boulevard theaters continued to attract middle-class audiences whereas others appealed to strictly working-class spectators, particularly those that staged melodramas on the eastern end of the boulevard du Temple. *The Theatre Industry in Nineteenth-Century France* (Cambridge: Cambridge University Press, 1993), 122–128.

83. On the destruction of "the people's boulevard du Temple," see Hemmings, *Theatre Industry,* 127–128; and Dominique le Roy, "Réflexions autour des processus d'élitisation, à propos de l'évolution de la production et de la consommation théâtrale à Paris au XIXe siècle," in *Oisiveté et loisirs dans les sociétés occidentales au XIXe siècle,* ed. Adeline Daumard (Abbeville: F. Paillart, 1983), 238–239.

## 4. Sex and Politics in Provincial Theaters

1. ADR 4M 478, commissaire général de police to prefect, 3 Dec. 1811. On the politicization of the "time-honored privilege" of the *sifflet* (whistle) during the French Revolution, see Paul Friedland, *Political Actors: Representative Bodies and Theatricality in the Age of the French Revolution* (Ithaca: Cornell University Press, 2002), 258–267.

2. On the *tricoteuses,* see Dominique Godineau, *The Women of Paris and Their French Revolution,* trans. Katherine Streip (Berkeley: University of California Press, 1998), xviii, 211–212.

3. See Sheryl Kroen, *Politics and Theater: The Crisis of Legitimacy in Restoration France, 1815–1830* (Berkeley: University of California Press, 2000) and F. W. J. Hemmings, "Applause for the Wrong Reasons: The Use of *Applications* for Political Purposes in Paris Theaters, 1780–1830," *Theater Research International* 14 (1986): 256–270. On politicized theatrical disorders in London during the same period, see Marc Baer, *Theatre and Disorder in Late Georgian London* (Oxford: Clarendon Press, 1992).

4. F. W. J. Hemmings, *Theatre and the State in France, 1760–1905* (Cambridge: Cambridge University Press, 1994), 136.

5. Willam B. Cohen, *Urban Government and the Rise of the French City: Five Municipalities in the Nineteenth Century* (New York: St. Martin's Press, 1998), 127–128.

6. Ibid., 129.

7. AML 89 WP 1, Delisle (theater director) to mayor, 12 Feb. 1810.

8. ADLA 177 T 1, mayor to prefect, 20 Jan. 1807. Legislation passed in 1806 and 1807 limited the number of theaters in Paris to eight and most provincial cities to one. Only Lyon, Bordeaux, Marseille, Nantes, and Turin had the right to two permanent theaters. Hemmings, *Theatre and the State,* 144. The 1807 legislation is also summarized in the entry "Théâtres," in Alfred Fierro, André Palluel-Guillad, and Jean Tulard, *Histoire et dictionnaire du Consulat et de l'Empire* (Paris: Robert Laffont, 1995), 1120.

9. Quoted in Daniel Rabreau, "Théâtre à Nantes ou l'urbanisme mis en scène," *Monuments historiques* 18 (1980): 48. See Stendhal's account of his visit to

Nantes in *Mémoires d'un touriste,* vol. 1, in volume 15 of his *Œuvres complètes* (Paris: Champion, 1968), 419.

10. Between 1791 and 1806, the years when theatrical controls were at their weakest, several smaller theaters competed with the Célestins. See Louis Trénard, "Le théâtre lyonnais sous le Consulat et l'Empire," *Cahiers d'histoire* 2 (1958): 165–189; and Trénard, *Lyon de l'Encyclopédie au préromantisme* (Paris: Presses Universitaires de France, 1958), 2: 557–572. Lists of plays performed at each theater were created annually and can be found in numerous places in both the municipal and departmental archives, including AML 89 WP 1. Hemmings says that in Lyon "the Célestins concentrated on straight plays, the Grand-Théâtre on musicals, mainly opera and comic opera; elsewhere there was one theatre that tended to draw on the more cultivated section of society, and a second one patronized mainly by the working classes." *Theatre and the State,* 145. He seems to be suggesting that unlike other cities, the same social groups attended both of Lyon's theaters. This conclusion disagrees with Trénard's findings and with the assumptions of contemporaries who associated the Célestins with melodramas and vaudevilles, and who expected those genres to appeal to less educated spectators than the classical genres performed at the Grand Théâtre.

11. One reference to a "maison de débauche" (brothel) in the vicinity of the Célestins appears in AN F$^7$ 3686 (8), police report dated 20 June 1819.

12. *Journal du commerce,* no. 9, 31 Dec. 1823.

13. In 1834, when the city proposed moving the Célestins, business owners in the neighborhood of the Célestins reacted immediately, claiming that they and their employees would suffer immeasurably from such a change. ADR T 426, "Observations sur la translation projetée du Théâtre des Célestins dans un autre quartier de la ville de Lyon," 1834.

14. Rabreau, "Théâtre à Nantes," 37–41.

15. ADLA 177 T 1, letter to mayor, from the directors of the two theaters, 31 Dec. 1811. Their names suggest that the directors were sisters-in-law: Dames Richer veuve Tarvouillet and Tarvouillet veuve Laruefrancis.

16. ADLA 178 T 1, annual lists of plays in the theaters' repertories.

17. In her memoirs, Julie Pellizzone recorded positive reactions to melodramas performed at Marseille's Théâtre-Français in 1811. *Souvenirs,* vol. 1 *(1781–1815),* transcribed and annotated by Hélène Échinard and Georges Reynaud (Paris: Indigo and Côté-femmes, 1995), 267–269. Her list of plays performed there in 1821 also included melodramas and vaudevilles. Pellizzone, *Souvenirs: Journal d'une Marseillaise,* vol. 2 *(1815–1824)* (Paris: Indigo and Côté-femmes, 2001), 316–318.

18. *Le véridique,* 7 March 1820, quoted in Pierre Jourda, *Le théâtre à Montpellier 1755–1851* (Oxford: Voltaire Foundation, 2001), 211.

19. ADLA 177 T 1, directors of theaters of Nantes to prefect, 28 June 1806.

20. ADLA 177 T 2, miscellaneous correspondence. A woman, Madame Jausseraud, the widow of the previous director, was Nantes' director of theaters during the early 1820s. Another woman offered her services as director in 1817, though she was never hired. In her work on eighteenth-century provincial theaters, Lauren Clay has found that female directors were commonplace and that the financial difficulties described here were a frequent occurrence then as well. See Clay, "Provincial Actors, the Comédie-Française, and the Business of Performing in Eighteenth-Century France," *Eighteenth-Century Studies* 38 (2005): 651–679. The material on women appears on p. 664. An 1824 law made it illegal for women to hold the position of director. See Hemmings, *Theatre and the State,* 162.

21. AN F$^7$ 6770, report to minister of the interior from prefect, 16 Jan. 1827, informing him that the theater had closed earlier that month. Similar problems arose in Montpellier after 1824. See Jourda, *Théâtre à Montpellier,* chs. 5 and 6. Cohen gives statistics on the similarly brief careers of theater directors in other provincial cities in *Urban Government,* 140.

22. Coulet, *Observations succinctes adressées à messieurs les membres du Conseil Général de la commune de Lyon* (Lyon: Pelzin, 1812). Held in BML, Collection Coste 114582.

23. *Chronique parisienne, ou revue politique, morale, littéraire et théâtrale, par une société de gens de lettres* (Paris: Herhan, 1817), 96.

24. AML 89 WP 1, Rapport fait dans l'assemblée générale des sociétaires du Grand Théâtre de Lyon par l'un d'eux, n.d.; and undated letter from Delisle to mayor. In fact, Madame Lobreau (Michelle Destouches-Lobreau) received virtually no financial support, only the right to use the theater for free. I am grateful to Lauren Clay for providing this corrective to me based on her research on eighteenth-century provincial theaters. See her "Theater and the Commercialization of Culture in Eighteenth-Century France" (Ph.D. diss., University of Pennsylvania, 2003), 260–266.

25. Antoine Sallès, *Les théâtres lyonnais en 1827–1828* (Paris: Jobert, 1927), 40–41.

26. AML 89 WP 1, prefect's decree, 15 Feb. 1811. Authorities in Marseille made a similar proposition in 1807. They hoped to save that city's Grand Théâtre by closing down the secondary theater, which appealed to the least educated classes, and thus continue to provide entertainment to "the class of citizens that appreciates good theater and music." AN F$^7$ 8748, commissionnaire général de police (Marseille) to the conseiller d'état chargé du 2ème arrondissement de la police générale de l'Empire (Paris), 20 Oct. 1807.

27. ADLA 179 T 1, Jausseraud (theater director) to prefect, 20 Jan. 1819. He made these complaints despite earlier legislation that required owners of *petits spectacles* to give one-fifth of their gross receipts to the director of the Grand Théâtre. "Théâtres bourgeois" referred to performances staged in people's

homes or in small theaters or cafés rented for an evening. They were usually organized by *jeunes gens* (youth) as a way to entertain their friends on winter evenings. On the eighteenth-century origins of these amateur theater companies, as well as a discussion of the different terms used to describe them, see Antoine Lilti, "Public ou sociabilité: Les théâtres de société au XVIIIe siècle," in *De la publication: Entre renaissance et lumières,* ed. Christian Jouhaud and Alain Viala (Paris: Fayard, 2002), 281–300. Hemmings describes the early Restoration craze for *théâtre de société* or *théâtre bourgeois* in *Theatre and the State,* 232.

28. Quoted in Hemmings, *Theatre and the State,* 146.

29. AML 88 WP 1, undated letter to prefect (c. 1810) from a commandant de la Légion d'Honneur.

30. Cohen, *Urban Government,* 133–134. On the significance of theater for teaching social norms and even language use, see René Merle, "Fonction sociale du théâtre français et du théâtre dialectal dans le sud-est, de la fin de l'Ancien Régime à 1840," *Provence historique* 40 (1990): 157–172.

31. Circular sent to prefects by the minister of instruction, Rœderer, 7 Messidor Year X (26 June 1802) quoted in Jourda, *Théâtre à Montpellier,* 42–43.

32. AML 89 WP 2, yearly prospectus for Grand Théâtre, 1813–1814.

33. Cohen, *Urban Government,* 138.

34. Malcolm Crook, *Toulon in War and Revolution* (Manchester: Manchester University Press, 1991), 207.

35. ADLA 177 T 1, statement by theater directors (Dames Thérèse Richer veuve Tarvouillet and Marie Tarvouillet veuve Laruefrancis), 31 Dec. 1811.

36. Cohen, *Urban Government,* 131.

37. AN F$^7$ 6770, Rapport sur la situation morale, politique et administrative du département de la Loire Inférieure, 16 Jan. 1827.

38. Virtually all the archival documents I found dealing with *petits spectacles* date from the Restoration, not the Empire.

39. *Journal du commerce,* 29 Sept. 1824, quoted in Antoine Sallès, "Anecdotes et souvenirs d'autrefois: Le Grand Théâtre de Lyon et le public lyonnais," *Revue du Lyonnais* 2 (1922): 97.

40. *Journal du commerce,* no. 166, 12 Jan. 1825.

41. ADR T 435, carton 4, Tableau raisonné de situation du théâtre des Célestins dit variétés, 31 Oct. 1807.

42. Ibid., 1 April 1808. On *pièces féeries* and other popular genres, see John McCormick, *Popular Theaters of Nineteenth-Century France* (London: Routledge, 1993), 113–200. Lauren Clay notes the large repertories of provincial theaters in the eighteenth century, too. In one month in 1773, "the Bordeaux theater staged more than fifty *different*" plays of various sorts. "Provincial Actors," 655–656.

43. *Chronique parisienne,* 110–111.

44. F. W. J. Hemmings argues that a club-like atmosphere dominated in Parisian theaters as well. *The Theatre Industry in Nineteenth-Century France* (Cambridge: Cambridge University Press, 1993), 16.

45. *Journal du commerce*, no. 14, 11 Jan. 1824 (emphasis added).

46. Ibid., no. 102, 8 Aug. 1824.

47. BML MS. 6346, Correspondance de Mme Arthaud, vol. 2, doc. 21, 12 July 1801.

48. AML Fonds Vitet, 84 II 12, letters from Catherine Arnaud-Tizon née Deschaux (in Rouen) to Pierre and Amélie Vitet (in Paris), 30 July 1808 and 15 Sept. 1814. On the popularity (and enormous salaries) of Parisian actors appearing at provincial theaters, see Clay, "Provincial Actors," 666. Trénard discusses their appeal as well. *Lyon de l'Encyclopédie au préromantisme*, 565–566.

49. *Journal de Nantes*, no. 121, 3 May 1823.

50. *Le véridique*, 10 Dec. 1818, quoted in Jourda, *Théâtre à Montpellier*, 156. The "other species" must be a reference to prostitutes.

51. ADLA 177 T 1, commissaire général de police to prefect, 30 Frimaire Year IX (21 Dec. 1800).

52. This lack of numbering was true in Paris as well as in the provinces. See Hemmings, *Theatre Industry*, 29–30.

53. ADLA 177 T 1–4, miscellaneous posters from the entire period.

54. Martine de Rougemont, *La vie théâtrale en France au XVIIIe siècle* (Paris: Honoré Champion, 1988), 294. Jeffrey Ravel presents similar findings in his examination of provincial theater riots during the reign of Louis XVI. *The Contested Parterre: Public Theater and French Political Culture 1680–1791* (Ithaca: Cornell University Press, 1999), 170–184. His work makes clear that staging protests in theaters predated the Revolution.

55. Cohen, *Urban Government*, 134.

56. *Chronique parisienne*, 110.

57. James H. Johnson, *Listening in Paris: A Cultural History* (Berkeley: University of California Press, 1995).

58. AMN I¹ 53, dos. 2, commissioner of police to mayor, 8 Floréal Year XII (27 April 1804). Ravel noted increased criticism of police beginning in the mid eighteenth century. *Contested Parterre*, 136.

59. Ravel, *Contested Parterre*, 183.

60. Pellizzone, *Souvenirs*, 2: 231–232.

61. AMN I¹ 53, dos. 3, prefect to mayor, 13 Oct. 1808. In his response to the mayor's request for details, the commissioner of police could only confirm that "several remarks addressed to the parterre had come from the boxes above [and that] the parterre responded to them." He added that he had heard that one of the men involved was an officer who had since departed for Rennes. Ibid., commissioner of police to mayor, 15 Oct. 1808.

62. ADR 4M 449, commissioner of police to leutenant général de police, 21 May 1818. Also, ADR 4M 176, commissioner of police to mayor and mayor to commissioner of police, 21 May 1818. On May 22, the mayor suggested that twelve gendarmes be placed in the parterre. The man's quotation is in ADR 4M 176, commissioner of police to mayor, 26 May 1818.

63. ADR 4M 176, "Observations," 22 and 24 May 1818. Documents pertaining to similar disturbances in the early 1820s appear in AML 89 WP 3 and AML 88 WP 1.

64. AML 89 WP 1, police report, 19 Nov. 1810.

65. ADLA 177 T 3, mayor to prefect, 28 May 1822.

66. ADLA 177 T 3, report from Gendarmerie Royale, 28 May 1822.

67. AMN I¹ 53, dos. 4, report on theater, 27 May 1822 and AN F⁷ 4051, report to minister of police générale, May 1822. Three whistlers *(siffleurs)* and three others who were believed to be their accomplices were arrested.

68. Jourda, *Théâtre à Montpellier*, 57.

69. Ravel, *Contested Parterre*, 210–224.

70. AN F⁷ 8381, letter dated 12 May 1806. The stated author of the letter, a Parisian whose information supposedly came from a friend who had recently visited him from Nantes, argued that Nantes' inhabitants were far from fervent supporters of Napoleon. He seemed to be implying that these youthful outbursts had political motives.

71. AMN I¹ 53, dos. 3, commissioner of police to chief of police, 20 Oct. 1806.

72. Ibid., commissioner of police to mayor, 8 Dec. 1806.

73. Lenard Berlanstein, *Daughters of Eve: A Cultural History of French Theater Women from the Old Regime to the Fin-de-Siècle* (Cambridge, Mass.: Harvard University Press, 2001), 103. On actresses' "outcast status" from 1815 to 1848, see ch. 4. Berlanstein argues that actresses seemed less threatening once a bourgeois order was fully established, particularly after 1830. Although they could be viewed as "feminine" and to a certain extent tamed in comparison to the Old Regime and the revolutionary period, they continued to be seen as fallen women who needed to be segregated from "respectable women."

74. In 1805, "scandalous whistles . . . were directed at Madame Joanny who found herself forced to abandon the stage. . . . Seven or eight unknown men" were believed to have been at the heart of the disturbance. AMN I¹ 53, dos. 2, commissioner of police to mayor, 11 Floréal Year XIII (1 May 1805). An account of a similar incident appears in ADLA 177 T 4, mayor to prefect, 25 May 1825.

75. AMN I¹ 53, dos. 4, police report, 31 May 1818.

76. ADLA 177 T 3, mayor to prefect, 3 Aug. 1821.

77. Similar struggles are at the core of Ravel's study of eighteenth-century audiences. He argues that "after 1750, . . . observers began to conceive of the

parterre as part of larger, more politicized notions such as the 'public' or the 'nation.'" *Contested Parterre,* 11.

78. AMN I¹ 53, dos. 4, police report, 2 Jan. 1819. Kroen found examples of people exploding what she calls "stink bombs" in churches in the mid-1820s. These may have been similar explosives. *Politics and Theater,* 241. On Mellinet and her paper, see Alain Chatreau, "Camille Mellinet, sa famille, et son temps," *Bulletin de la Société Archéologique et Historique de Nantes et de la Loire-Atlantique* 120 (1984): 139–141.

79. AN F⁷ 8381, Anaudin to comte de Réal, conseiller d'état, 24 Oct. 1813. The letter's purpose was to draw the minister's attention to the incompetence of the recently appointed prefect, Prosper Barante. Among the letter-writer's complaints was his view that Madame Barante "is not afraid to demonstrate to the public that she interferes with the administration [of the department]." He then recounts his experiences while at the theater when the prefect responded inappropriately to some disorderly behavior by calling for the lighting to be extinguished. This supposedly inept prefect would go on to an illustrious career. See Antoine Denis, *Amable-Guillaume-Prosper Brugière de Barante (1782–1866): Homme politique, diplomate et historien* (Paris: H. Champion, 2000).

80. Pellizzone, *Souvenirs,* 2: 119–120.

81. Ibid., 307.

82. AMN I¹ 51, dos. 1, confidential letter from prefect to mayor, 22 Sept. 1826.

83. ADR T 435, carton 4, Tableau raisonné de situation du théâtre des Célestins dit variétés, 31 Oct. 1807. The director made a similar request in the 1808 Tableau raisonné in which he argued that "personnes honnêtes" would attend the theater in larger numbers if prostitutes sat in a designated area of the theater. ADR T 435, carton 4, 1 April 1808.

84. AML 89 WP 1, prefect to mayor, 9 Nov. 1809. Definitions of theatrical terms like "parquet" can be found in Hemmings, *Theatre Industry.*

85. AMN I¹ 52, dos. 6, mayor's draft of law, 17 Aug. 1816.

86. According to Jann Matlock, prostitution would become "*the* social issue . . . by the early years of the July Monarchy." *Scenes of Seduction: Prostitution, Hysteria, and Reading Difference in Nineteenth-Century France* (New York: Columbia University Press, 1994), 22. On the new regulations of the late 1820s and early 1830s, see Alain Corbin, *Women for Hire: Prostitution and Sexuality in France after 1850* (Cambridge, Mass.: Harvard University Press, 1990), 3–16. See also the discussions of the term "femme publique" in Susan P. Conner, "Politics, Prostitution, and the Pox in Revolutionary Paris, 1789–1799," *Journal of Social History* 22 (1989): 718; and W. Scott Haine, *The World of the Paris Café: Sociability among the French Working Class, 1789–1914* (Baltimore: Johns Hopkins University Press, 1996), 183.

87. AMN I$^1$ 52, dos. 6, letter from Adolphe Quonjaz (name partially illegible) to theater director, 6 Feb. 1821.

88. ADR 4M 226, draft letters to mayor, theater director, and director of police from prefect, 27 Sept. 1814.

89. ADR 4M 426, poster dated 21 July 1815. This was shortly after the reinstatement of the Bourbons following the Hundred Days.

90. AMN I$^1$ 53, dos. 4, commissioner of police to mayor, 5 Dec. 1815. I have been unable to uncover any particular significance for the use of cooked pears, other than their consistency, which would have left a sticky mess on the eagle statues. They may have been a reference to Louis XVIII's large girth, as would be the case more famously when pears were used to caricature Louis-Philippe after 1830. See Elise K. Kenney and John M. Merriman, *The Pear: French Graphic Arts in the Golden Age of Caricature* (South Hadley, Mass.: Mount Holyoke College Art Museum, 1991). Emilienne Leroux discusses efforts to rid the town of Napoleonic symbols in her *Histoire d'une ville et de ses habitants* (Nantes, 1984), 126. Sheryl Kroen refers to such efforts as the symbolic *mise-en-place* of the Restoration, or the politics of *oubli*. See her "Revolutionizing Religious Politics during the Restoration," *French Historical Studies* 21 (1998): 32 and her *Politics and the Theater*. On the continued presence of Napoleonic imagery during the Restoration and later, see Barbara Ann Day-Hickman, *Napoleonic Art: Nationalism and the Spirit of Rebellion in France (1815–1848)* (Newark: University of Delaware Press, 1999). Maurice Agulhon comments on Restoration attempts to replace Napoleonic symbols with Bourbon ones in "Politics and Images in Post-Revolutionary France," in *Rites of Power: Symbolism, Ritual and Politics Since the Middle Ages,* ed. Sean Wilentz (Philadelphia: University of Pennsylvania Press, 1985), 190.

91. Hemmings, *Theatre and the State,* 155. Hemmings discusses the frequent disorders staged by Bonapartists during the early Restoration in *Theatre Industry,* 83–86.

92. AMN I$^1$ 53, dos. 4, police report, 8 Nov. 1817. (The events took place on the fourth.) Victor Mangin et fils was one of the city's print shops. Beginning in 1819, they published the newspaper *L'ami de la Charte: Journal politique, littéraire et d'avis, de Nantes,* a liberal publication. Victor Mangin *fils* wrote all the articles on the theater.

93. AN F$^7$ 3686 (8), monthly report from head of the Gendarmerie Royale to minister of the interior, June 1820, and police report for first half of June.

94. Kroen, *Politics and Theater,* 4.

95. Ibid., 258.

96. AN F$^7$ 6770, dos. 3, report to minister of the interior, 4 Jan. 1826.

97. Kroen, *Politics and Theater,* 237 (the quotation), 250–256.

98. *Gazette universelle de Lyon,* no. 257, 1 Nov. 1826.

99. Ibid.

100. AN F⁷ 6770, Rapports sur la situation . . . du département de la Loire Inférieure, 16 Feb. and 1 March 1827.

101. At the Théâtre Français in Paris, this sense of intimacy went to its furthest extreme in the *baignoires,* boxes located "behind the pit and below the first
gallery . . . [where a] good deal of fondling and kissing went on" because they
obscured all but the heads of their occupants. Hemmings, *Theatre Industry,* 32.

102. AML Fonds Vitet, 84 II 12, letter from Catherine Arnaud-Tizon to her son-in-
law, Pierre Vitet, 15 Sept. 1814. In 1813, an incident involving someone taking
seats that did not belong to him at the Célestins left a record of two ladies
*(dames)* at the theater alone together. AML 89 WP 1, police report, 11 Sept. 1813.

103. For a parallel argument on the shift from mixed-sex salons to male clubs during the July Monarchy, see Steven Kale, *French Salons: High Society and Political Sociability from the Old Regime to the Revolution of 1848* (Baltimore: Johns
Hopkins University Press, 2004), ch. 6.

## 5. Building Solidarity

1. *Feuille nantaise,* no. 108, 15 Nivôse Year IX (5 Jan. 1801).

2. One important form of associational life not included in this chapter is
freemasonry, a huge topic that has received extensive attention from historians and deserves even more. See Margaret C. Jacob, *Living the Enlightenment:
Freemasonry and Politics in Eighteenth-Century Europe* (Oxford: Oxford University Press, 1991) and Jacob's review of Pierre-Yves Beaurepaire, *L'Europe
des francs-maçons, XVIIIe–XXIe siècles* (Paris: Belin, 2002), *H-France Review* 3
(Oct. 2003). Of particular relevance is Janet M. Burke and Margaret C. Jacob,
"French Freemasonry, Women, and Feminist Scholarship," *Journal of Modern
History* 68 (1996): 513–549, which makes a case for women's active involve-
ment in the Enlightenment through freemasonry.

3. On the longevity of the "corporate idiom," see William H. Sewell, Jr., *Work and
Revolution in France: The Language of Labor from the Old Regime to 1848*
(Cambridge: Cambridge University Press, 1980). For an example of a "corpo-
rate outlook," see Robert Darnton, "A Bourgeois Puts His World in Order: The
City as a Text," in *The Great Cat Massacre and Other Episodes in French Cul-
tural History* (New York: Vintage, 1984), 107–143.

4. Of course it is nothing new to argue that class and gender need to be considered together. "There is no choice between a focus on class or on gender; each
is necessarily incomplete without the other." Joan Wallach Scott, *Gender and
the Politics of History* (New York: Columbia University Press, 1988), 66.

5. *Journal des dames et des modes,* vol. 7, no. 61, 5 Thermidor Year XI (25 July
1803), 489.

6. Maurice Agulhon, *Le cercle dans la France bourgeoise 1810–1848* (Paris: Armand Colin, 1977), 17, 32.

7. Serge Charléty, "La vie politique à Lyon sous Napoleon Ier," *Revue d'histoire de Lyon* 4 (1905): 378; and Agulhon, *Le cercle*, 21.

8. Agulhon, *Le cercle*, 52, emphasis in original. Jean Tulard agrees with Agulhon on the masculine nature of the cercle: "Born of the anglomania and the misogyny of the society of the Civil Code (women were excluded from cercles) it [the cercle] tended to replace salons. The cercle brought together a narrow, exclusively masculine elite whose concerns were essentially male *(virile)* and whose [remarks] were freer *(plus libres)*." *La vie quotidienne des Français sous Napoléon* (Paris: Hachette, 1978), 209–210.

9. Louis Trénard, "Culture et sociabilité dans l'espace rhodanien à l'aube du XIXe siècle," in *Le Rhône: Naissance d'un département* (Lyon: Conseil Général du Rhône, 1990), 114. A Cercle de Bellecour existed before the Revolution and was dissolved during the Terror. It had 107 members in 1793. See Antoine Sallès, *L'ancien Cercle de Bellecour: Sa dissolution et sa liquidation après le siège de Lyon en 1793* (Lyon: Salut Public, 1923). The vagueness of the terms "cercle," "société," and "salon" during the eighteenth century comes across in Antoine Lilti, "Sociabilité et mondanité: Les hommes de lettres dans les salons parisiens au XVIIIe siècle," *French Historical Studies* 28 (2005): 417–418.

10. AML I² 46, Règlements du Cercle de Bellecour; and ADR 4M 827, membership list for Cercle de Bellecour, 1811. Son of a lyonnais businessman, Jordan was a monarchist and vehement Catholic who was one of the leaders of the 1793 revolt in Lyon. When he returned to France after the Eighteenth Brumaire, he did not hide his hostility toward Bonaparte's government, but he avoided political activity until the Restoration when he joined the constitutional opposition. Biographical information on Jordan is available in J. Tulard, J. F. Fayard, and A. Fierro, *Histoire et dictionnaire de la Révolution française,1789–1799* (Paris: Robert Laffont, 1987), 902. Louis Trénard counts Jordan among a group of liberals that also included Madame de Staël and Madame Récamier. *Lyon de l'Encyclopédie au préromantisme*, vol. 2 (Paris: Presses Universitaires de France, 1958), 716–719.

11. Agulhon, *Le cercle*, 52–53 (includes the quotation from the prefect). Agulhon's "galante à la française" brings to mind Mona Ozouf's argument about "French singularity," in *Women's Words: Essay on French Singularity* (Chicago: University of Chicago Press, 1997). Agulhon postulates that the phrase "vieille galanterie française" (old-style French gallantry) dates from 1830 or so, as people complained about the new "sociabilité anglomane" that left women at home (*Le cercle*, 52).

12. Charléty, "La vie politique à Lyon," 378.

13. According to Carol E. Harrison, cercles were required to prohibit gambling in their bylaws, when in fact it was one of the most common activities of members

and virtually the raison d'être of some organizations. *The Bourgeois Citizen in Nineteenth-Century France: Gender, Sociability, and the Uses of Emulation* (Oxford: Oxford University Press, 1999), 94.

14. AML I² 46, Article 12, Règlements du Cercle de Bellecour. This stipulation is apparently what led Trénard to assume that women brought their daughters to find them husbands. I was unable to find any other evidence that would lead to such a conclusion.

15. On the continuation of salons into the nineteenth century see Steven Kale, *French Salons: High Society and Political Sociability from the Old Regime to the Revolution of 1848* (Baltimore: Johns Hopkins University Press, 2004) and his articles "Women, the Public Sphere, and the Persistence of Salons," *French Historical Studies* 25 (2002): 115–148 and "Women, Salons, and the State in the Aftermath of the French Revolution," *Journal of Women's History* 13 (2002): 54–80. See also Anne Martin-Fugier, *La vie élégante, ou la formation du Tout-Paris, 1815–1848* (Paris: Fayard, 1990), ch. 3; and Adeline Daumard, "La vie de salon en France dans la première moitié du XIXe siècle," in *Sociabilité et société bourgeoise en France, en Allemagne et en Suisse, 1750–1850*, ed. Etienne François (Paris: Editions Recherche sur les Civilisations, 1986), 81–92.

16. W. D. Edmonds, *Jacobinism and the Revolt of Lyon, 1789–1793* (Oxford: Clarendon Press, 1990).

17. Balzac, *Le contrat de mariage* ([1835] Paris: Gallimard, 1973), 114.

18. Trénard, "Culture et sociabilité," 114. Such organizations probably posed no serious threat. "Were the notables able to discuss in their cercles those subjects on which the press remained silent? . . . In fact, cercles were watched as closely as the official associations." Jacques Prévosto, "Les événements, la politique et les hommes," in *Histoire de Lyon des origines à nos jours*, vol. 2, *Du XVIe siècle à nos jours*, ed. Françoise Bayard and Pierre Cayez (Le Coteaux: Horvath, 1990), 282.

19. On elite women and Napoleonic politics, see Kale, "Women, Salons, and the State," 63–67.

20. BML MS. 6346, Correspondance de Mme Arthaud, vol. 2, doc. 21, 12 July 1801.

21. AML I¹ 155, "Liste des messieurs et des dames composant le Cercle des Dames;" ibid., "Liste des personnes invitées au bal donné chez le préfet le 15 février 1807"; AML I² 46, "L'ancien Cercle des Dames prend la dénomination du Cercle du Midi," 29 Feb. 1812.

22. P. J. Charrin, *Le conteur des dames, ou les soirées parisiennes* (Paris: Veuve Lepetit, 1821), title page. The phrase played on eighteenth-century pornographic pamphlets that stated, "La mère en proscrira la lecture à sa fille." The Marquis de Sade used the same phrase, but replaced "proscrira" with "prescrira." I am grateful to Lynn Hunt for making me aware of this parallel language.

23. Charrin, *Conteur des dames*, xi–xii.

24. Germaine de Staël, "Des femmes qui cultivent les lettres," in *De la littérature considérée dans ses rapports avec les institutions sociales,* vol. 2 ([1800] Geneva: Droz and Paris: Minard, 1959), 336. Of course, French stereotypes of British gender relations did not necessarily reflect reality. One only needs to think of the novels of Jane Austen to see mixed-sex sociability taking place on the other side of the channel. See Robert B. Shoemaker, *Gender in English Society, 1650–1850: The Emergence of Separate Spheres* (London: Longman, 1998), 42.

25. Charléty, "La vie politique," 378 and *Almanach historique et politique de la ville de Lyon et du département du Rhône pour l'année 1811* (Lyon: Balanche, n.d.), 280–281.

26. ADR 33 J 12 a*, Procès-verbal du Cercle littéraire, 1807 (emphasis in original). Balzac mentioned these "caricatures entitled 'Jadis et aujourd'hui,' that had so much success during the Empire" in *Le contrat de mariage,* 156.

27. AN BB 18 692 Reg. C, no. 3164, 16 May 1808.

28. ADR 4M 827, "Tableaux des noms & professions de messieurs les membres du Cercle des Terreaux" (undated but most likely from the1811 investigation) and AML I² 46 (microfilm 44), "Extrait des Règlements du cercle du Commerce à Lyon," 31 March 1811.

29. Charléty, "La vie politique," 378–379.

30. *Histoire de la France urbaine,* vol. 3, *La ville classique de la Renaissance aux révolutions,* ed. Georges Duby (Paris: Seuil, 1981), 601–602.

31. Complaining about the unfortunate loss of the documents from the 1811 *enquête* (investigation) for the north and west of France, Agulhon expresses the possibility that western France may have been ahead of other regions with regard to this "practice of male clubs devoted to leisure." *Le cercle,* 34. Trénard assumes that cercles had existed prior to the Revolution in Lyon as well. "Culture et sociabilité," 114. On the history of cercles and other kinds of clubs in Nantes, see G. Martin, "Les chambres littéraires de Nantes," *Annales de Bretagne* 37 (1925–1926): 347–365.

32. AMN I² 32, dos. 1, police reports to mayor, 29 Oct. 1808, 15 and 16 March 1819, and June 1820. The last document provides the most complete information on the clubs, including their newspaper subscriptions and the length of time they had existed.

33. Several subscription reading rooms existed in Lyon, many of which were run by women. AN F⁷ 6872, "Etats des journaux et brochures mis en lecture dans les cercles et cabinets du département du Rhône pendant le mois d'août 1820." See Trénard, "Culture et sociabilité," 115; and Françoise Parent-Lardeur, *Lire à Paris au temps de Balzac: Les cabinets de lecture à Paris, 1815–1830,* 2nd ed. (Paris: Editions de l'Ecole des Hautes Etudes en Sciences Sociales, 1999), 107–113. Although literary references to women borrowing books from *cabinets de lecture*

abound, no archival records list women as clients, only as owners and employees. See Martyn Lyons, *Readers and Society in Nineteenth-Century France* (Basingstoke: Palgrave, 2001), 81–86.

34. AMN I² 32, dos. 14, prefect to mayor, 11 Nov. 1817 and 26 Dec. 1817, and mayor to commissioner of police, 30 Dec. 1817.

35. AN F⁷ 6872, prefect of the Rhône to minister of police, and accompanying report, 23 Sept. 1820.

36. See Sarah Maza, *The Myth of the French Bourgeoisie: An Essay on the Social Imaginary, 1750–1850* (Cambridge, Mass.: Harvard University Press, 2003), ch. 5; and Jeremy D. Popkin, *Press, Revolution, and Social Identities in France, 1830–1835* (University Park: Pennsylvania State University Press, 2002), ch. 2.

37. *Journal du commerce*, no. 9, 31 Dec. 1823.

38. On the political affiliations of Lyon's newspapers, see Popkin, *Press, Revolution, and Social Identities*, 29–33.

39. AN F⁷ 6770, extrait du rapport général sur la situation morale, politique et administrative du département de la Loire-Inférieure pendant l'année 1826.

40. The historiography on salons is enormous. Among the more influential studies are Carolyn C. Lougee, *Le Paradis des Femmes: Women, Salons, and Social Stratification in Seventeenth-Century France* (Princeton: Princeton University Press, 1976); Dena Goodman, "Enlightenment Salons: The Convergence of Female and Philosophic Ambitions," *Eighteenth-Century Studies* 22 (1989): 329–350; and Jolanta T. Pekacz, *Conservative Tradition in Pre-Revolutionary France: Parisian Salon Women* (New York: Peter Lang, 1999). Earlier work often assumed that salons came to an end in the early nineteenth century. However, in *French Salons*, Kale argues that they continued much longer, through the July Monarchy and beyond. Martin-Fugier makes this point as well in *La vie élégante*, 91–100, as does Philip Mansel in *Paris Between Empires: Monarchy and Revolution, 1814–1852* (New York: St. Martin's Press, 2003), 120–140.

41. BML MS. 6449, letter from Voght to Mme Récamier, 18 June 1812. The letter writer must have been Baron von Voght, a philanthropist who corresponded with Madame de Staël. *La Correspondance de Madame de Staël et du baron Voght*, ed. Otto Kluth (Geneva, 1958). On Madame Semérzy (née Clémence d'Audignac), see Trénard, *Lyon*, 2: 756–757. Trénard identifies most of those listed in this letter; they represented Lyon's literary and intellectual elite.

42. Trénard, *Lyon*, 717–718; and Prévosto, "Les événements," 283. See the biography by Françoise Wagener, *Madame Récamier, 1777–1849* (Paris: Jean-Claude Lattès, 1986), 225–231.

43. AMN R² 5, dos. 5, petition to mayor from group of businessmen expressing gratitude for the new library and requesting a change in hours of operation, 18 March 1809. On the perceived importance of a town having a library, see Harrison, *Bourgeois Citizen*, 69–71.

44. AN F$^7$ 6770, report dated 1 March 1827.

45. Harrison, *Bourgeois Citizen*, 64.

46. Catherine Blanlœil, "De l'Institut Départemental à la Société Académique de la Loire-Inférieure: Une société savante de province au XIXe siècle (1798–1914)" (thèse de doctorat, Université de Nantes, 1992), 179. According to an 1835 study, the Nantais who most cultivated poetry were women: Madame Dufrénoy, la princesse de Salm-Dyck, and Elisa Mercoeur. A. Hugo, *France pittoresque, topographique et statistique des départements et colonies de la France . . . Département de la Loire-Inférieure, Nantes* (Paris: Delloye, 1835), 162.

47. *Journal de Nantes*, no. 245, 2 Sept. 1821.

48. AN F$^7$ 6770, report dated 1 March 1827.

49. Catherine Duprat, *Usage et pratiques de la philanthropie: Pauvreté, action sociale et lien social, à Paris, au cours du premier XIXe siècle*, vol. 2 (Paris: Association pour l'Etude de l'Histoire de la Sécurité Sociale, 1997) and Christine Adams, "Constructing Mothers and Families: The Society for Maternal Charity of Bordeaux, 1805–1860," *French Historical Studies* 22 (1999): 65–86. Two of the most significant studies of Anglo-American women's charitable work are Lori D. Ginzberg, *Women and the Work of Benevolence: Morality, Politics, and Class in the Nineteenth-Century United States* (New Haven: Yale University Press, 1990) and Martha Vicinus, *Independent Women: Work and Community for Single Women, 1850–1920* (Chicago: University of Chicago Press, 1985).

50. A thorough discussion of its formation and functioning can be found in Duprat, *Usage et pratiques de la philanthropie*, 616–635. See also Duprat, "Le silence des femmes: Associations féminines du premier XIXe siècle," in *Femmes dans la cité, 1815–1871,* ed. Alain Corbin, Jacqueline Lalouette, and Michèle Riot-Sarcey (Grâne: Créaphis, [1997]), 79–100; and Stuart Woolf, "The Société de Charité Maternelle, 1788–1815," in *Medicine and Charity before the Welfare State,* ed. Jonathan Barry and Colin Jones (London: Routledge, 1991), 102–105. Duprat makes little mention of the extension of this organization into the provinces and pays no attention whatsoever to non-Parisian activities. On the provinces, see Adams, "Constructing Mothers and Families," and Jean-Pierre Chaline, "Sociabilité féminine et 'maternalisme,' les Sociétés de Charité Maternelle au XIXe siècle," in *Femmes dans la cité,* 69–78.

51. ADR 4M 523. These specifications were included in directions to prefects dated 8 April 1812.

52. In December 1812, the deputy mayor of Bordeaux, Charles Fieffé, donated 25 francs to that city's Société de Charité Maternelle. AMB, Fonds Fieffé 31 S 61.

53. These trends parallel larger Napoleonic developments including the system of prefects and the incorporation of former nobles with bourgeois notables into the administration of the nation. See Edward A. Whitcomb, "Napoleon's Prefects," *American Historical Review* 79 (1974): 1089–1118; Jacques Godechot,

*Les institutions de la France sous la Révolution et l'Empire* ([1951] Paris: Presses Universitaires de France, 1989), 589–592, 696–701; and Jean Tulard, *Napoléon et la noblesse de l'Empire* (Paris: Tallandier, 1986). For a revision of these views, see Rafe Blaufarb, "The Social Contours of Meritocracy in the Napoleonic Officer Corps," in *Taking Liberties: Problems of a New Order from the French Revolution to Napoleon*, ed. Howard G. Brown and Judith A. Miller (Manchester: Manchester University Press, 2002), 126–146.

54. ADR 4M 523, "Règlement pour la Société de la Charité Maternelle" (Paris, 1811). This carton contains extensive correspondence between Lyon and Paris regarding the organization. On the new attention to breastfeeding, beginning in the late eighteenth century, see Elizabeth Badinter, *L'amour en plus: Histoire de l'amour maternel (XVIIe–XXe siècle)* (Paris: Flammarion, 1980), 196–198. On the controlling aspects of "benevolent" acts see Jacques Donzelot, *The Policing of Families,* trans. Robert Hurley ([1977] Baltimore: Johns Hopkins University Press, 1997). As her title suggests, in "Constructing Mothers and Families," Adams also emphasizes the mechanisms of control that accompanied charitable efforts.

55. BML Collection Coste, MS. 948, letter to Monsieur le comte Dejean (the prefect) from la comtesse de Bondy, 11 Feb. 1813.

56. On the Parisian association, which took its inspiration from the Lyonnais model, see Duprat, *Usage et pratiques de la philanthropie,* 698–700; and Duprat, "Le Silence des femmes," 85–95.

57. ADR 4M 523, undated letter to prefect, his response acknowledging receipt of the bylaws dated Nov. 1818, and the bylaws themselves. These women's names connect them to Lyon's most prominent families. "Rewarding virtue" was the language used by the soon-to-be-established "Montyon" prize as well.

58. ADR 4M 523, Règlement de la Société des Jeunes Economes.

59. Maurice Garden, *Histoire économique d'une grande entreprise de santé: Le budget des hospices civils de Lyon, 1800–1976* (Lyon: Presses Universitaires de Lyon, 1980), 13–14, 51–52.

60. AN F[7] 3686 (7), Police générale, Year V—1807, prefect, Compte de situation (Rhône), 10 May 1807.

61. AML 742 WP 2. Letters to mayor from women expressing their regret at being unable to participate, dated 17 April 1827.

62. Sarah A. Curtis, *Educating the Faithful: Religion, Schooling, and Society in Nineteenth-Century France* (DeKalb: Northern Illinois University Press, 2000), 35. On secular schools, see Sharif Gemie, *Women and Schooling in France, 1815–1914: Gender, Authority, and Identity in the Female Schooling Sector* (Keele: Keele University Press, 1995). On the growth in women's religious orders after the Revolution, see James H. McMillan, *France and Women, 1789–1914: Gender, Society, and Politics* (London: Routledge, 2000), 54–56.

On trends in primary education under the Napoleonic and Restoration regimes, see Isser Woloch, *The New Regime: Transformations of the French Civic Order, 1789–1820s* (New York: Norton, 1994), ch. 7.

63. Charléty, "La vie politique," 432–433.

64. AML 306 WP 4, letter to mayor from one of the dames religieuses Ursalines, 18 Nov. 1817. On the ambiguous position of women religious in postrevolutionary France, see Caroline Ford, *Divided Houses: Religion and Gender in Modern France* (Ithaca: Cornell University Press, 2005).

65. AML 306 WP 4, prefect to mayor, 10 Oct. 1817. In a response to an 1815 questionnaire held in the same carton, the Ursalines described their goals as "the instruction of *jeunes demoiselles* and the instruction of poor *jeunes filles.*" Such language replicates that used in other settings: "demoiselles" were young "ladies" from wealthy families whereas "jeunes filles" were young girls from poor backgrounds. Status, not age, determined the terminology chosen. The construction of the sentence in two parts suggests that the two groups received different kinds of instruction.

66. According to André Latreille, women's orders were reestablished after 1815 more easily than those for men because the latter were hampered by "legislation and by prejudices inherited from the Revolution." "La vie politique et le mouvement des idées de 1815 à 1905," in *Histoire de Lyon et du Lyonnais,* ed. André Latreille (Toulouse: Privat, 1975), 342.

67. *Journal de Nantes,* no. 19, 19 Jan. 1821.

68. ADLA 1M 669, poster: "Le maire de la ville de Nantes à ses administrés," 12 August 1808.

69. *Règle et coutumier de l'institut des religieuses hospitalières de la providence de Nantes* (Nantes: C. Marson, 1834), 146–147. Despite the government's support of female religious communities, concerns about their potential economic power arose in debates regarding their legal reestablishment in 1825. See Caroline Ford, "Private Lives and Public Order in Restoration France: The Seduction of Emily Loveday," *American Historical Review* 99 (1994): 42.

70. ADLA 78 V 1, undated letter, as well as other related documents from 1828–29 addressed to prefect.

71. See the discussion of Napoleonic festivals in Chapter 1.

72. Claude Langlois, *Le Catholicisme au féminin: Les congrégations françaises à supérieure générale au XIXe siècle* (Paris: Cerf, 1984), ch. 2. Elizabeth Rapley traces the seventeenth-century rise and eighteenth-century decline of the three main teaching orders in *A Social History of the Cloister: Daily Life in the Teaching Monasteries of the Old Regime* (Montreal: McGill-Queens University Press, 2001).

73. *Journal de Nantes,* no. 2389, 31 July 1819 and *Journal du commerce,* no. 68, 19 May 1824.

74. *Etrennes mignonnes lyonnaises . . . pour 1829* (Lyon: J. M. Barrett), 47 (held in ADR, Fonds Léon Galle F. 588). In *Le contrat de mariage,* which takes place in Bordeaux in the 1820s, Balzac depicts the old-fashioned notary, Mathias, as honorable and trustworthy. He was an active member of the hospice committee and the benevolent committee, and neither he nor his wife had a carriage. Balzac contrasts Mathias to Solonet, the younger notary, who has a carriage, goes to balls and the theater, buys paintings, and plays card games, activities that prove his lack of worth. *Le contrat de mariage,* 153–156. Balzac's portrayal confirms findings that serving on charitable committees brought honor and dignity to the men who held such positions. See David Garrioch, *The Formation of the Parisian Bourgeoisie, 1690–1830* (Cambridge, Mass.: Harvard University Press, 1996), 7–8; and Harrison, *Bourgeois Citizen,* 2–14.

75. Maurice Garden, *Lyon et les Lyonnais au XVIIIe siècle* (Paris: Société d'Edition les Belles-Lettres, 1970); 595.

76. See Claire Goldberg Moses, *French Feminism in the Nineteenth Century* (Albany: SUNY Press, 1984), 41; and Popkin, *Press, Revolution, and Social Identities,* chs. 3–4. Popkin's analysis of social identities has many connections to the spaces and activities examined in this chapter.

## 6. Drinking, Dancing, and the Moral Order

1. *Journal des dames et des modes,* vol. 7, no. 39, 15 Germinal Year XI (5 April 1801), 313–314.

2. On inverting the social order in early modern carnival festivities, see M. M. Bakhtin, *Rabelais and His World,* trans. Hélène Iswolsky (Bloomington: University of Indiana Press, 1984). On the evolution of festival traditions in nineteenth-century industrial society, see Peter Stallybrass and Allon White, *The Politics and Poetics of Transgression* (Ithaca: Cornell University Press, 1986); and E. P. Thompson, "Rough Music," in *Customs in Common* (New York: New Press, 1993), 467–538.

3. ADLA 1M 494, poster with laws regarding observance of Sundays and holidays, Paris, 7 June 1814. The same law was broadcast in cities around the country. A copy of it is held in in ADR 4M 478.

4. *Les paysans* first appeared in serial form in *La presse* in 1844. On the subversive possibilities of working-class drinking establishments, see James C. Scott, *Domination and the Arts of Resistance: Hidden Transcripts* (New Haven: Yale University Press, 1990), 120–124.

5. On Parisian drinking establishments, see W. Scott Haine, *The World of the Paris Café: Sociability among the French Working Class, 1789–1914* (Baltimore: Johns Hopkins University Press, 1996); Thomas Brennan, *Public Drinking and Popular Culture in Eighteenth-Century Paris* (Princeton: Princeton University Press,

1988); and Daniel Roche, "Le cabaret parisien et les manières de vivre du peuple," in *Habiter la ville XVe–XXe siècles,* ed. Maurice Garden and Yves Lequin (Lyon: Presses Universitaires de Lyon, 1984). On the contrast between cafés and cabarets, see James Van Horn Melton, *The Rise of the Public in Enlightenment Europe* (Cambridge: Cambridge University Press, 2001), 235–240.

6. *Journal de Nantes et du département de la Loire-Inférieure,* no. 22, 22 Oct. 1813. In a report to the minister of the interior, the prefect stated that the guilty parties "made plans in a café to force the director to appear on stage and to throw apples at him." He went on to describe their tumultuous behavior (AN F⁷ 8381, report dated 2 Nov. 1813). Michael Sibalis discusses numerous examples of the surveillance and even closing of cafés in Paris and around the country due to political outbursts and other incidents in "The Napoleonic Police State," in *Napoleon and Europe,* ed. Philip G. Dwyer (Harlow: Longman, 2001), 86–87.

7. This was a period of unprecedented growth for the silk industry. According to Robert J. Bezucha, the "middle years of the Restoration" saw "rapid expansion" in the silk industry before "the severe crisis of the late 1820s." *The Lyon Uprising of 1834: Social and Political Conflict in the Early July Monarchy* (Cambridge, Mass.: Harvard University Press, 1974), 28.

8. Maurice Garden, *Lyon et les Lyonnais au XVIIIe siècle* (Paris: Société d'Edition les Belles-Lettres, 1970), 544–545. A letter written by a journalist in the late 1820s assumes that cafés were prime locations for newspaper reading. ADR 4M 449, copy of undated letter to minister of the interior from M. Pitrat.

9. AN F⁷ 4143, *Rapport mensuel,* Oct. 1822. According to Scott Haine, Restoration authorities assumed that politics was the main focus in bourgeois cafés, whereas working-class cafés remained sites of "traditional" pursuits. *World of the Paris Café,* 212–213.

10. Carol E. Harrison, *The Bourgeois Citizen in Nineteenth-Century France: Gender, Sociability, and the Uses of Emulation* (Oxford: Oxford University Press, 1999), 90. On political disturbances in Lyon, see Guillaume de Bertier de Sauvigny, *The Bourbon Restoration,* trans. Lynn M. Case (Philadelphia: University of Pennsylvania Press, 1966), 151–152, 172.

11. Jeremy D. Popkin cites 1820s police reports from Lyon commenting on the practice of reading newspapers aloud in cafés. *Press, Revolution, and Social Identities in France, 1830–1835* (University Park: Pennsylvania State University Press, 2002), 59.

12. ADR 4M 77, commissioner of police to prefect, "Observations sur l'esprit public," "first semester" of 1822.

13. Sarah Maza, *The Myth of the French Bourgeoisie: An Essay on the Social Imaginary, 1750–1850* (Cambridge, Mass.: Harvard University Press, 2003), 161.

14. ADR 4M 645, letter from mayor of Villefranche to lieutenant general of police (Lyon), 18 Feb. 1818.

15. ADR 4M 645, chief of Gendarmerie Royale to lieutenant of police (Lyon), 23 January 1818, and letter from prefect to lieutenant of police, 27 Jan. 1818.

16. AMT Don Lamouzèle 5 S 117, police commissioner to mayor, 18 May 1820.

17. Both of these examples are cited in Sheryl Kroen, *Politics and Theater: The Crisis of Legitimacy in Restoration France, 1815–1830* (Berkeley: University of California Press, 2000), 341 n. 63.

18. AN F⁷ 6636, prefect to minister of the interior, 18 Feb. 1823.

19. Scott Haine recounts the story of Paris' "Belle Limonadière," and other "comely or famous young women" who worked behind Parisian café counters. However, he emphasizes that female café owners, who usually worked along-side their husbands, were "more than just a pretty face behind the counter." They tended to play "the roles of financier, cashier, and accountant." Haine, *World of the Paris Café*, 183–185. Among references to female café owners in Lyon is an 1820 discussion of an incident that took place in the café Billiet run by the *dame* Billiet. AN F⁷ 6636, letters from lieutenant de police de Lyon to director general, 27 and 31 March 1820.

20. On the relationship between sexuality, morality, and class identities, see Anna Clark, *The Struggle for the Breeches: Gender and the Making of the British Working Class* (Berkeley: University of California Press, 1995).

21. *Journal du commerce,* no. 11, 4 Jan. 1824, and no. 14, 11 Jan. 1824.

22. *Journal du commerce,* no. 59, 18 April 1824. First published privately in 1823, *Ourika* went through four editions and reprints in 1824. Four plays based on the novel were also staged that year. Joan DeJean and Margaret Waller, Intro-duction to Claire de Duras, *Ourika*, trans. John Fowles (New York: MLA Press, 1994), viii. See also the French version and its accompanying discussion in Claire de Duras, *Ourika*, ed. Roger Little (Exeter: University of Exeter Press, 1993), as well as Alison Finch, *Women's Writing in Nineteenth-Century France* (Cambridge: Cambridge University Press, 2000), ch. 7.

23. *Journal du commerce,* no. 60, 30 April 1824.

24. Jean Tulard, *La vie quotidienne des Français sous Napoléon* (Paris: Hachette, 1978), 177. Though exact numbers are not available, one study estimates that four thousand to five thousand black people were present in France in the late eighteenth century. Sue Peabody, *"There Are No Slaves in France:" The Political Culture of Race and Slavery in the Ancien Régime* (Oxford: Oxford University Press, 1996), 4. At least one man of color was active in the 1831 insurrection in Lyon: "Stanislas the Negro" appears in several sources, including an engraving of the period. See Popkin, *Press, Revolution, and Social Identities*, 223.

25. See Edward Said, *Orientalism* (New York: Pantheon, 1978). On French atti-tudes toward slavery and people of color during this period, see Léon-François Hoffmann, *Le nègre romantique: Personnage littéraire et obsession col-lective* (Paris: Payot, 1973) and William Cohen, *The French Encounter with*

*Africans: White Response to Blacks, 1530–1880* (Bloomington: Indiana University Press, 1980), 184–191.

26. *Journal du commerce,* no. 60, 30 April 1824.

27. Maurice Garden, "Effacement politique, contradictions culturelles et tensions sociales," in *Histoire de Lyon et du Lyonnais,* ed. André Latreille (Toulouse: Privat, 1975), 278.

28. AN F$^7$ 3686 (8), police report for second half of March 1819.

29. ADR 4M 171, mayor of Irigny to prefect, 26 Dec. 1810, and AML I$^2$ 33, police report, 15 June 1816. In the latter, the shouting took place in a cabaret on rue de la Barre in central Lyon, near the place Bellecour.

30. AMN I$^1$ 50, dos. 1, notice from the police to "Citoyens de cette commune qui tiennent auberge, café ou salle de danse publics," 22 Pluviôse Year VIII (11 Feb. 1800) and poster listing regulations of 29 Oct. 1808.

31. Ibid., dos. 6, poster with extracts of laws published by city hall, 30 Nov. 1819.

32. In 1828, La Guillotière had a population of thirteen thousand and contained "wide, paved boulevards." John Merriman, *The Margins of City Life: Explorations on the French Urban Frontier, 1815–1851* (New York: Oxford University Press, 1991), 47.

33. Merriman, *Margins of City Life,* 66.

34. AN F$^7$ 3686 (8), mayor of Lyon to minister of the interior, 5 Aug. 1809.

35. *Journal du commerce,* no. 39, 10 March 1824.

36. AML I$^1$ 156, draft copy of letter from mayor to minister of police, 10 July 1810.

37. AN F$^7$ 9865, prefect to conseiller d'état chargé du 2eme arrondissement de la police, 12 Nov. 1813. On policing issues, see Merriman, *Margins of City Life,* 221–223.

38. Mayor of Nantes, quoted in Christophe Patillon and Jean-Luc Souchet, *Chantenay: Histoires illustrées d'une ville devenue quartier* (Nantes: C.D.M.O.T., 1993), 74. The image of fathers drinking all day brings to mind the quotation in Chapter 4 about fathers being better off at the theater than drinking in a cabaret.

39. AMN I$^1$ 50, dos. 6, prefect to mayor, 12 April 1826.

40. AML 4 WP 56, prefect to mayor of La Guillotière, 10 April 1818.

41. AN F$^7$ 3686 (8), report from Gendarmerie Royale, 18 May 1819.

42. AML 4 WP 56, police commissioner to mayor of La Guillotière, 1 March 1822.

43. Merriman, *Margins of City Life,* 62. Merriman's argument parallels that of Louis Chevalier, *Laboring Classes and Dangerous Classes in Paris during the First Half of the Nineteenth Century,* trans. Frank Jellinek (New York: H. Fertig, 1973). For a critique of Chevalier, see Barrie M. Ratcliffe, "Classes laborieuses et classes dangereuses pendant la première moitié du XIXe siècle? The Chevalier Thesis Reexamined," *French Historical Studies* 16 (1991): 542–574.

44. AML 4 WP 56, law announced 21 March 1829.

45. *L'ami de la Charte: Journal politique, littéraire et d'avis de Nantes,* no. 50, 10 Nov. 1819. The rest of the article contains an anecdote meant to portray the workers who went to these places as ignorant and naive. One worker sees another as he is leaving the neighborhood to return to the city at 5:30 in the evening. He asks, "Is there some pressing matter that is making you leave so soon?" "No," the other replies, "I am going to the theater; they are performing *La Petite Ville,* and you see, it's surely the Ville-en-Bois that I will see there." The poster announced that the play would be followed by *Le Rossignol.* The workers' limited experience kept them from understanding that these were simply the titles of plays and that they had nothing to do with a guinguette in the Ville-en-Bois.

46. ADR 4M 455, mayor to prefect, 6 Aug. 1806.

47. ADR 4M 171, mayor to prefect, 3 Dec. 1810. Prostitutes were commonly victims of abuse. Julie Pellizzone recounts a story of a prostitute being left in a cave outside of Marseille by some *compagnons* (journeymen artisans). It was only by chance that some hunters heard her cries, but that was after she had spent more than twenty-four hours trapped in the darkness. Pellizzone, *Souvenirs,* vol. 1 *(1781–1815),* transcribed by Hélène Echinard, presented and annotated by Pierre Echinard, Hélène Echinard, and Georges Reynaud (Paris: Indigo and Côté-femmes, 1995), 254.

48. AMN I$^2$ 29, police report, 1 Feb. 1823.

49. J.-P.-R. Cuisin, *Les cabarets de Paris, ou l'homme peint d'après nature* (Paris: Delongchamps, 1821), 14–16. Cuisin's publications include *Les bains de Paris et des principales villes des quatres parties du monde, ou le Neptune des dames, avec anecdotes, galanteries décentes, etc.* (Paris: Verdière, 1821); *Clémentine orpheline et androgyne, ou les caprices de la nature et de la fortune* (Paris, 1819); *Le conjugalisme, ou l'art de se bien marier* (Paris: Mansut, 1823); and *Le guide des épouseurs pour 1825, ou le conjugalisme: Etrennes aux futures par un homme qui s'est marié sept fois* (Paris, 1824).

50. AMM 1I 4, letter to mayor from femme Frontin née Tinel, undated but attached to police report dated 14 July 1829.

51. AMN I$^1$ 50, dos. 1, lists of cabarets in Nantes by arrondissement. These lists include information on what amenities the cabarets offered their customers.

52. ADR 4M 478, prefect to mayor, 14 Feb. 1811, and mayor to prefect, 18 Feb. 1811.

53. François Gasnault, *Guinguettes et lorettes: Bals publics à Paris entre 1830 et 1870* (Paris: Aubier, 1986), 14.

54. L'abbé Ernest Sevrin, *Les missions religieuses en France sous la Restauration (1815–1830),* vol. 1, *Le missionnaire et la mission* (Saint-Mandé: Procure des Prêtres de la Miséricorde, 1948), 273.

55. Mercier, *Le nouveau Paris* (Paris: Fuchs, [1799]), 130, 150, 154. According to a synthetic work on French urban history, "balls, public and private, *mondains*

*et populaires,* were hugely successful." Guy Chaussinand-Nogaret, "La ville jacobine et balzacienne," in *Histoire de la France urbaine,* vol. 3, ed. Georges Duby (Paris: Seuil, 1981), 607 (in caption for image of a costume ball at the Paris Opera). A study of eighteenth-century leisure practices in the small city of Laval in the Loire valley includes dancing as one of the most popular activities, along with going to cabarets. See Frédérique Pitou, "Les pratiques de divertissement à Laval au XVIIIe siècle," *Histoire urbaine* 1 (2000): 87–104.

56. Gerard Pernon, *Fêtes et spectacles au temps de la Révolution* (Rennes: Ouest France, 1988), 26.

57. AMN I¹ 43, police regulations on masked balls, 17 Pluviôse Year VIII (6 Feb. 1800).

58. *Journal de Nantes,* no. 456, 1 Jan. 1815. The use of the English term "vauxhall" suggests continued "anglomania" in this period. See Josephine Grieger, *Anglomania in France, 1740–1789: Fact, Fiction, and Political Discourse* (Geneva: Droz, 1985).

59. *Journal de Nantes,* no. 469, 15 Jan. 1815.

60. David Garrioch, *The Making of Revolutionary Paris* (Berkeley: University of California Press, 2002), 244–245. Garrioch also describes the guinguettes of the Parisian suburbs, which grew in number and popularity in the second half of the eighteenth century.

61. BML, Collection Coste 114592, announcement of new dance hall called "l'Harmonie," 13 May 1810.

62. AMN I¹ 52, dos. 12, "Entrepreneurs des bals de wauxall to citoyen president et officiers municipaux de la ville de Nantes," 16 Frimaire Year VI (6 Dec. 1797).

63. AMN I¹ 43, declaration of Marie Faupin, 26 Pluviôse Year XII (15 Feb. 1804) and police report, 20 Pluviôse Year XII (9 Feb. 1804).

64. AMN I² 29, police report, 26 Aug. 1822.

65. Mercier, *Le nouveau Paris,* 158.

66. "Ouverture des redoutes," *Journal de Nantes,* no. 447, 23 Dec. 1814.

67. *Journal du commerce,* no. 166, 12 Jan. 1825.

68. *Journal de Paris,* 8 July 1807, quoted in Alphonse Aulard, *Paris sous le Premier Empire: Recueil de documents pour l'histoire de l'esprit public à Paris,* vol. 3 (Paris: Barbier, 1923), 241–242.

69. Julien-Joseph Virey, *De la femme, sous ses rapports physiologique, moral, et littéraire* (Paris: Crochard, 1825), 242. Carla Hesse analyzes the postrevolutionary emphasis on biology to prove women's mental incapacity in *The Other Enlightenment: How French Women Became Modern* (Princeton: Princeton University Press, 2001), 130–134.

70. Adélaïde-Gillette Billet Dufrénoy, *La petite ménagère, ou l'éducation maternelle* (Paris: A. Eymery, 1816), 2: 101. On Dufrénoy, see Hesse, *Other Enlightenment,* 51.

71. This is the argument I make in "*Bonnes Lectures:* Improving Women and Society Through Literature in Post-Revolutionary France," in *The French Experience from Republic to Monarchy, 1792–1824: New Dawns in Politics, Knowledge and Culture,* ed. Máire F. Cross and David Williams (Basingstoke: Palgrave, 2000), 155–171.

72. *Eve en France où les plus ressemblantes copies de ce premier modèle des femmes abondent plus qu'en tout autre pays du globe terrestre* (Lyon: André IDT, n.d. [circa 1825]), 1–2. I appreciate the efforts of the staff at the Lyon Municipal Archives in bringing this fascinating and largely unknown pamphlet to my attention.

73. The term "grisette" dates from the eighteenth century and refers to the coarse gray dresses of working women. See Valerie Steele, *Paris Fashion: A Cultural History,* 2nd ed. (Oxford: Berg, 1998), 68–69. Victoria E. Thompson examines changing representations of grisettes in *The Virtuous Marketplace: Women and Men, Money and Politics in Paris, 1830–1870* (Baltimore: Johns Hopkins University Press, 2000), 39–46.

74. In his study of student life during the Restoration and the July Monarchy, Jean-Claude Caron discusses the prevalence of the grisette if not in reality at least in the minds of bourgeois students. According to Caron, during the Restoration the term signified "the companion of a worker"; it was only after 1830 that it came to mean a young girl who lived in the Latin Quarter with a student. "Neither prostitute nor kept woman, the grisette is generally glorified for her disinterestedness." *Générations romantiques: Les étudiants de Paris et le quartier latin (1814–1851)* (Paris: Armand Colin, 1991), 205–206. I have found "grisette" used to mean the working-class girlfriend of a wealthy young man as early as 1801, in the anecdote that opens this chapter. Describing eighteenth-century Parisian taverns, Daniel Roche depicts "a grisette deceiving a dandy" in *The People of Paris: An Essay in Popular Culture in the Eighteenth Century,* trans. Marie Evans (Berkeley: University of California Press, 1987), 254. This portrayal suggests that even before the Revolution the term signified a lower-class woman with a wealthy lover.

75. August Ricard, *La grisette* ([1827] Stuttgart: Belser Verlag, 1989).

76. Gasnault, *Guinguettes et lorettes.* On their history in the eighteenth century, see Brennan, *Public Drinking,* 175–186; and Melton, *Rise of the Public,* 23–37. Brennan provides a detailed description of eighteenth-century Parisian guinguettes: "The space available in the suburbs meant that guinguettes could be much larger than cabarets. The guinguettes had larger rooms and buildings, but more importantly they offered gardens and greens where customers could sit and drink, dance or play boulles" (177).

77. ADR 4M 478, mayor of Vaise to prefect, 19 June 1811.

78. Ibid., prefect to sous-préfet of Lyon, 21 June 1811.

79. Ibid., mayor of Tassin to sous-préfet, 26 June 1811.

80. AML 4 WP 56, sous-préfet to mayor of La Guillotière, 29 May 1812.

81. ADR 4M 478, mayor of La Croix-Rousse to prefect, 23 Nov. 1817.

82. ADR 4M 455, mayor of Vaise to prefect, 15 July 1823.

83. ADR 4M 155, police lieutenant to prefect, 29 July 1819.

84. ADR 4M 479, poster published by mayor of La Croix-Rousse, 10 Oct. 1829. *Fêtes baladoires* evolved out of the tradition of young men walking along the boundaries of their village or neighborhood staking their claim to the territory. An exhibition called "Lyon en fêtes" held at Lyon's Musée Gadagne in 2003 treated these events.

85. ADR 4M 478, prefect to mayor, 31 May 1811.

86. *Journal du commerce*, no. 77, 11 June 1824. A source in which exaggeration is less likely, a report from the Gendarmerie Royale, includes the same comparison to Longchamp, an annual festival in Paris. AN F[7] 3686 (8), report, 5 May 1819. On Longchamp, see Martin-Fugier, *La vie élégante, ou la formation du Tout-Paris, 1815–1848* (Paris: Fayard, 1990), 331.

87. Garden, "Effacement politique," 279. The term "vogue" also appeared in western Provence. See Michel Vovelle, *Les métamorphoses de la fête en Provence de 1750 à 1820* (Paris: Aubier/Flammarion, 1976), 38. For a brilliant analysis of the "social-moral economy" of youthful misbehavior in an eighteenth-century German context, see Hans Medick, "Village Spinning Bees: Sexual Culture and Free Time among Rural Youth in Early Modern Germany," in *Interest and Emotion: Essays on the Study of Family and Kinship*, ed. Hans Medick and David Warren Sabean (Cambridge: Cambridge University Press, 1984), 317–339. One sees many parallels to the lyonnais practice of vogues, both among their participants and in the reactions of authorities.

88. *Journal du commerce*, no. 88, 7 July 1824.

89. ADR 4M 478, mayor of Irigny to sous-préfet, 30 July 1813.

90. Authorities described tensions aroused by statements made in cabarets and quarrels at dances that escalated into "petites guerres" between the youth of neighboring villages. AN F[7] 3686 (8), police report, Gendarmerie Royale, 5 May 1819.

91. Quoted in Sevrin, *Les missions religieuses*, 1: 275.

92. Natalie Zemon Davis, "Women on Top," in *Society and Culture in Early Modern France* (Stanford: Stanford University Press, 1975), 124.

93. ADR 4M 478, curé of Chaponost to prefect, 18 Sept. 1816.

94. Ibid. I do not have the prefect's response to the priest, but a letter from the mayor of Chaponost to the prefect suggests that the latter had asked him to address the concerns of the curé. The mayor stated that while it was true that "a dance took place every Sunday in an isolated part of the community," the diverse disorders described by the priest as well as the cabaret component were pure inventions. ADR 4M 478, mayor of Chaponost to prefect, 3 Oct. 1816.

95. Martyn Lyons, "Fires of Expiation: Book Burnings and Catholic Missions in Restoration France," *French History* 10 (June 1996): 240–266; Kroen, *Politics and Theater*, 91; and Sevrin, *Les missions religieuses*, 1: 272–288.

96. ADR 4M 478, mayor of La Guillotière to prefect, 10 Sept. 1818. The prefect attempted to soothe the mayor's concerns by insisting that the curé's comments should not be taken as a personal attack, and that he knew that the mayor was going a good job. He insisted on only one point: that *fêtes patronales* must not be allowed to continue until late into the night. ADR 4M 478, prefect to mayor of La Guillotière, 15 Sept. 1818.

97. ADR 4M 478, prefect to mayor of La Guillotière, 8 Oct. 1818. Same letter held in AML 4 WP 55.

## Conclusion

1. See William H. Sewell, "A Theory of Structure: Duality, Agency, and Transformation," *American Journal of Sociology* 92 (1992): 1–29; and Sharon Hays, "Structure and Agency and the Sticky Problem of Culture," *Sociological Theory* 12 (1994): 57–72.

2. Louis-Damien Eméric, *De la politesse, ouvrage critique, moral et philosophique* (Paris: Delauney, 1819), 43.

3. Julien-Joseph Virey, *De la femme, sous ses rapports physiologique, moral et littéraire* (Paris: Crochard, 1825), 264. Earlier in his career, Virey devoted his attentions to the issue of race in *Histoire naturelle du genre humain* (Paris: F. Dufart, 1800). William Cohen refers to Virey as "the most ardent developer of eighteenth-century racism." *The French Encounter with Africans: White Response to Blacks, 1530–1880* (Bloomington: Indiana University Press, 1980), 98. Robert A. Nye analyzes *De la femme* in his *Masculinity and Male Codes of Honor in Modern France* (Berkeley: University of California Press, 1997), 59–62.

4. See Claire Goldberg Moses, "'Difference' in Historical Perspective: Saint-Simonian Feminism," in *Feminism, Socialism, and French Romanticism*, ed. Claire Goldberg Moses and Leslie Wahl Rabine (Bloomington: Indiana University Press, 1993).

# List of Primary Sources

## Unpublished Sources

### *Archives Nationales, Paris*

Judicial records
  BB 18 447–452 (Loire-Inférieure), 688–693 (Rhône)
Police records
  F⁷ 3681 (7), F⁷ 3686 (7), F⁷ 3686 (8), F⁷ 4051, F⁷ 4143, F⁷ 6636, F⁷ 6770,
  F⁷ 6872, F⁷ 6951, F⁷ 8381, F⁷ 8748, F⁷ 9695, F⁷ 9865

### *Archives Départementales de la Loire-Atlantique, Nantes*

Family papers
  133 J 43 Fonds Louis Bouchaud
Police records
  1M 468, 1M 494, 1M 669, 1M 670, 1M 671
Cultural institutions and education
  161 T 1, 177 T 1, 177 T 2, 177 T 3, 177 T 4, 178 T 1, 179 T 1
Religion
  78 V 1

### *Archives Départementales du Rhône, Lyon*

*Section ancienne* (private papers)
  33J 12 a*
  Fonds Léon Galle F. 588
*Section moderne*
  Police records

4M 77, 4M 78, 4M 155, 4M 171, 4M 176, 4M 226, 4M 426, 4M 449, 4M 455, 4M 475, 4M 478, 4M 479, 4M 523, 4M 645, 4M 827

Cultural institutions and education

T 426, T 435

### Archives Départementales de la Seine-Maritime, Rouen

1M 364, 1M 365 (police)

1Mi 1137, Souvenirs d'Alélaïde Bauche

### Archives Municipales de Bordeaux

734 $I^1$ (police)

Fonds Fieffé 31 S 61

### Archives Municipales de Lyon

Old classification—police records

$I^1$ 155, $I^1$ 156, $I^1$ 157, $I^1$ 157A, $I^2$ 33, $I^2$ 46

New classification—various

4 WP 55, 4 WP 56, 4 WP 94, 85 WP 1, 88 WP 1, 89 WP 1, 89 WP 2, 89 WP 3, 306 WP 4, 742 WP 2

Family papers

Fonds Vitet 84 II 11, 84 II 12

Microfilmed posters

2 Mi 52

### Archives Municipales de Montpellier

1I 4 (police)

### Archives Municipales de Nantes

Police

$I^1$ 11, $I^1$ 29, $I^1$ 30, $I^1$ 43, $I^1$ 50, $I^1$ 51, $I^1$ 52, $I^1$ 53

$I^2$ 29, $I^2$ 32

Religion

$P^1$ 8

Cultural institutions and education

$R^2$ 1, $R^2$ 5

*Archives Municipales de Toulouse*

Don Lamouzèle 5 S 117

*Bibliothèque Municipale de Lyon, département de fonds anciens*

Collection Coste
   MS. 948
   various ephemera in bound volumes
General Collection
   MS. 6205 (12), MS. 6346, MS. 6449

## Newspapers

*L'ami de la Charte: Journal politique, littéraire et d'avis de Nantes*
*Courrier des spectacles*
*Feuille nantaise*
*Gazette de France*
*Journal du commerce de Lyon et du département du Rhône*
*Journal des dames et des modes*
*Journal de Nantes et du département de la Loire-Inférieure*
*Journal de Rouen et du département de la Seine-Inférieure*
*Le miroir des spectacles, des lettres, des mœurs et des arts*

## Published Books and Pamplets

*Almanach historique et politique de la ville de Lyon et du département du Rhône pour l'année 1811.* Lyon: Balanche, n.d.

Auger, Hyppolyte. *Physiologie du théâtre.* 3 vols. Paris: Didot Frères, 1839.

Avrillon, Marie-Jeanne-Pierette. *Mémoires de Mlle Avrillon première femme de chambre de l'impératrice sur la vie privée de Joséphine, sa famille et sa cour.* 1833. Reprint. Paris: Mercure, 1986.

Balzac, Honoré de. *Le contrat de mariage.* 1835. Reprint. Paris: Gallimard, 1973.

———. *Les paysans.* 1844. Reprint. Paris: Gallimard, 1975.

[Bayle-Mouillard, Elisabeth-Félicie]. *La bonne cousine, ou conseils de l'amitié par Mme Elisabeth Celnart.* Paris: Villet, 1822.

Beaulieu, C. F. *La Révolution de France, considérée dans ses effets sur la civilisation des peuples, et ses rapports avec les circonstances actuelles.* Paris: Dentu, 1820.

Brazier, Nicolas. *Histoire des petits théâtres de Paris.* 2 vols. Paris: Allardin, 1838.

Camel, Jean-Baptiste-Louis. *De l'influence des théâtres et particulièrement des théâtres secondaires sur les mœurs du peuple.* [Paris]: Nouzou, 1822.

Charlemagne, Armand. *Le mélodrame aux boulevards: Facétie littéraire, historique et dramatique.* Paris: L'Imprimerie de la rue Beaurepaire, 1809.

Charrin, P. J. *Le conteur des dames, ou les soirées parisiennes.* 2 vols. Paris: Veuve Lepetit, 1821.

*Chronique parisienne, ou revue politique, morale, littéraire et théâtrale par une société de gens de lettres.* Paris: Herhan, 1817.

*Le cicérone, ou l'indicateur de Paris.* Paris: Debray, 1811.

Coulet. *Observations succinctes adressées à messieurs les membres du Conseil Général de la commune de Lyon.* Lyon: Pelzin, 1812.

Cuisin, J.-P.-R. *Les bains de Paris et des principales villes des quatres parties du monde, ou le Neptune des dames, avec anecdotes, galanteries décentes, etc.* Paris: Verdière, 1821.

———. *Les cabarets de Paris, ou l'homme peint d'après nature.* Paris: Delong-champs, 1821.

———. *Clémentine, orpheline et androgyne, ou les caprices de la nature et de la fortune.* Paris, 1819.

———. *Le conjugalisme, ou l'art de se bien marier.* Paris: Mansut, 1823.

———. *Le guide des épouseurs pour 1825, ou le conjugalisme: Etrennes aux futures par un homme qui s'est marié sept fois.* Paris, 1824.

*Discours sur le prix de vertu prononcé dans la séance publique du 25 août 1824 par le comte de Sèze, directeur.* Paris: Firmin Didot, 1824.

Dufrénoy, Adélaïde-Gilette Billet. *Biographie des jeunes demoiselles, ou vies des femmes célèbres depuis les Hébreux.* 2 vols. Paris: Eymery, 1816.

———. *La petite ménagère, ou l'éducation maternelle.* 4 vols. Paris: A. Eymery, 1816.

Dufrénoy, Adélaïde-Gillette Billet, and Amable Tastu. *Le livre des femmes, choix de morceaux extraits des meilleurs écrivains français sur le caractère, les mœurs et l'esprit des femmes.* 2 vols. Gand: G. de Busscher, 1823.

Duras, Claire Dufort de. *Ourika.* Edited by Roger Little. Exeter: University of Exeter Press, 1993.

———. *Ourika: An English Translation.* Translated by John Fowles. Introduction by Joan DeJean and Margaret Waller. New York: Modern Languages Association Press, 1994.

Eméric, Louis-Damien. *De la politesse, ouvrage critique, moral et philosophique.* Paris: Delauney, 1819.

*Essai sur l'état actuel des théâtres de Paris et des principales villes de l'Empire, leurs administrations, leurs acteurs, leur répertoire, les journalistes, le conservatoire, etc. etc.* Paris: L'Huillier, 1813.

*Etrennes mignonnes lyonnaises . . . pour 1829.* Lyon: J. M. Barrett, n.d.

*Eve en France où les plus ressemblantes copies de ce premier modèle des femmes abondent plus qu'en tout autre pays.* Lyon: André IDT, n.d. (circa 1825).

Guépin, A., and E. Bonamy. *Nantes au XIXe siècle: Statistique topographique, industrielle et morale.* 1835. Reprint. Nantes: Université de Nantes, 1981.

*Guide de l'étranger dans Paris.* Paris: Barba, 1805.

*Le guide du voyageur à Paris.* Paris: Dabo, 1814.

Hapdé, Jean Baptiste Augustin. *De l'anarchie théâtrale, ou de la nécessité de remettre en vigueur les lois et règlemens relatifs aux différens genres de spectacles de Paris.* Paris: J. G. Dentu, 1814.

Hervé, Peter. *How to Enjoy Paris: Being a Guide to the Visitor of the French Metropolis.* 2 vols. London, 1816.

Hugo, A. *France pittoresque, topographique et statistique des départements et colonies de la France . . . Département de la Loire-Inférieure, Nantes.* Paris: Delloye, 1835.

Legouvé, Gabriel. *Le mérite des femmes.* Paris: Louis, an IX (1801).

*Madame la duchesse d'Angoulême à Nantes les 19, 20, 21 22 septembre 1823.* Nantes: Mellinet-Melassis, 1823.

Mercier, Louis-Sébastien. *Le nouveau Paris.* Paris: Fuchs, [1799].

———. *Panorama of Paris: Selections from Le "Tableau de Paris."* Based on translation by Helen Simpson, edited by and new translation by Jeremy D. Popkin. University Park: Pennsylvania State University Press, 1999.

Montigny, Louis Gabriel. *Le provincial à Paris: Esquisses des mœurs parisiennes.* 3 vols. Paris: Ladvocat, 1825.

Morgan, Lady [Sydney]. *France.* 2 vols. Philadelphia: M. Thomas, 1817.

*Naissance de S.A.R. le duc de Bordeaux, fils de France, né à Paris le 29 septembre 1820.* Nantes: Mellinet-Melassis, 1820.

*Nouveau Parisium, ou curiosités de Paris.* Paris: Marchand, 1810

*Paris as It Was and as It Is, Illustrative of the Effects of the Revolution.* London: C. and R. Baldwin, 1803.

Pellizzone, Julie. *Souvenirs.* Vol. 1 *(1781–1815).* Transcribed by Hélène Echinard. Presented and annotated by Pierre Echinard, Hélène Echinard, and Georges Reynaud. Paris: Indigo and Côté-femmes, 1995.

———. *Souvenirs: Journal d'une Marseillaise.* Vol. 2 *(1815–1824).* Transcribed by Hélène Echinard. Presented and annotated by Pierre Echinard, Hélène Echinard, and Georges Reynaud. Paris: Indigo and Côté-Femmes, 2001.

Pixérécourt, René-Charles Guilbert de. *Cœlina ou l'enfant de mystère.* Paris, 1801.

———. *Guerre au mélodrame!!!* Paris: Delaunay, 1818.

———. *Tékéli, ou le siège de Montgatz.* Paris: Barba, 1804.

———. *Théâtre choisi.* 4 vols. Paris: Tresse, 1841.

*Procès-verbal de l'arrivée et du séjour à Lyon de SAR le comte d'Artois le frère du roi.* Lyon, 1814.

*Règle et coutumier de l'institut des religieuses hospitalières de la providence de Nantes.* Nantes: C. Marson, 1834.

*Relation des fêtes données par la ville de Paris et de toutes les cérémonies qui ont eu lieu dans la capitale à l'occasion de la naissance et du baptême de son altesse royale Monseigneur le duc de Bordeaux.* Paris: Petit, 1822.

Rémusat, Claire de. *Mémoires de Madame de Rémusat.* Paris: Les Amis de l'Histoire, 1968.

Ricard, August. *La grisette.* 1827. Reprint. Stuttgart: Belser Verlag, 1989.

Ruggieri, Claude. *Précis historique sur les fêtes, les spectacles et les réjouissances publiques.* Paris: L'Auteur, 1830.

Salm, Constance de. *Œuvres complètes.* 4 vols. Paris: Firmin Didot, 1842.

Staël, Germaine de. *De la littérature considérée dans ses rapports avec les institutions sociales.* 2 vols. 1800. Reprint. Geneva: Droz and Paris: Minard, 1959.

Stendhal. *Œuvres complètes.* Paris: Champion, 1968.

*Traité du mélodrame, par MM. A! A! A! !* [Abel Hugo, Armand Malitourne, J. Adler.] Paris: Delaunay, 1817.

Villiers, P. *Manuel du voyageur à Paris, ou Paris ancien et moderne.* Paris: Delaunay, 1811.

Virey, Julien-Joseph. *De la femme, sous ses rapports physiologique, moral et littéraire.* Paris: Crochard, 1825.

———. *De l'influence des femmes sur le goût dans la littérature et les beaux-arts pendant le XVIIe et XVIIIe siècle. Discours qui a remporté le prix sur cette question proposée par la Société des Sciences, Lettres et Arts de Mâcon en 1809.* Paris: Deterville, 1810.

*Le vœu accompli: Vers adressés aux dames de Lyon, qui ont fait un vœu pour le retour du Roi, et récités au Grand-Théâtre de Lyon le 25 août 1815.* Lyon, 1815.

*Voyage descriptif et historique de Paris.* 2 vols. Paris: L'Auteur, 1814.

# Index

Harvard University Press is a member of Green Press Initiative
(greenpressinitiative.org), a nonprofit organization working to
help publishers and printers increase their use of recycled paper
and decrease their use of fiber derived from endangered forests.
This book was printed on 100% recycled paper containing
50% post-consumer waste and processed chlorine free.